W9-DFK-218

Miles Hewstone is Lecturer in Psychology at the University of Bristol and editor of *Attribution Theory*. **Rupert Brown** is Lecturer in Social Psychology at the University of Kent and editor of *Intergroup Processes*.

Contact and Conflict in Intergroup Encounters

Social Psychology and Society
General Editors: Howard Giles and Miles Hewstone

Contact and Conflict in Intergroup Encounters

Edited by
Miles Hewstone and Rupert Brown

Basil Blackwell

British Library Cataloguing in Publication Data

Contact and conflict in intergroup
   encounters.— (Social psychology and
   society)
   1. Social interaction   2. Social groups
   I. Hewstone, Miles   II. Brown, Rupert   III. Series
   302.4   HM291
   ISBN 0-631-14074-3

Library of Congress Cataloging in Publication Data

Contact and conflict in intergroup encounters.
   (Social psychology and society)
   Bibliography: p.
   Includes index.
   1. Interpersonal relations. 2. Social groups.
3. Social conflict. I. Hewstone, Miles. II. Brown,
Rupert. III. Series. [DNLM: 1. Conflict (Psychology)
2. Interpersonal Relations. HM 132 C759]
HM132.C627 1986   302.3   86-6165
ISBN 0-631-14074-3

Typeset by Columns of Reading
Printed in Great Britain by
The Camelot Press Ltd, Southampton

To Claudia and Lyn

It has sometimes been held that merely by assembling people without regard for race, color, religion, or national origin, we can thereby destroy stereotypes and develop friendly attitudes. The case is not so simple.

Gordon W. Allport, *The Nature of Prejudice* (1954)

It is a peculiar property of intergroup contacts that the role of one person vis-à-vis another is not determined solely by personal qualities, nor even by social prescriptions about roles that cut across group lines, such as occupational or educational functions. The salient factor is the standing of the two groups.

Muzafer Sherif, *Group Conflict and Cooperation* (1966)

Whenever the underlying structure of social divisions and power or status differentials is fairly resilient, it is not likely to be substantially affected by piecemeal attempts at reform in selected situations of 'contact'.

Henri Tajfel, *Annual Review of Psychology* (1982)

Contents

Foreword

Social psychology began the 1970s in a so-called state of 'crisis'. In particular, critics questioned our ability to generalize from laboratory experiments to natural settings. The response to this crisis since that time has been impressive and constructive with regard to empirical and theoretical developments, many of which have been reflected in a steady growth of new journals and a vast increase in authored and edited volumes. Although not wishing to imply that all in the garden is now rosy, this series aims to reflect one major aspect of our emergence from this crisis – the relationship between social psychology and society. This has always been the *raison d'être* of a social psychology – an integration of individual and wider social analyses.

Contemporary research on the social psychology of intergroup relations is, perhaps, exemplary of the most positive type of response to the late Henri Tajfel's famous claim in 1972, that much of the discipline was concocted in a 'social vacuum'. In the area of intergroup relations, social-psychological factors have been, and must be, married to economic, political and historical factors; social psychology here cannot be divorced from society.

We believe that Tajfel's vacuum has now been replaced by a volatile gas, by a social psychology (for a growing number of scholars) that really is concerned with social problems and social life outside the laboratory. As such it confronts issues of sometimes burning current interest (e.g. racism and fascism), as well as areas of fundamental human concern (e.g. delinquency and health). Given such topics, this series aims to confront squarely the relationship between social psychology and its sociostructural determinants, and to speak directly to the policy implications of much social-psychological research.

Contact and Conflict in Intergroup Encounters is a good starting point to this series for many reasons, not least of which includes the contributors' focus on real-life 'blood and guts' issues, rather than on abstracted laboratory experiments. Indeed, these are issues, which, if they remain unresolved and poorly understood, will long continue to divide our societies. Intergroup contact occurs against a complex backdrop of quite diverse societal conditions. Such complexity and cultural variety is well represented in the chapters which follow. Moreover, a framewoιk is provided for understanding the dynamics of and processes underlying many other intergroup contact situations not examined here (e.g. inter-generational communication, inter-professional encounters).

We are not, of course, so blind as to believe that social psychology, let alone this series or this particular book, holds out a panacea for all societal ills; in this vein, we still embrace the healthy self-criticism of the 1970s. What we hope to do is to convince students, colleagues, other professionals and policy makers of the contribution to such social issues that can be made by a social-psychological approach.

Howard Giles and Miles Hewstone
May 1986

Preface

The focus of this book is the long-held view that *contact* between members of different groups will improve relations between them. This view goes back at least as far as Gordon Allport's classic book *The Nature of Prejudice* (1954) and is premised partly on the assumption that intergroup contact should increase the accuracy of intergroup images, if opportunities arise to perceive intergroup similarities. It has furthermore been the basis of many social policy decisions advocating (racial) integration in schools, housing and sport. Despite the seeming simplicity of this nostrum, it is susceptible to multiple interpretations. *Type* of contact may be between individuals or groups; between different or equal-status parties; in intimate or casual settings. Alternatively, contact may be seen as effective only in the context of other socio-structural changes that hit out against institutionalized discrimination.

Notwithstanding the high hopes held out for the 'contact hypothesis', the reported effects have been inconsistent. Many studies have failed to find reduction of prejudice or discrimination by interracial contact between individuals of equal social or occupational status; while others have yielded more positive findings. A persistent problem dogs all such studies – whether dealing with integrated schools, housing, sports, combat conditions, work experience or other settings – will the findings generalize? Racist norms in the wider society seem often to have prevailed, thus restricting positive outcomes to specific encounters between individuals. This point is vividly illustrated by one of the participants in a television programme (BBC 2 *Horizon, Are you a racist?*) that brought together four self-described racists and four black victims of racism. At one point a white woman states: 'I could never change, you know. I mean I talk to you and these [black people present], but when I go back, my attitude will still be the same.' It appears especially problematic to generalize from interpersonal situations to what people do when their group memberships become salient (especially when groups vary in terms of power, status, wealth, religion and so on). In these latter conditions behaviour may be altogether different, because feelings, thoughts and behaviour are determined by social group memberships, and not by interpersonal characteristics.

Given these problems, this book seeks to assess the contact hypothesis in situations of *intergroup* encounter. This approach provides a much sterner test of the hypothesis, but yields a more realistic picture of social-psychological contributions to the reduction of intergroup conflict. The book also pays close attention to the durability of reported positive effects, in a further attempt to ascertain the real strengths and shortcomings of research and policy in this mould. Short-term effects may be dramatic, but the real test remains whether harmony between groups endures in the future and outside the setting of the intervention.

A further dimension of this book is the widely ranging national backgrounds of the contributors and their topics. Evaluating the contact hypothesis in relation to such a diverse set of conflicts – including Catholics and Protestants in Northern Ireland, Jews and Arabs in Israel, blacks and whites in Britain and the United States – results in a more rigorous and eclectic assessment than heretofore. The aim here is to reflect the nature of intergroup relations in a variety of cultures whose distinct social fabrics will, of necessity, broaden the base of research and thinking on intergroup relations. We are therefore not so much interested in replication, and the comparison between different cultures, as in the factors associated with intergroup contact found in a variety of extremely different contexts. This cultural dimension underlines the need to discuss social-psychological factors (our domain of expertise) alongside other determinants. Realistic treatments of intergroup relations in a wide variety of cultures must inevitably consider economic, historical, religious, political and other dimensions of intergroup conflict.

Hostile intergroup relations represent one of the most challenging problems for contemporary society. This volume concentrates firmly on the reduction of intergroup conflict, but does not imply that all social conflicts are necessarily harmful. The focus on conflict reduction is, rather, a counterweight to the volume of work on the development and maintenance of conflict, and an acknowledgement of the fact that the contribution of social psychology will be judged by the acid test of applicability: can its theorizing contribute towards the reduction of socially divisive conflicts between certain groups in society? The answer presented in the following pages is both positive and cautious: intergroup contact can help to improve intergroup relations, but the traditional contact hypothesis is too narrow.

Miles Hewstone gratefully acknowledges the financial support of the Alexander von Humboldt-Stiftung, whose Fellowship allowed him to pursue research at the Universität Tübingen, including the first stages of this book. Another debt of gratitude is also due to Wolfgang Ströbe, host professor at the Psychologisches Institut, for his friendship and encouragement during two very happy years. The authors would also like to thank Bernd Simon for his careful work on the references and indexes.

M. H. and R. J. B

Contributors

Peter Allen, Social Psychology Research Unit, University of Kent, England.

Yehuda Amir, Department of Psychology, Bar-Ilan University, Israel.

Jeannette Bellerose, Department of Psychology, McGill University, Canada.

Rachel Ben-Ari, Department of Psychology, Bar-Ilan University, Israel.

Rupert Brown, Social Psychology Research Unit, University of Kent, England.

Lise Dubé, Department of Psychology, McGill University, Canada.

Gillian Finchilescu, Department of Psychology, University of Natal, Republic of South Africa.

Don Foster, Department of Psychology, University of Cape Town, Republic of South Africa.

Miles Hewstone, Department of Psychology, University of Bristol, England.

Uwe Machleit, Psychologisches Institut, Ruhr-Universität, West Germany.

Thomas F. Pettigrew, Adlai E. Stevenson College, University of California, USA.

Stephen Reicher, Department of Psychology, University of Exeter, England.

Janet Ward Schofield, Learning Research and Development Center, University of Pittsburgh, USA.

Donald M. Taylor, Department of Psychology, McGill University, Canada.

Karen Trew, Department of Psychology, The Queen's University of Belfast, Northern Ireland.

Uli Wagner, Psychologisches Institut, Ruhr-Universität, West Germany.

1 Contact is not Enough: An Intergroup Perspective on the 'Contact Hypothesis'

Miles Hewstone and Rupert Brown

> When Darwin went ashore with the sailors they clustered round him, patting his face and his body with great curiosity, and they were extraordinarily good mimics; every gesture he made and every word he uttered was perfectly imitated. When he made faces at them they grinned and made faces back at him . . .
>
> Alan Moorehead, *Darwin and the Beagle* (1969)

PRELIMINARY CONSIDERATIONS

Darwin's first encounter with the natives of Tierra del Fuego was, sadly, distinctly atypical. Contact between members of different groups – whether 'racial', ethnic or other – has long been a focus of social-scientific research (e.g. Brown, 1934; Frazier, 1957; Lieberson, 1961; Park, 1950; Price, 1950), but frequently more negative outcomes have been reported. As Blalock wrote about 'frontier-contact situations':

It has been almost universally true that white contacts with simple hunting and gathering bands or with cultures at the hoe-agriculture level of development have resulted in either the annihilation or expulsion of the tribe in question or its complete disappearance through assimilation into the dominant culture. (Blalock, 1967, p. 76)

Such outcomes transpire, at least partly, because one group is typically in a superior position economically, politically or militarily and thus able to force the other group into a subordinate position (see Rothstein, 1972).

Our aim in this book is to examine intergroup encounters from a social-psychological perspective. In particular, we are concerned with the 'contact hypothesis' – the long and widely held belief that interaction between individuals belonging to different groups will reduce ethnic prejudice and intergroup tension. It is our belief that a properly social-psychological approach has much to contribute to these issues, particularly in elucidating the individual and social processes implicated in contact experiences. At the same time, in taking this rather narrow perspective we would also emphasize that it is but one of a number of valid approaches to the study of intergroup contact. Clearly, most social conflicts have their origins deep in historical, political and economic divisions in the society in which they occur, and it would be foolish to pretend that in this area social psychology by itself had any exclusive rights to wisdom. Indeed, with Billig (1976), we would argue that to place psychology too much in the 'driving seat' – as it were – is to run a serious risk of trivializing our analyses of, and prescriptions for, particular social problems. It is for this reason that all the contributors to this book have been asked to set their arguments against the wider social background of the phenomena they are considering.

In chapter 1 we examine the 'contact hypothesis' in some detail. We begin by outlining three classic positions on the role of contact. This leads us into a preliminary assessment of the hypothesis in the light of three decades of empirical research. From that review we identify five major limitations of traditional theorizing in this area. The most central of these from our perspective is a complete neglect of the important distinction between interpersonal and intergroup contact. Once that distinction is accepted it is possible to suggest a number of methods by which the effects of contact may be augmented. This we do on pages 22–28. Then on pages 28–32 we analyse the origins and effects of some cognitive processes which are at work in intergroup encounters. Finally, we develop a new conceptual framework for analysing contact situations from which we derive some policy implications.

CLASSIC STATEMENTS OF THE CONTACT HYPOTHESIS

Allport

In its earliest form the contact hypothesis posited simply that association with persons from a disliked group leads to the growth of liking and respect for that group (Cook, 1978). But even Allport (1954/1979)[1] in his classic statement acknowledged that 'the case is not so simple' (p. 261)[2] and he accepted that contact could increase, as well as decrease, prejudice. Allport emphasized the 'nature of contact' and saw that its effect would depend on the kinds of people and situations involved. Perhaps his greatest contribution at this early stage was the provision of a taxonomy of relevant factors which, today, over 30 years later, is just as striking and useful as it was then (Allport, 1954/1979, pp. 262–3).

Kinds of Contact

Quantitative aspects of contact:

(a) Frequency
(b) Duration
(c) Number of persons involved
(d) Variety

Status aspects of contact:

(a) Minority member has inferior status
(b) Minority member has equal status
(c) Minority member has superior status
(d) Not only may the individuals encountered vary thus in status; but the group as a whole may have relatively high status (e.g., Jews) or relatively low status (e.g., Negroes).[3]

Role aspects of contact:

(a) Is the relationship one of competitive or cooperative activity?
(b) Is there a superordinate or subordinate role relation involved; e.g., master-servant, employer-employee, teacher-pupil?

Social atmosphere surrounding the contact:

(a) Is segregation prevalent, or is egalitarianism expected?
(b) Is the contact voluntary or involuntary?
(c) Is the contact 'real' or 'artificial'?
(d) Is the contact perceived in terms of intergroup relations or not perceived as such?
(e) Is the contact regarded as 'typical' or as 'exceptional'?
(f) Is the contact regarded as important and intimate, or as trivial and transient?

Personality of the individual experiencing the contact:

(a) Is his initial prejudice level high, low, medium?
(b) Is his prejudice of a surface, conforming type, or is it deeply rooted in his character structure?
(c) Has he basic security in his own life, or is he fearful and suspicious?
(d) What is his previous experience with the group in question, and what is the strength of his present stereotypes?
(e) What are his age and general education level?
(f) Many other personality factors may influence the effect of contact.

Areas of contact:

(a) Casual
(b) Residential
(c) Occupational
(d) Recreational
(e) Religious
(f) Civic and fraternal

(g) Political
(h) Goodwill intergroup activities

We shall, below, follow up the implications of several points raised by Allport. It is worth emphasizing here however, given our intergroup perspective, Allport's points (d) and (e) under the heading 'Social atmosphere surrounding the contact': 'Is the contact perceived in terms of intergroup relations or not perceived as such?' 'Is the contact regarded as "typical" or as "exceptional"?' As we shall attempt to show, these issues are central to a proper understanding of situations of intergroup contact.

On the basis of this taxonomy Allport grouped together studies done in a wide variety of settings and was able to summarize the effects of particular types of contact; he concluded that the outcome of contact would be favourable when participants were of equal status, pursuing common goals and backed by social and institutional support (Allport, 1979, p. 281).

Cook

Cook has dedicated his working life to the elaboration and testing of the contact hypothesis in an impressive number of laboratory and field studies (see Cook, 1978, 1984 for reviews). Having earlier acknowledged the complexity of variables in studies of the contact hypothesis (Cook and Selltiz, 1955), Cook was one of the first to move towards the much more specific and more fruitful question: 'In what types of contact situations, with what kinds of representatives of the disliked group, will interaction and attitude change of specific types occur – and how will this vary for subjects of differing characteristics?' (Cook, 1962, p. 76). Cook (1978, p. 97) predicts that less derogatory outgroup attitudes will result when individuals have personal contact with members of a group they dislike, but under the following five conditions:

1 Participants from the two groups have equal status within the confines of the contact situation.
2 The characteristics of outgroup members with whom contact takes place disconfirm the prevailing outgroup stereotype.
3 The contact situation encourages, or perhaps necessarily requires, co-operation in the achievement of a joint goal.
4 The contact situation has high 'acquaintance potential' (i.e. it enables individuals to get to know each other as individuals, rather than as stereotypical outgroup members).

5 The social norms within and surrounding the contact situation favour 'group equality' and 'equalitarian intergroup association'.

After contact under these conditions, individuals did tend to report more favourable evaluations of the individual outgroup members they had come to know. The rationale Cook developed for the above criteria is derived from a theory of interpersonal attraction: contact between members of different groups allows individuals to discover that they have, after all, many similar values and attitudes. This discovery, according to theories of interpersonal attraction (e.g. Byrne, 1969), will lead to mutual understanding and liking and will eventually – given time, repeated experiences of contact and the above favourable conditions – neutralize the negative relationship that formerly existed between the two groups.

Unfortunately, as Cook recognizes, the persistent problem with such studies is that of generalization. Notwithstanding his optimism about the change in attitudes towards specific individuals, Cook does not deny that there is little or no change in attitudes towards outgroups in general. This is a point we return to on pages 16–20, with the claim that an intergroup approach to contact could help to overcome this problem.

Pettigrew

The characteristics of the contact situation to which Pettigrew attaches most importance are based on Allport's (1954) work. Thus, the interacting individuals should be of equal status and be co-operatively interdependent with one another in the pursuit of common goals. They should also enjoy the positive support of authorities, laws or customs (Pettigrew, 1971, p. 275). Pettigrew seems primarily concerned that too much contact is with low-status minority group members and it is contact with high-status individuals from the outgroup that will have the greatest impact on attitudes. Thus he cites the study by Mackenzie (1948), comparing the attitudes of white war veterans who had contact with 'Negroes' of either lower, equal or higher occupational status than themselves. Results showed reduction of prejudice only when contact had been with 'Negroes' of equal or higher status.

Despite Pettigrew's concern, there seem to be two main problems here. First, the above-mentioned problem of generalization, that is that such contact will, in most cases, have implications only for attitudes towards high-status outgroup members (and not blacks in general). Second, the introduction of successful, qualified outgroup members can sometimes backfire. The real bigot may be enraged at educated blacks in their large houses, or new cars; or, as Pettigrew's (1979) more recent work on intergroup attribution has shown, the success of such 'token' blacks is seen as further proof that blacks in general are *not* oppressed or discriminated against, but are just 'too lazy'.

Pettigrew basically supports the extrapolation of interpersonal attraction theory (as seen above in the work of Cook). The positive influence of contact is interpreted in the light of Newcomb's (1956, 1961) work. Contact leads to the perception of increased similarity of attitudes, which in turn leads to an increase in positive attraction. Referring to the work of Newcomb, and of Rokeach (1960), Pettigrew argued that Allport's four conditions reduce prejudice because they maximize the probability that shared values and beliefs will be demonstrated and perceived and will therefore provide the basis for interpersonal attraction between ingroup and outgroup members. The interpersonal basis of the Cook–Pettigrew version of the contact hypothesis is thus explicit.

ASSESSMENTS OF THE CONTACT HYPOTHESIS

Research based on the contact hypothesis has yielded an impressive, if sometimes bewildering, array of data derived from a wide range of social situations. There have been studies in the armed services (e.g. Landis, Hope and Day, 1984; Roberts, 1953; Stouffer et al., 1949), in educational settings (e.g. Johnson, Johnson and Maruyama, 1984; Schwarzwald and Amir, 1984), in the workplace (e.g. Harding and Hogrefe, 1952; Minard, 1952) and in places of residence (e.g. Deutsch and Collins, 1951; Jahoda and West, 1951; Wilner, Walkley and Cook, 1952). Perhaps because of this diversity of settings, and the predominance of field – rather than laboratory – studies, the reported effects of contact have been inconsistent. Positive results (reduction of prejudice) have been found in some studies, while negative results (increased prejudice for members of the majority group and an increased sense of isolation and decreased self-esteem for members of the minority group) have emerged from others (see reviews by Amir, 1976, 1969; Harding et al., 1969; Katz, 1970; McClendon, 1974; Riordan, 1978; Simpson and Yinger, 1972). This inconsistency has made clear the need to know what conditions are necessary for intergroup contact to produce positive results and it has led to more careful analyses of the relevant *dimensions*, as well as *domains*, of contact.

The most comprehensive reviews of the contact literature are those of Amir (1969, 1976). Because some of these points are (at our request) reiterated by Ben-Ari and Amir in chapter 2, it suffices here to dwell on a few major points. Amir focused his reviews on a number of specific dimensions of the contact situation and systematized the available evidence on: the principle of equal status; contact with high-status representatives of a minority group; co-operative and competitive factors; casual versus intimate contact; institutional support; personality factors; the direction and intensity of initial attitude. The crux of Amir's (1969, pp. 338–9) painstaking assessment can be seen in his summary of some of the favourable conditions that tend to reduce prejudice (1969, p. 338), and some of the unfavourable conditions that tend to strengthen prejudice (1969, pp. 338–9).[4] The favourable conditions were:

(a) When there is equal status contact between members of various ethnic groups.
(b) When the contact is between members of a majority and *higher* status members of a minority group.
(c) When an 'authority' and/or the social climate are in favor of and promote the intergroup contact.
(d) When the contact is of an intimate rather than a casual nature.
(e) When the ethnic intergroup contact is pleasant or rewarding.
(f) When the members of *both* groups in the particular contact situation interact in functionally important activities or develop common goals or superordinate goals that are higher ranking in importance than the individual goals of *each* of the groups.

The unfavourable conditions were:

(a) When the contact situation produces competition between the groups.
(b) When the contact is unpleasant, involuntary, tension laden.
(c) When the prestige or status of one group is lowered as a result of the contact situation.
(d) When members of a group or the group as a whole are in a state of frustration . . . .
(e) When the groups in contact have moral or ethnic standards which are objectionable to each other.
(f) In the case of contact between a majority and a minority group, when the members of the minority group are of lower status or are lower in any relevant characteristic than the members of the majority group.

Despite the clarity of Amir's review, which was influential in directing the thrust of later research, a number of scholars have commented on the difficulty of attributing the outcome of contact unambiguously and confidently to discrete aspects of contact alone (see Cook, 1978). Illustrative of this problem is the debate on the role of equal status between interacting individuals.

The paramount distinction here is between equal status *within* and *beyond* the specific contact situation (see Amir, 1969; McClendon, 1974) and there is still some debate about which type of equal status is more important. One view (held by Allport, 1954; Kramer, 1950; and Pettigrew, 1971) emphasizes equal status within the contact situation. According to McClendon, this variable is important, because it increases the probability that common beliefs will be perceived. Its manipulation certainly makes research more practicable, but its use makes generalization beyond the specific situation more problematic. Furthermore, Riordan (1978) contends that equal status (interracial) contact, although a valued ideal, is non-existent in a racist society and quite difficult, if not impossible, to implement. In other words, intergroup disparities outside the experimental context may be so vast and divisive as to rule out the manipulation of equal status within this setting (see pages 20–22 and 27–28 below). As the opponents of sporting contact in South Africa insist, 'No equal sport in an unequal society' (see chapter 7).

There would seem to be merit in both interpretations of equal status and, as Riordan (1978) writes, they are not mutually exclusive, but rather interrelated and overlapping. However, both views should be made explicit and an integration sought; too often research has tended to reify its manipulation of intra-situational variables while underplaying, or seemingly ignoring, the real differences of status between groups whose interrelations are sufficiently conflictual to require contact.

In addition to the problem of attributing effects to discrete aspects of contact, there is sometimes a very real problem of concluding whether contact has had any effect at all. Hamilton and Bishop (1976) studied the response of white suburban home-owners to the initial 'integration' of their previously all-white neighbourhood by *one* black family. At the outset these authors accepted that contact between residents in a suburban neighbourhood was frequently of a superficial nature and their supposition was proved correct. Although the salience of a new black family was high after three months, only 11 per cent of the white respondents knew the last name of their black neighbours (the figure was 60 per cent for new white neighbours). As Hamilton and Bishop wrote: 'This pattern of results suggests that when a black family moves into a previously all white neighbourhood, the residents are less concerned about who they are than about what they're like' (p. 60). Despite this pessimistic finding, one year after the black family had moved in interviewees who lived near them had significantly less racist attitudes. While this looks, at first glance, like support for the contact hypothesis, Hamilton and Bishop rule out such an explanation for two reasons. First, the frequency of self-reported interaction with the new black neighbours was so low that it could not seriously be proposed as a mediating variable. Second, after one year, residents in the integrated neighbour-hoods had less racist attitudes *irrespective of whether they had, or had not, interacted with their black neighbours*. Living in an integrated setting was apparently the crucial variable, rather than interpersonal contact with black individuals.

Hamilton and Bishop's study underlines the importance of cautious interpretation of data in this field; it also touches on an important theme picked up in several chapters of this book (see chapters 3, 4, 6 and 7): interaction within the same ethnic group is more frequent than cross-ethnic interaction (see also Gerard, Jackson and Connolley, 1975; Johnson et al., 1984; Shaw, 1973). Indeed, as Taylor et al. argue in chapter 6, it seems that intergroup contact is often *avoided* (see also Bradburn, Sudman and Gockel, 1971; Cagle, 1973; Jakobsen, 1977). This absence of contact is all the more remarkable when there does seem to be institutional support for integration, as in the study reported by Rogers et al. (1984); despite parental support for school desegregation, black and white schoolchildren 'resegregated' themselves by ethnic group during their classroom and school-break activities. This group patterning of social interaction is discussed in some detail by Schofield in chapter 4. The basis of such avoidance is an interesting issue in itself (e.g. expectations of intergroup differences in roles and norms; see Landis et al., 1984), but its mere existence is a reminder of how the odds seem sometimes stacked against any simple interpretation of the contact hypothesis.

MAJOR LIMITATIONS OF RESEARCH ON THE CONTACT HYPOTHESIS

Thus far we have considered some of the points emerging from critical assessment of the contact hypothesis. This section is devoted to a more detailed exposition of what we regard as the five fundamental limitations of research to date. In some cases we have merely tried to build on the pioneering work of Allport (1954); to acknowledge this fact, relevant quotations have been used to illustrate each point.

The role of ignorance and misperceptions of dissimilarity

The contact hypothesis seems to assume that much prejudice is caused by ignorance about the outgroup. Indeed, Stephan and Stephan (1984) dedicate their chapter to the resurrection of the hypothesis that ignorance causes prejudice, a view that was emphasized in classic contributions by Myrdal (1944) and Williams (1947). Yet, reviewing early work on the relationship between ignorance and prejudice, Stephan and Stephan can report only moderate correlations between knowledge of a different group and attitudes towards that group. This question of intergroup knowledge is discussed by Allen in chapter 8 of this book, where he examines the different correlates of 'accurate' or 'erroneous' attitude-attributions in the context of industrial conflict.

It is because ignorance has been held to be so important that many studies have examined the efficacy of propaganda in improving intergroup relations. The central issue, according to Stephan and Stephan, has been the extent to which programmes for improving intergroup relations should focus on group similarities or differences. While some work has emphasized group differences, this is in contrast to multi-cultural curricula that tend to deny that group differences exist. As Stephan and Stephan point out, the major problem for the former lies in presenting differences in a non-evaluative way. There is a very real danger that *any* group differences will be interpreted as implying that one group is inferior to another (see work on the evaluative connotations of descriptive language; e.g. LeVine and Campbell, 1972; Peabody, 1970). This risk must be weighed against the view that it is better to explain and acknowledge differences than to ignore them.

Researchers see advantages and disadvantages in the decision to stress similarities or differences between groups. On the one hand, Stephan and Stephan argue that an emphasis on similarities is reasonable (given that black and white people for example do share a number of basic values; see Triandis, 1972) and that this focus may capitalize on the tendency for perceived similarity to be associated with liking for others who are similar (Byrne, 1969). On the other hand, it would surely be both naïve and wrong to teach people that others are similar in all respects and to gloss over fundamental differences. This will only lead to a shocking disconfirmation of expectations when differences do occur (as for example when Muslim schoolgirls in the UK appear for gym lessons wearing long trousers, while everyone else is wearing shorts). These issues are explored further in several chapters of this book. Schofield discusses the relative merits of a 'colour-blind' policy in education as compared to a multicultural policy which makes group differences explicit; Trew also touches on the same theme in the context of Northern Ireland; Allen warns of the danger of overindulgent misperceptions in industrial relations.

Furthermore, one of the assumed consequences of contact – i.e. the discovery of similarity between groups – is sometimes rather unlikely to occur. For the groups concerned may often, in reality, turn out to have rather *dissimilar* values and attitudes (see Ashmore, 1970). According to Harding et al. (1969), it is reasonable to believe that frequently contacts with members of other groups increase the salience of attitudes towards those groups. Thus, as Salamone and Swanson (1979) maintain, 'It is from contact with other groups that groups find the need to reaffirm or redefine themselves' (p. 169). For example, Jaspars and Warnaeon's (1982) study of intergroup relations in Indonesia found that ingroup favouritism and outgroup discrimination were both more marked when different ethnic groups lived alongside each other in the capital, Jakarta, than when they lived separately on outlying islands. This *dis*similarity is particularly likely to become obvious when groups are characterized by what Brewer and Campbell (1976) call 'convergent boundaries' (i.e. where group identities are reinforced by the coincidence of many different distinctions, such as religious, economic and political factors; indeed, this book is full of examples of such groups). Contact in cases such as these is likely to reveal these differences and hence, according to the causal process alleged to underlie the contact hypothesis (i.e. similarity-attraction), should result in *less*, not more, intergroup liking.

We would agree with Stephan and Stephan's conclusion (based on a review of cross-cultural studies) that knowledge and understanding of differences *as well as* similarities between groups is important in reducing prejudice. Information about real differences should respect the customs and traditions of other groups and should be supported by information which explodes myths about false differences.[5] Notwithstanding this view of the content of educational programmes, we still wish to de-emphasize the importance of knowledge. Although Stephan and Stephan present a path-analytic model that *does* include a direct path between knowledge of outgroup culture and attitude towards the outgroup (for Anglo-American students' ratings of 'Chicanos' in the US) there is now ample evidence to show that intergroup discrimination and hostility are often caused by factors *other* than mere lack of knowledge or inaccurate perceptions. Thus, as Sherif's (1966) work shows, objective conflicts of interest between groups are a potent source of mutual derogation. Alternatively, the mere fact of categorization may be sufficient to trigger discrimination, as Tajfel and his colleagues have shown (Tajfel et al., 1971). Or again, factors which affect the identity of group members –

whether through altering the stability or legitimacy of status relations, the minority status of the ingroup or power relations – have all been shown to be influential in changing intergroup attitudes (see Tajfel, 1978, 1982a). All these factors, rooted as several of them are in objective features of the environment, are unlikely to be affected by mere contact between groups, even under the ideal conditions listed earlier. Thus, expectations for the effects of increasing knowledge through contact should, we argue, be more modest.

The direction of causality

It is true that the *causal* factor in studies of this type is not entirely clear. (Allport, 1954, p. 267)

In evaluating the contact hypothesis reviewers have noted that many studies have methodological inadequacies that make it difficult to determine what variables mediated any observed differences in attitudes. The central problem is that it is generally unclear from the data whether the favourable attitude or the contact came first. The studies are *ex post facto* in nature, or 'after only', involving attitude measures taken at only one point in time and with contact already under way. Thus there is reliance on retrospective reports of contact experiences (in this respect, some of the research reported by Taylor et al. in chapter 6 can also be criticized) and the possibility of subject-selection biases. For example, one explanation of Brophy's (1946) study on merchant seamen is that the people who were least prejudiced to begin with may have *sought out* interracial contact on board ship (Pettigrew, 1971). Thus there may have been 'selective entry'. Alternatively, or additionally, there may have been 'selective withdrawal' of highly prejudiced subjects (see Cook, 1978, 1984; and the earlier discussion of contact *avoidance*). As Amir (1969) reports, the early work of Williams (1964) seemed to show that 'the more prejudiced a person is and the more vulnerable his personality make-up, the less likely he is to have inter-ethnic contacts' (Amir, 1969, p. 323).

The issue of causal direction is well discussed by Wagner and Machleit (chapter 3) and they demonstrate exemplary caution in the interpretation of results. Stephan and Rosenfield (1978), using a cross-lagged correlational design, found that contact prior to school desegregation was related to attitude measures after desegregation, but that pre-segregation attitudes were *not* correlated with post-segregation contact. These findings indicate that the stronger direction of causality is *from* contact *to* attitudes, as the contact hypothesis predicts. However, such pre- and post-measures should be correlated in other settings before confident conclusions are made. For the time being it seems safer to assume a dynamic relationship, or mutual causality, and to interpret results in this light.

Interpersonal or intergroup contact?

Is the contact perceived in terms of intergroup relations or not perceived as such? (Allport, 1954, p. 263)

This is, we argue, an issue of fundamental importance and one that has been omitted, overlooked or blurred in previous research on contact. Consider Miller and Brewer (1984). In a foreword Hoffman (1984) refers to the contact hypothesis in its simplest form as the idea that 'attitudes toward a disliked *social group will become more positive with increased interpersonal* interaction' (p. xiii, emphases added). In apparent contradiction, the editors themselves describe, in their preface, the contact hypothesis as the idea 'that prejudice and hostility between *members of segregated groups* can be reduced by promoting the frequency and intensity of *intergroup* contact' (p. xv, emphases added). However, a few pages later, the same authors summarize the contact hypothesis as the idea that 'one's behaviour and attitudes towards *members of a disliked social category* will become more positive after direct *interpersonal* interaction with them' (p. 2). This looseness of terminology is at best careless, and at worst confusing for any reader trying to decide how best to implement a programme of intergroup contact. Such laxity also glosses over the theoretically important distinction between 'interpersonal' and 'intergroup' behaviour.

The polarities of interpersonal and intergroup behaviour have their origin in the work of Tajfel (e.g. 1978). He suggested that interpersonal and intergroup behaviour could be distinguished by three criteria. First, the presence or absence of at least two clearly identifiable social categories, for example black and white, Catholic or Protestant. Second, whether there is low or high *inter*subject variability of behaviour or attitude within each group (intergroup behaviour is typically homogeneous or uniform, while interpersonal behaviour shows the normal range of individual differences). Third, whether there is low or high *intra*subject variability in relation to other group members (does the same person react similarly to a wide range of different others – as in the case of stereotyping – or does he or she show a differentiated response to them?). Thus, in summary, as Sherif (1966a) observed, intergroup behaviour occurs 'whenever individuals belonging to one group interact, collectively or individually, with another group or its members *in terms of* *their* group identification' (p. 12). Interpersonal behaviour, by contrast, is where the interaction is determined by the individual characteristics and personal relationships between participants (Tajfel, 1978b; Brown and Turner, 1981). This distinction is nicely caught by Harris's (in press) anthropological study of 'Ballybeg' in Northern Ireland. She comments on a switch from a view of each neighbour as an individual with a mixture of traits to a categorical view of 'our fellows' and 'their fellows' (see chapter 5). In the first case the people's religious category memberships seem rather insignificant; in the second they have become overwhelmingly important.

What are the psychological components of intergroup behaviour? Turner (1982) has proposed that underlying the shift from interpersonal to intergroup behaviour is a transition from personal to social identity. Personal identity, in his view, refers to self-definitions in terms of personal or idiosyncratic characteristics, while social identity denotes definitions in terms of category memberships. Along with these self-definitions, according to Turner, go self-assignments of the common or critical attributes of these group memberships. So not only do individuals see outgroup members in stereotyped ways, they also see *themselves* as relatively interchangeable with ingroup members.[6] Thus, intergroup behaviour is more uniform both within the group and towards outgroups because individuals develop their attitudes and actions on the basis of those common group attributes. It should be clear therefore that it is not simply a matter of numbers of people that distinguishes the two kinds of behaviour. Both interpersonal and intergroup behaviour are the actions of individuals, but in one case they are the actions of individuals *qua* individuals, while in the other they are actions of individuals *qua* group members.

It is unnecessary to review the empirical evidence that supports this distinction; suffice it to say that there is a growing body of research that suggests that people's behaviour is indeed qualitatively different in group settings (see Brown and Turner, 1981; Wilder, 1984; but cf. Reid and Sumiga, 1984 for some contrary evidence). Perhaps more relevant are the theoretical implications that follow from an acceptance of the distinction. The first is that theories that attempt to explain intergroup phenomena by reference to interpersonal relations – for example similarities of attitudes – are unlikely to be very predictive because they cannot cater for the widespread uniformity that is characteristic of those phenomena. One Catholic may taunt a Protestant or several Protestants in ignorance of, or in spite of, many personal attributes that they may or may not have in common. Where more than one Catholic is involved, the multiplicity and complexity of interpersonal relations may be enormous and yet the behaviour is often quite uniform. The conclusion therefore is that we need different kinds of theories to make sense of that uniformity.

Consider again Turner's proposed demarcation between personal and social identity. The key feature of the latter, he argues, is its self-stereotypic nature – a depersonalization of the individual in the group. Once this starts to happen, it follows that what affects the group as a whole has implications for the individual and his or her behaviour. Thus, what are likely to affect intergroup behaviour are not inter*personal* relations, but inter*group* relations of status, power, material interdependence and so on (variables that characterize the situations described in all the following chapters). On this account theories of intergroup behaviour must formulate independent variables concerning people's social relations as group members, and not as individual persons (see e.g. Sherif's, 1966a, realistic conflict theory with its emphasis on functional or goal relations between groups; and Tajfel's, 1978a, social identity theory with its stress on intergroup comparisons and pressures towards group distinctiveness).

We see the distinction between interpersonal and intergroup behaviour as fundamental to intergroup relations in general, and the contact hypothesis in particular. In addition to the reasons cited above, this distinction seems to interact with many of the other relevant variables. Consider for example some specific differences with regard to the effects of similarity in interpersonal and intergroup domains (see Brown and Turner, 1981). While similarity may have attractive or convergent properties in the former domain (e.g. Byrne, 1971), once one moves to the intergroup level the picture is more complex. For instance, it appears that groups that converge too far towards similarity may precipitate intergroup discrimination when their distinctiveness is threatened (Lemaine, Kastersztein and Personnaz, 1978). This is likely to be the case particularly when the situation is competitive and/or the dimensions of intergroup comparison are evaluative (e.g. Brown and Abrams, 1986; Mummendey and Schreiber, 1984; Turner, 1978). On the other hand in more co-operative contexts and on more affective dimensions it does appear that intergroup similarity results in enhanced attraction towards the outgroup (Brown, 1984; Brown and Abrams, 1986). Amir (1976) has also warned that, paradoxically, equal-status contact may itself be the basis for intergroup threat and may thus produce negative attitudinal change. This could occur when a higher-status ethnic group is threatened by the social advances made by a previously lower-status group (see Ghosh and Huq, 1985).

· These considerations raise the question of whether an inappropriate methodology has so far been used to assess an improvement in relations after contact. Whitley, Schofield and Snyder (1984) argue that the hypothesized process of individuation through contact operates within individuals and is the result of dyadic relationships between individuals. One should therefore select a statistical technique that focuses on the relationships between individuals, rather than on the number of responses divided by the number of respondents. Such an analysis may reveal little change in preference for classmates of a different ethnic group, but an increase in liking for specific individuals based on the quality of interpersonal relationships with those individuals (Whitley et al., 1984).

Notwithstanding such statistical refinements, and a not insignificant improvement in some interpersonal relationships, we believe the interpersonal-intergroup distinction has one other major implication for research on the contact hypothesis. Unless the contact can be characterized as intergroup (i.e. between individuals as group representatives or *qua* group members), any such positive outcomes will be primarily cosmetic, in the sense that they will leave divisive and conflictual intergroup relations unchanged. This assertion leads us to a discussion of the key concept, generalization.

Generalization of attitude change

People may come to take for granted the particular situation in which the contact occurs but fail completely to generalize this experience. (Allport, 1979, p. 276)

The problem of generalization is one that has dogged research in this area (see Amir, 1969; Katz, 1970; McClendon, 1974; Pettigrew, 1971, chapter 6). First, attitude change is often limited to the specific situation which produced it. For example, in Harding and Hogrefe's (1952) study of department store employees in the US, equal-status work contact was found to increase whites' willingness to work with blacks, but did not produce any change in willingness to engage in other types of association (e.g. eating at the same table in a cafeteria). In another early study Minard (1952) described a mining community in West Virginia. Underground in the mine, black and white miners worked harmoniously in mixed teams, with white miners sometimes even working under black supervisors. Above ground however the two groups went their separate ways with segregated restaurants, neighbourhoods and so on. Clearly, in these cases, non-intimate contact at work (even if for eight hours a day) did not generalize beyond the specific setting (see also Palmore, 1955; Reed, 1947; Saenger and Gilbert, 1950). Part of the explanation for this lack of generalizability beyond specific situations has to do with the different kinds of social and institutional support for desegregation available in the different settings (Allport, 1954). In the workplace, the way the work is organized or the existence of trade unions cutting across ethnic divisions may help to redefine the intergroup relationship between blacks and whites. The result is a reduction of discrimination, not just in one or two individuals, but generalized across the whole group. Remove these source of influence and the intergroup relationship reverts to the original conflictual definition deriving from a different set of authorities. Viewing contact in terms of intergroup relations in this way thus allows the possibility of more widespread change – or resistance to change – than is conceivable from just focusing on the multiplicity of interpersonal relations.

A second key issue for contact researchers has also been how far the positive attitudes promoted by the contact experience will generalize to include other members of the outgroup not actually present in the contact situation. The consensus from a number of studies seems to be rather pessimistic on this point (see Amir, 1976). To take one instance, as noted earlier Cook's programme of research on interracial contact found consistent evidence of positive attitude change towards outgroup *participants*, but little sign of attitude change towards the outgroup as a whole (Cook, 1978).

Not all studies have reported this failure to generalize, whether across situations or across individuals. Consider some of the optimistic results of studies on bi-racial housing projects in the US (e.g. Deutsch and Collins, 1951). Housewives in two types of housing project were interviewed: 'building integrated' and 'area segregated'. It was found that almost half of the women in the integrated projects (but hardly any in the segregated projects) reported some type of regular intimate contact with Negro neighbours and a fairly close relationship with at least one Negro resident. Respondents in the integrated projects had more favourable attitudes towards all Negroes in the project *and* towards Negroes 'in general' (see also Brophy, 1946; Stouffer et al., 1949a and b; Wilner et al., 1952). What is therefore needed for contact experiences to generalize? According to Cook:

attitude change will result from cooperative interracial contact only when such contact is accompanied by a supplementary influence that promotes the process of generalization from favourable contact with individuals to positive attitudes toward the group (from which the individual comes). (Cook, 1978, p. 103)

In Cook's study the supplementary influence was to bolster pleasant experiences with black individuals by means of information relating explicit peer-group norms supporting equal-status race relations. A well-liked black co-worker's accounts of discrimination were immediately followed by another member of the ingroup who advocated desegregation and racial equality. According to Cook, this peer-group support served as a 'cognitive booster' for generalization to ethnic attitudes at the intergroup level. Interestingly, Stephan and Stephan (1984) also ascribe high value to peer-group (rather than parental) attitudes, and report a high positive correlation between outgroup contact and friends' positive attitudes towards the outgroup.

Obviously, the failure to generalize positive attitudes to outgroup members in general is a critical weakness in traditional contact theory, and we propose that the present intergroup approach can provide some pointers as to how generalization might be achieved. Recall our above criticism, that interpersonal interaction and attraction could tell us little about intergroup attitudes. It follows that if the interaction takes place on an inter*group* basis, and also if some of the various qualifying conditions for successful contact are present, then there *is* a chance that any positive attitudes so engendered will be seen as applying not just to those present, but to others in the same category.[7] To be successful in changing the evaluation of an outgroup, favourable contact with an outgroup member *must* be defined as an inter*group* encounter. A weak association between the contact-partner and the outgroup (i.e. if the target is an *a*typical outgroup member) will define the contact situation as an interpersonal, rather than an intergroup, encounter. This view is based on fundamental principles of psychology, i.e. that generalization is a function of stimulus-similarity (Kimble, 1961). Thus, the more cues that indicate the group membership of a target, the greater should be the generalization (Ashmore, 1970). Somewhat paradoxically, this means making the group affiliations *more* salient and not less and ensuring that in some way the participants in the contact encounters see each other as representatives of their groups and not merely as 'exceptions to the rule' (Pettigrew, 1979b).

Although this idea may seem counter-intuitive, there is some evidence to support it. The most relevant is an experiment by Wilder (1984) in which the prototypicality of the outgroup member in the contact situation was systematically varied. In one set of conditions the outgroup member, who in this case belonged to a rival college, was made to fit some of the subjects' stereotypes of that college. In another set of conditions, the same person appeared to be rather atypical of the outgroup in question. The nature of the contact was also varied in line with traditional theorizing on contact. Thus, the contact person behaved either in a pleasant and supportive way towards the real participants or in a less pleasant and more critical fashion. The interaction took place over a co-operative task. Wilder predicted that only in the combined conditions where the interaction was pleasant *and* the partner could be seen as typical of her college would ratings of the outgroup college become more favourable. Where the interaction was unpleasant or the partner atypical, then either there would be no positive change or there would be no basis on which to extend the attitude change from that particular individual to her colleagues at the college. Wilder's results were exactly in line with his prediction. Only one condition showed a significant improvement in the evaluation of the outgroup as a whole: the pleasant encounter with the typical outgrouper.

Further supportive evidence for the importance of prototypicality has come from a study of stereotype change by Weber and Crocker (1983). They proposed that individuals resist information contrary to their stereotypes by 'sub-typing' the discrepant information. Thus 'exceptions' to stereotypes are classified as a subset of the outgroup and, by implication, are seen as unrepresentative of the outgroup as a whole. Weber and Crocker (1983) found that people's stereotypes about certain occupational groups changed most when they were presented with counter-stereotypic information about *representative* members of those groups. The same information, when associated with *a*typical members of the category in question, had much less effect in modifying attitudes.[8]

Summarizing the issue of generalization, it seems that as long as individuals are interacting *as* individuals, rather than as group members, there is no basis *either* for expecting any attitude change to be generalized throughout the group *or* for one person to extrapolate the positive attitudes towards one individual to other outgroup members (see Schwarzwald, Cohen and Hoffman, 1985). All we can expect, if the contact remains on an interpersonal basis, is that a few personal relationships will change but the intergroup situation will remain unaltered. There is also something of a paradox in this, in that intimate interpersonal relationships will usually involve a wider range of settings (hence generalization across situations), but will tie responses to a particular outgroup member (hence generalization across persons will be rendered unlikely). Yet, Rose (1981) argues that because an intimate relationship offers the possibility of multiple disconfirmations of the stereotype from the behaviour of only one outgroup member, such intimate relationships may be more effective in changing the stereotype (see Gurwitz and Dodge, 1977). Allport (1954) was well aware of what happens when categories conflict with the evidence: 'special cases' are excluded and the category is held intact. Allport called this a 're-fencing' device, saying: 'When a fact cannot fit into a mental field, the exception is acknowledged, but the field is hastily fenced in again' (Allport, 1979, p. 23). This state of affairs is encapsulated in the remark, 'Some of my best friends are blacks/Jews/Catholics, etc.', an expression which has become a cliché for ethnic or religious prejudice. The remark itself is an example of what Williams (1964) called an 'exemption mechanism', 'one of the ways in which established systems of discrimination and supporting prejudices are maintained against the erosion of interpersonal acquaintances and friendship' (p. 337).

The wider social context

It is of course a truism that any social behaviour must be located in a social context. However, it seems well worth reiterating some of the wider social influences on intergroup contact to which we alluded briefly at the beginning of this chapter. Their importance should be clear to us from classic studies (e.g. Minard, 1952), and can also be illustrated from fictional sources. Consider the shock of Ralph Ellison's *Invisible Man* on travelling from the American South to the North and 'seeing a black policeman directing traffic – and there are white drivers in the traffic who obeyed his signals as though it was the most natural thing in the world. Sure I had heard of it, but this was *real*' (Ellison, 1952/1965, p. 132).

The chapters in this book are full of illustrations of the significance of wider social factors. Some of the most powerful of these are rooted in the social and economic structure of society itself. This is the underlying theme of Allen's argument in chapter 8, which reminds us that any effects of contact between workers and managers must be viewed against the inherent conflict between employer and employee which exists in Western industrial societies. Writing of 'Gastarbeiter' in West Germany, Schönbach et al. argued that 'The living conditions of workers from abroad and their families still isolate these people in essential respects from German society at large' (1981, p. 4). This isolation relates back to the avoidance, or absence, of contact noted earlier. In other words, owing to the location and type of housing, contact is often limited from the start (see chapters 3 and 5). Considering the conditions in which the same 'Gastarbeiter' live, an interview in the collection edited by Klee (1972) is titled, 'Diese neun Monate haben wir wie Hunde gelebt' ('These nine months we lived like dogs'), which emphasizes the sometimes appalling accommodation to which migrant workers are consigned, whether for financial reasons, fears of racist attacks and/or discrimination (see Castles, Booth and Wallace, 1984). It is worth recalling Allport's point that such segregation into poor districts may be largely responsible for the stereotype of some minority groups as filthy, diseased and criminally inclined: 'What is due to segregation in housing is falsely ascribed to race' (Allport, 1954, p. 269). At its vilest extreme this segregation and economic exploitation becomes institutionalized into the very constitution of a country, as in South Africa (see chapter 7). Sadly, however, even outside official apartheid systems, housing segregation is one of the most persistent aspects of racism (see Hamilton, Carpenter and Bishop, 1984) and one which must have an especially powerful effect on attempts to integrate schools (see chapter 4).

Housing conditions generally co-vary with other social roles, so that one is often faced with a situation of multiple disadvantage, which in turn creates self-fulfilling prophecies. As Hartmann and Husband (1974) have argued, as long as it appears 'normal' for some groups to be badly housed, employed in menial work and socially disadvantaged, it will be 'normal' for other groups to expect preferment over them. As a number of contributors to this book also acknowledge, political factors in general and immigration policy in particular can have a powerful bearing on how minority groups are perceived (see chapters 3 and 9). Contact must be considered against the wider social background of racism in the form of media campaigns against immigrants, the articulation of fears of 'foreign swamping' of the national culture, racist attacks, the growth of neo-Nazi organizations and the increasing emphasis on 'racial' problems in the policies of major political parties (Castle et al., 1984, p. 5); this is a point central to Reicher's thesis in chapter 9. He suggests that the very existence of 'racial' categories at all derives not from any natural or *a priori* divisions in the world but can be traced to the political interests of ruling elites.

Another aspect of the wider social context that deserves mention, for it has been the subject of some debate in contact literature, are the policies of assimilation versus pluralism (see chapter 4). This debate centres on the extent to which the goal of intergroup contact is seen as one of trying to absorb the minority groups into the larger culture or, alternatively, as one of trying to ensure that they can retain their distinctive identities in a climate of tolerance. Assimilation is the process whereby different cultural groups adopt the culture of the mainstream, whereas pluralism refers to the maintenance or development of separate cultures or distinctive ethnic identities in a given society (see Berry, 1984; Triandis, 1976; Ward and Hewstone, 1985). This debate has been given a further impetus by an implication which can be drawn from our interpersonal-intergroup distinction and related theorizing on categorization and identity. This is that an effective factor for promoting intergroup harmony is to find policies which subsume existing group categorizations into a single, larger category (e.g. Turner, 1981; Worchel, 1979; chapter 9). Indeed, Turner has gone so far as to suggest that *the* most effective strategy for conflict resolution is 'through the creation of common or superordinate identifications' (Turner, 1981, p. 99), that is, for the groups concerned effectively to amalgamate.

Although this new version of the assimilationist position may seem plausible from one social-psychological perspective – and, indeed, there is some evidence to support it (Brown, 1984; Worchel et al., 1978) – it is doubtful whether it will always be the wisest policy. For it may simply not be feasible owing to groups' long history of, and allegiances to, their own culture and its values. Away from the laboratory environment, where group affiliations are usually weak and transitory, we may find that groups will strenuously resist the loss of distinctiveness which is implied by the assimilationist policy (see Tajfel, 1981). For example, in the Northern Ireland context it seems unlikely that Protestants and Catholics would lightly give up their religious identities in favour of some new, all-embracing category (see chapter 5), although they have, at least temporarily, united in their support for national sporting figures such as the boxer, Barry McGuigan. For situations such as these it would seem that the pluralist alternative of allowing groups to retain their diversity and of seeking ways to increase ingroup members' awareness and tolerance of that diversity is the preferable one.

Of course, such a policy is fraught with dangers, not least because the maintenance of existing group boundaries always carries with it the potential for conflict owing to categorization and the processes by which group identity is maintained (Turner, 1981). However, we should beware of overemphasizing the negative attributes of intergroup behaviour at the expense of the positive rewards accrued through group membership. Kidder and Stewart (1975) list a number of 'quasi-therapeutic' effects of intergroup conflict – for example the heightening of morale, increased satisfaction, improved mental health and ingroup solidarity – which tend to be ignored in solutions that require the individual to be cleaved from the group (e.g. Allen and Wilder, 1975). We will return, below, to this issue in proposing an intergroup approach to contact, but before doing that we consider some possibilities for augmenting the effects of contact.

AUGMENTING THE EFFECTS OF CONTACT

A number of scholars have argued that the contact hypothesis, even when contact is based on carefully specified dimensions, remains the offshoot of a simple theory of social engineering. It is in short unlikely that two groups can be brought together and that harmony will ensue unless contact is augmented or boosted by additional factors. Consequently, where contact appears to have produced successful outcomes, these may be attributed to other factors rather than to contact *per se* (Riordan, 1978). Given the nature of intergroup attitudes, perhaps it is hardly surprising that researchers have sought to bolster the effects of contact. In this section four such factors to augment contact are considered: superordinate goals, co-operation, cross-cutting categories and the manipulation of 'expectation states'.

Superordinate goals

Sherif's (1966a) research on the reduction of intergroup conflict is clearly distinct from any narrow interpretation of the contact hypothesis. In the famous summer camp studies, attempts to reduce intergroup conflict merely by bringing boys from two opposing groups into contact in pleasant surroundings resulted in further hostile exchanges (Sherif and Sherif, 1965; see also Diab, 1970). Sherif therefore concluded that there needed to be some positive and functional interdependence between groups before conflict between them would subside. This he created in the form of a superordinate goal, a goal which neither group can attain on its own and which supersedes other goals each group may have. Significantly, Sherif also reported that a single superordinate goal was not sufficient to reduce intergroup conflict; a series of cumulative superordinate goals was required (see also Wilder and Thompson, 1980). Thus we see one clear example of how contact may have to be augmented in order to succeed in reducing prejudice. In this case, contact-plus-superordinate-goals is based on what McClendon (1974) calls the 'utilitarian rationale', that is intergroup attitudes will improve when each group has utility for the other.

Despite this apparent success, Sherif's methods have been criticized. Both Billig (1976) and Tajfel (1978b) point out that when superordinate goals are finally introduced, the conflict is to all intents and purposes, over. Success appears to have been achieved by fusing together the two conflictual groups. Indeed, according to Feshbach and Singer (1957), superordinate goals reduce intergroup prejudice by creating a *new* ingroup (see Ashmore, 1970; Turner, 1981). In this respect it can be argued that the situation is no longer an intergroup one at all. While conflict may appear to have been reduced, or even resolved, we should also recall that the groups used in this study were *ad hoc*, formed at a summer camp for a short period of time. As such, they had no future beyond that context (Turner, 1981), and such results may be of limited relevance to more enduring conflicts between natural groups or situations in which groups retain their separate identities (as in the case of pluralism). For example, bringing together Catholics and Protestants (see chapter 5) or Arabs and Jews (see chapter 2) for the purposes of joint problem-solving may have some short-term effects, but the litmus test remains whether this harmony will endure in the future and outside the setting of the intervention.[9]

Moving beyond Sherif's work, and attempting to overcome some of these problems, recent thinking suggests that the ways that groups actually allocate the labour in the achievement of their co-operative goal may be an important factor in determining the nature of subsequent intergroup attitudes (Turner, 1981). Arguing from a 'social identity' perspective, with its emphasis on groups' needs to retain distinctive aspects of their identity, it can be suggested that co-operative encounters in which the groups' roles or contributions were not clearly recognizable might represent a threat to those groups' identities. A reaction to that threat might be increased intergroup differentiation or dislike, as the groups seek to reassert their distinctiveness.

Support for this idea was found in two experiments (Brown and Wade, 1986; Deschamps and Brown, 1983). In both, groups of college students were asked to undertake a co-operative task for real rewards. The groups' roles in undertaking this task were however experimentally varied. In the first experiment they were given *either* very similar jobs to do *or* each group's role was made rather different. In fact, *increases* in dislike were observed after co-operation when the groups had similar roles. This was confirmed in a second experiment in which an even more ambiguous condition was added, where the groups' roles were completely unallocated. The liking for the outgroup was directly related to the distinctiveness of the two groups' roles (these findings also link with our earlier discussion of the role of similarity in intergroup relations).

Thus superordinate goals can reinforce the positive effects of contact, and these effects may be generalized to include future intergroup encounters when care is taken to maintain, rather than blur, intergroup distinctiveness.

Co-operation

Superordinate goals often generate strong motivations for co-operation, which in many applied settings has been used to reduce intergroup conflict. In addition to Cook's extensive work, discussed earlier, co-operation has also been employed in class-rooms to reduce tensions between ethnic groups (see Aronson et al., 1978; Johnson et al., 1984). Worchel (1979) reviews the evidence for the effectiveness of co-operation and reports that it can increase intergroup attraction and communication, reduce tension and lead to greater trust and increased satisfaction with group products. Specifying the conditions under which co-operation does decrease conflict, Worchel's analysis starts from the assumption that groups in a state of conflict will attempt to accentuate mutual differences and to delineate group boundaries. It is then proposed that the presence of variables permitting group members to make intergroup discriminations will probably weaken the positive effects of co-operation. Indeed, they may even exacerbate conflict.

The outcome of co-operation – success or failure – is one variable that has received close attention in the literature as a possible factor in maintaining conflict (e.g. Blanchard, Adelman and Cook, 1975; Worchel, Andreoli and Folger, 1977). When co-operation between previously competitive groups ends in failure, the result may be outgroup derogation in the form of scapegoating (Heider, 1944). The outgroup is blamed unless subjects are provided with some other viable explanation for the result (such as unsuitable physical setting; see Worchel and Norvell, 1980) in which case the salience of intergroup differences is increased, whereas Worchel et al. (1978) propose that cooperation should increase intergroup attraction to the extent that it reduces the salience of group boundaries or distinctions.

Despite the apparent success met by co-operative techniques, we remain unconvinced of *how* they should function. Worchel's work emphasizes that co-operation will not necessarily improve intergroup attitudes, unless the ingroup-outgroup division is eliminated. The claim that co-operation increases inter*group* attraction to the extent that it reduces the salience of group boundaries gives us little faith in this 'cure'. Like other approaches considered above, such a solution can surely have little effect on groups that will never merge, whose distinctions are insurmountable and whose daily lives are lived out in contexts that strengthen intergroup distinctions.

Multi-group membership and cross-cutting social categories

A feature of real societies, unlike the very simplified (sometimes 'minimal') *us-them* dichotomies created in our laboratories, is that they contain many different groups. Furthermore, many societies, both peasant and industrialized, are characterized by the existence of crosscutting dimensions of categorization. Thus at the same time as a person may be Catholic (or Protestant), she or he may also be a trade-unionist (or an employer), a member of one occupational group (rather than another) and of course a woman (or a man). Each of these secondary classifications is independent of the original category division. LeVine and Campbell (1972) discuss anthropological evidence (e.g. Evans-Pritchard, 1940) showing that in tribal societies the 'crossing' of group memberships may help to control the incidence of intergroup conflict. When ties of loyalty have 'pyramidal-segmentary' ('socially divisive', LeVine and Campbell) structures, individuals are members of groups that are in turn segments of larger collectivities. Thus each individual is a member of several units increasing in scope and effectiveness, and loyalty to sub-groups must be ranked. This kind of social structure is associated with more frequent combat than is the 'cross-cutting' ('socially integrated', LeVine and Campbell) social structure. In this case each male individual for example owes loyalty to more than one group (such as his local group and his groups based on common descent and age). Individuals find themselves belonging to one group on the basis of one set of criteria and to another group (sometimes traditionally hostile) in terms of other criteria, consequently this social structure is associated with less fighting (see also Giles and Johnson, 1981).

There is some experimental evidence that if alternative categorizations can be brought into play, these may help to reduce the conflict surrounding the original division. Of course, one must make very certain that these alternative categories do not perfectly overlay and hence reinforce the original divide (Brown and Turner, 1979), and that one category does not become the dominant basis for social identity in a particular setting (Brewer and Miller, 1984). Deschamps and Doise (1978) introduced such 'criss-cross' categorizations and found a decrease in intergroup discrimination. Subjects were asked to evaluate groups of people assigned to opposite categories according to one criterion, and belonging to the same category according to another criterion. The perceived differences between groups in the latter condition were smaller than in the strictly dichotomous condition.[10]

Despite their findings, Deschamps and Doise are aware that such results are often specific to a particular situation (see Doise, 1978; Minard, 1952). One must also, like Tajfel (1982), ask how useful and valid such manipulations are. Commins and Lockwood (1978) introduced transient experimental categorizations to try to decrease intergroup discrimination between Catholics and Protestants in Northern Ireland. They found only a non-significant tendency in the direction of decreased discrimination. Thus, once again, doubts remain about the utility of such an intervention in the context of pervasive and realistic group loyalties.

Achieving equal status by the manipulation of 'expectation states'

As a final example of how the effects of contact can be augmented, we consider the manipulation of so-called 'expectation states'. The important role of equal-status contact has been seen already; however, it was noted that the manipulation of equal status within a contact setting may be very difficult and sometimes impossible to achieve. Cohen (1982, 1984) has re-formulated the equal-status concept in terms of expectation states (or status characteristics) theory (Berger, Cohen and Zelditch, 1972). This theory emphasizes that status is seen as a basis for generating *expectations* about oneself and others in social interaction. According to Cohen the theory can be used to describe the process by which members of a high-status group come to dominate intergroup interaction (see also Katz, 1964). Thus it has been found that white Americans tend to be more active and influential than black Americans in interethnic interaction and to dominate them on valued intellectual tasks. This tendency is obviously undesirable for black individuals, both in the sense that others dominate them and that they themselves come to have low expectations of their own performance. This results in less effort being exerted and, via a self-fulfilling prophecy, lower actual achievement.

Cohen's contribution, by means of 'expectation training', has been to boost experimentally the individual status of members of the lower-status group (see also Riordan and Ruggiero, 1980) and thus to overcome the negative expectations of blacks and whites before interaction. Cohen and Roper (1972) found that they had to overcome an initial anti-black view, held by white children, concerning the ability of black children. This was done by assigning an especially high level of competence to blacks in their study. Interestingly, Cohen and Roper demonstrated that it was not just a matter of raising the black childrens' expectations of themselves, but also of improving white children's expectations of their black counterparts' abilities.

The importance of this work is that once again it suggests that contact *per se* – in this case contact without prior alteration of the expectations of, for example, black and white schoolchildren – will probably be ineffectual, and may even make things worse. One should note however that as with other solutions the manipulation of expectancies is no foolproof panacea. First, research on programmes of affirmative action (e.g. Garcia et al., 1981) has shown that members of minority groups who do achieve high status may still be downgraded, because the positive discrimination aimed at their benefit is perceived as unfair (see also Norvell and Worchel, 1981) and possibly also as threatening to members of the high-status group (Tajfel, 1978a). The member of the minority group accorded such high status may also be perceived as atypical, and his or her behaviour explained in these terms (see below); in this case we are faced with the familiar problem of generalizing beyond the experimental setting and improving evaluations of outgroup members in general.

In sum, it is clear that intergroup contact can be, and in practice often is, boosted by the presence of other factors. The achievement of superordinate goals, co-operation, cross-cutting categories or the manipulation of expectation states appear to be the four main factors in this respect. While convinced of their utility, we have also noted grounds for caution in the application and interpretation of these factors. Further progress can perhaps also be made by considering in more depth the cognitive processes that occur in such intergroup encounters, in particular those (mis)perceptions that may seriously impede the desired outcome of intergroup contact.

COGNITIVE PROCESSES IN INTERGROUP CONTACT

What happens when, for example, black and white individuals come into contact for the first time? Katz (1970) has described the initial awkwardness in such encounters, and Weitz (1972) has proposed a 'repressed affect' model, based on the finding that those people with the *most* favourable attitudes towards blacks had the *least* friendly voice tone and behaviour towards blacks. As Johnson et al. (1984) propose, when initial contact is made, first impressions are formed on the basis of salient characteristics that dominate observed behaviour. Such impressions may become 'monopolistic' (taking account of only a few characteristics), 'static' (remaining unchanged across situations) and 'stereotyped'; or they may become 'differentiated' (taking account of many characteristics), 'dynamic' (in a constant state of change) and 'realistic'. As these authors put it, physical proximity among ingroup and outgroup members 'is the beginning of an opportunity, but like all opportunities it carries a risk of making things worse as well as the possibility of making things better' (Johnson et al., 1984, p. 190). As one approach towards a better understanding of the reasons why contact can accentuate or attenuate intergroup conflict, pages 28–32 follow Rose's (1981) focus on the social cognitive processes operating in the contact setting. This discussion considers quite briefly four major cognitive processes that have received attention in the recent literature (e.g. Hamilton, 1979, 1981; Hamilton and Trolier, in press) and that seem most pertinent.

Social categorization

Social categorization, by which is meant the segmentation and organization of the social world into social categories or groups, is a central cognitive process (see Tajfel, 1981). Social categorization serves several important functions: reducing the complexity of incoming information; facilitating rapid identification of stimuli; predicting and guiding behaviour (Bruner, 1957; Triandis, 1971). Allport (1954), because of these functions, recognized that categorical prejudgement and erroneous generalization were *natural and common* capacities of the human mind.

S.E. Taylor (1981) has shown some of the ways categorization functions. For example, the study by S.E. Taylor et al. (1978) showed that subjects could remember whether a black or a white member of a discussion group had spoken, but not which black or white individual. This suggests that subjects were organizing information around categories of group membership (in this case, black or white). Rose (1981) spells out one important implication of this finding: if all that people can remember is the race of an individual, they may easily and incorrectly assume that the act or attribute of one person is typical of the group as a whole. This categorization can have debilitating effects for members of minority groups, who see and feel that they are 'lumped together'. Such categorization effects are crucial for contact, given that some researchers see the aim of contact as being to 'individuate' outgroup members so that some lack of uniformity within the outgroup is perceived (Wilder, 1978). Given our previous discussion of generalization and the interpersonal–intergroup distinction, contact should have the dual aim of emphasizing typicality and creating a less monolithic, more differentiated view of the outgroup.

Stereotyping

Three essential aspects of stereotyping can be identified:

1 Other individuals are categorized, usually on the basis of easily identifiable characteristics such as sex or ethnicity.
2 A set of attributes is ascribed to all (or most) members of that category. Individuals belonging to the stereotyped group are assumed to be similar to each other, and different from other groups, on this set of attributes.
3 The set of attributes is ascribed to any individual member of that category (see Hewstone and Giles, 1986).

While it may be objected (see Brigham, 1971) that stereotypes are perforce 'bad' because they lead people to treat others as members of groups rather than as individuals, this view ignores the existence of *positive ingroup stereotypes* of which group members are proud (hence Turner's, 1982, discussion of *self*-stereotyping). Rather than aiming to do away with stereotypes, which do serve explicit psychological and social functions (see Tajfel, 1981), one should aim to enrich outgroup stereotypes. Outgroups are generally referred to as though they were 'homogeneous and monolithic', while ingroups are seen as 'variegated and complex' (Rothbart, Dawes and Park, 1984). Similarly, it has been reported that people perceive more variability within ingroups than within outgroups (Park and Rothbart, 1982; Quattrone and Jones, 1980), and that outgroup images are impoverished relative to ingroup images (Linville and Jones, 1980). However, it is possible that these effects are limited to majority groups' perceptions of minorities. An experiment by Simon (1985) suggests that when a minority is viewing either the majority or another minority, it is the *ingroup* that is seen as more homogeneous. More will be said about stereotypes, below, in our intergroup model of contact; at this stage, we support the view that contact should aim to increase the complexity of outgroup perceptions and to challenge the belief that most members of a group fit one, single stereotype (Stephan and Rosenfield, 1982).

Hypothesis-testing and the self-fulfilling prophecy

Further evidence of the role of social cognitions in contact is seen in Snyder's (1981) work on stereotypes and self-fulfilling prophecies. Snyder and Swann (1978a and b) examined how people tested a hypothesis they were given about another person. Results showed a strong tendency towards hypothesis-confirmation. For example, asked to test whether someone was an extrovert, people would ask questions to support, not disconfirm, the hypothesis. If this same process operates in intergroup encounters, and we suggest that it often does, then it is easily seen why contact so often fails to change attitudes. In short, stereotypes generate expectancies, and perceivers seem to want to see expectancies confirmed. This affects the behaviour of the perceiver and the interpretation of the target's action. People tend to see behaviour that confirms their expectancies, even when it is absent (Cooper and Fazio, 1979). When stereotypes set up expectations of behaviour, disconfirming evidence tends to be ignored, but confirming evidence remembered (Rothbart, Evans and Fulero, 1979).

Thus contact situations can so easily become self-fulfilling prophecies, and here we see the danger of emphasizing typicality. According to

Snyder's work, the more an individual is perceived as typical of the outgroup, the more expectations about the outgroup are likely to have an influence on information-processing in contact situations. So the benefits of stressing typicality, in terms of generalization, may be bought at the cost of increasing stereotypic perceptions. Once again, it will be necessary to precede contact with a careful analysis of how each group sees itself and relevant outgroups (see the discussion of auto- and hetero-stereotypes by Triandis and Vassiliou, 1967).

Intergroup attributions

For most contact theorists the aim of intergroup encounters is a positive outcome, whether perceived in terms of successful co-operation, superordinate goals or an enjoyable meeting. Unfortunately, while such outcomes may prove difficult to distort or deny, individuals can always retreat behind a wall of ingroup-serving and/or outgroup-derogating attributions. Such explanations are all the more likely the more ambiguous the situation (see Duncan, 1976) and have obvious implications for any analysis of contact. Jaspars and Hewstone (1982) argued that in an intergroup situation, behaviour that would normally be attributed to the situation was often attributed to particular participants because of the salience of social categorization. Such an effect, it was argued, will increase in strength, because the interaction that takes place between individuals belonging to different ethnic groups is very often highly selective in nature.

The role of expectancies, highlighted at several points in this chapter also has implications for attributions. Pyszczynski and Greenberg (1981) suggest that when perceivers see their expectancies confirmed, they may simply rely on dispositions implied by the stereotype, not even bothering to consider additional causal factors. Behaviour inconsistent with expectancies, on the other hand, tends to be attributed to external factors (e.g. Regan, Strauss and Fazio, 1974; Stephan and Rosenfield, 1982). At the level of attributions for in- and outgroup members (see Hewstone and Jaspars, 1982, 1984) these processes help to explain why stereotypes are so pervasive and difficult to change. Because stereotypes refer to people's assumptions about the *dispositional* attributes of in- and outgroup members, any behaviour that violates the stereotype could be avoided on the basis that it reflected *situational* influences and thus did not derive from the personal characteristics of the actor (Hamilton, 1979). In relation to this, Wilder (1984) reported that a single contact experience was not enough to change prevailing beliefs, which might be based on multiple confirming examples (Rothbart, 1981), about the outgroup as a whole. Rather than altering stereotypes, exceptions may simply reduce the likelihood of applying stereotypes in that setting. Ashmore (1970) has also argued that contact must be extensive enough, or involve a sufficiently large sample of outgroup members, so that counter-stereotypic behaviour cannot be explained in terms of situational demands or individual exceptions to the rule. Positive behaviour of outgroup members is problematic for prejudiced individuals and is dealt with by Pettigrew (1979b): given negative stereotypes, positive behaviour is likely to be interpreted as *atypical* and 'explained away' in terms of 'the special case', luck, high motivation and effort, or the situation. Thus Allport's (1954) 'fence mending' would appear to be mediated by intergroup attributions.

It now becomes clear that attributions are important independent, as well as dependent, variables. Different patterns of attribution could affect the nature of the interaction that develops and determine whether intergroup contact will in fact improve intergroup relations (Rose, 1981). Thus Worchel and Norvell (1980) suggest that if ingroup members can be prevented from blaming the outgroup, co-operation resulting in failure need not result in an even greater bias against the outgroup. In their study, failure still led to increased intergroup attraction as long as environmental conditions had been perceived as detrimental to success and therefore could have served as an explanation for the outcome.[11]

Allport (1954) referred to an 'insatiable hunger for *explanations*' (p. 170), and this hunger is seen as crucial in intergroup encounters (see also the references to attributions in chapters 4, 6 and 8). Researchers and practitioners must obviously learn to expect that all of the cognitive processes discussed above can interfere with their 'best laid schemes'. As Rose (1981) acknowledged: 'the person's existing beliefs and expectations about a group may be relatively unaffected as a result of intergroup contact and, in fact, they may actually be bolstered even when they have objectively been disconfirmed' (p. 273). Such cognitive processes may, furthermore, help to explain the chequered pattern of outcomes associated with contact, whereby contact sometimes improves and sometimes worsens intergroup relations.

BEYOND THE CONTACT HYPOTHESIS? AN INTERGROUP APPROACH

Writing in 1974, McClendon claimed that there had been little *theoretical* advancement in the area of intergroup contact since Allport's (1954) work. While we agree with this view, it is encouraging to report that the contact hypothesis is currently receiving renewed critical attention.

Brewer and Miller's model of 'decategorization'

Brewer and Miller (1984)[12] have also recently attempted to go beyond the contact hypothesis and, like the present authors, have based their approach on Tajfel's (1978a) social identity theory. However, their conclusions and recommendations from this shared theoretical starting-point are different in crucial respects from our own.

Brewer and Miller state explicitly their interest, and faith, in situations 'whereby category-based social interactions may be replaced by social relations that are more interpersonally oriented and more consistent with the goals of desegregation' (p. 286). This view is somewhat qualified, a few lines later, with the statement that the role of desegregation 'is not simply to redistribute members of different social categories, but to promote intergroup acceptance and to reduce the role that category membership plays in creating barriers to individual social mobility and to the development of positive interpersonal relationships' (p. 287). Thus apparently contact should improve intergroup and interpersonal relationships.

Brewer and Miller also clearly state their view that the reduction of category-based responding should be associated with social interactions based on increasing 'differentiation' and 'personalization'. By differentiation they mean that individual outgroup members are seen as distinct from one another, but that sub-groups formed in this way are still seen as parts of the larger social category. Personalization denotes that outgroup individuals are responded to in terms of their relationship to the ingroup individual's self, such that self-other interpersonal comparisons are made across category boundaries. Thus Brewer and Miller introduce three models of intergroup contact: category-based, differentiation and personalization. They appear to place their faith in the last, for such contact experiences are seen as 'more likely to generalize to new situations because extended and frequent utilization of alternative informational features in interactions undermines the availability and usefulness of category identity as a basis for future interactions with the same or different individuals' (pp. 288–9). This perspective has much in common with that taken by Ben-Ari and Amir in chapter 2. Like Brewer and Miller they also place much emphasis on developing interpersonal relationships across ethnic lines.[13]

Consistent with our earlier critical analysis of the contact hypothesis, this view is challenged on both theoretical and empirical grounds. First, the definition of personalization is somewhat vague; according to Brewer and Miller, it 'reduces information processing and interaction decisions that are category-based' (p. 288) and yet it does *not* 'necessitate that real differences or perceived distinctions between groups be eliminated' (p. 289). Given the importance we attach to the interpersonal-intergroup distinction, personalization appears something of a chimera. Second, in line with our strictures on generalization, and recent empirical evidence (Wilder, 1984), we would see the outcome of such contact in terms of person-based attributions and 'fence mending', rather than generalization across members of the outgroup. Recall Rose's (1981) paradox, that intimate relationships may generalize over a wide range of situations, but not over different persons.

Mutual intergroup differentiation

Our own approach to intergroup contact is inspired, on the one hand, by Tajfel's (1978a) social identity theory and, on the other hand, by Brown and Turner's (1981) analysis of interpersonal and intergroup behaviour. According to social identity theory, individuals define themselves to a large extent in terms of their social group memberships and tend to seek a positive social identity (or self-definition in terms of group member-ship). They achieve this by comparing their own group with other groups to establish a positively valued distinctiveness between the two groups. Claiming that motivational as well as cognitive factors underlie intergroup differentiation, the theory holds that positive comparisons (intergroup differences seen to favour the ingroup) provide a satisfactory social identity, while negative comparisons (differences which favour the outgroup) convey an unsatisfactory identity.

Brown and Turner extend Tajfel's distinction between interpersonal and intergroup behaviour and provide evidence for its empirical validity. The importance of this approach for intergroup contact is clear from Brown and Turner's forthright statement that:

to the extent that the contact takes places (sic) on an 'interpersonal' basis it is unlikely to modify intergroup attitudes and behaviour since the two domains are controlled, we suggest, by different psychological processes. What is more probable, if contact is confined to social interaction between individuals *qua* individuals, is that a few interpersonal relationships will change but that the intergroup situation will remain substantially unaltered. If, on the other hand, the contact can be characterized in 'group' terms, that is as interaction between individuals *qua* group members, or in ways that alter the structure of group relations, then genuine changes at the intergroup level may be expected. (Brown and Turner, 1981, p. 60)

Thus Brown and Turner argue that intergroup contact works, if and when it does, because it changes the nature and structure of the intergroup relationship – *not* because it permits and encourages interpersonal friendships between members of different groups. From this viewpoint, improvements and positive changes in interpersonal relations are viewed as an effect, rather than a cause, of a more general alteration in intergroup relations. What is needed therefore is an intergroup approach to contact, to which we now turn.

The essence of our intergroup approach to contact lies in the varying importance that members of different groups ascribe to dimensions of intergroup comparison, as conceived in social identity theory. Following Brewer (1979), intergroup differentiation will be maximized on dimensions where the ingroup's position is superior, but minimized when the ingroup's position is inferior. But the fact that attenuation of group differences occurs on some dimensions does not imply any reduction of accentuation on other dimensions. The implications of this argument are that research might usefully concentrate on establishing *mutual intergroup differentiation*, rather than swimming against the tide and attempting to deprive individuals of their valued group identities (Hewstone and Giles, 1984). This is very similar to what van Knippenberg (1984) advocates in his notion of 'social cooperation'. As Tajfel (1981) concludes in his discussion of minority groups: 'it may be useful to see in each intergroup situation whether and how it might be possible for each group to achieve, preserve, or defend its vital interests . . . in such a way that the self respect of other groups is not adversely affected at the same time' (Tajfel, 1981, p. 343).

There is evidence that perceived threat to individual and group distinctiveness may be resolved by making comparisons on new or different dimensions (see Lemaine et al., 1978) and that low-status groups may perceive differences between themselves and high-status groups on particular sets of traits, thus providing for positive social identities for in- and outgroups (van Knippenberg, 1978; van Knippenberg and van Oers, 1984). Turner (1981) underlines that comparative interdependence should not be seen as incompatible with positive distinctiveness, suggesting that the realization of superordinate goals may often call for 'a division of labour between cooperating groups, the differentiation and coordination of their activities into separate but complementary work-roles' (pp. 84–5). Mutual recognition of superiorities and inferiorities would characterize this mutual intergroup differentiation and would be reflected in group stereotypes. Each group would view itself positively *and* hold positive stereotypes of outgroups, consistent with those groups' autostereotypes (see Taylor and Simard, 1979). Thus each group is seen as it wishes to be seen, and desired differences are highlighted. This prescription for intergroup harmony fits nicely with Stephan and Stephan's (1984) discussion of whether similarities and/or differences should be the focus in educational and cross-cultural programmes, and their conclusion that presentation of fundamental similarities *and* group-specific differences should help to attack intergroup ignorance and improve intergroup relations. (A similar view is taken by Schofield in chapter 4). While this approach may seem merely optimistic, if not naive, there is some evidence to support it. Taylor and Simard (1979) make the valid point that outgroup stereotypes, in the context of pluralism rather than assimilation, may lead to the positive outcome of mutual social differentiation. They report that in Canada, despite tensions, mutual positive attitudes do prevail between ethnolinguistic groups (see also Berry, 1984).

There are of course still problems and dangers associated with this intergroup approach. For example, as Berry (1984) warns, one must apparently encourage a positive view of the ingroup, but beware of stoking the fires of ethnocentrism. Second, following recent work by Mummendey and Schreiber (1983, 1984) and van Knippenberg and van Oers (1984), there is still a danger of sometimes more subtle outgroup discrimination, in that ingroups may try to appropriate the most valued, task-relevant or status-stressing dimensions for their own group. Third, reiterating the point made by Stephan and Stephan (1984), the discussion and presentation of differences must be carried out with great care to avoid the perception that one group is inferior to another.

A model of intergroup contact

Notwithstanding these reservations, a new theoretical framework for intergroup contact is presented (see figure 1.1). This model is as yet untested; nonetheless, it provides a systematic distillation of the major arguments put forward in this chapter and attempts to guide future research to those questions that need answers most. The model can be viewed as nine blocks or stages, each of which is briefly addressed. These stages have been arranged as a kind of flow chart, but assumptions about causal order are certainly more complex than depicted. Brewer and Miller (1984) have suggested a number of alternative process models of contact, and we agree with them that complex reciprocal causal relationships (as opposed to unidirectional causality) would probably best represent the processes underlying intergroup contact.

I   The first stage of the model does no more than list some of the wider social factors that impinge on any contact situation involving realistic groups (see pages 20–22). The impact of these factors can be seen in every one of the following chapters.

II   Stage two lists the five central dimensions of classic work on the

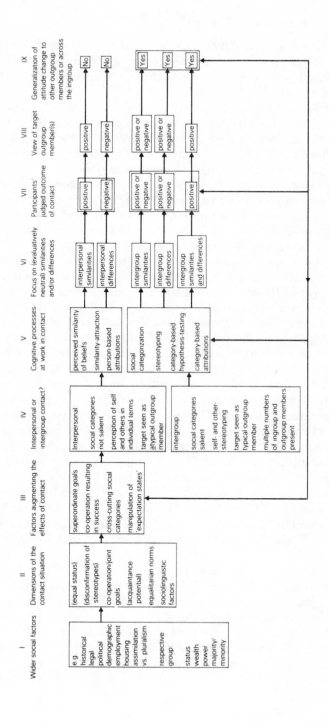

Figure 1.1 A model of intergroup contact

contact hypothesis (see pages 2–6). Some of these are dealt with in the chapters in this book. For instance power and status differences are a central theme in chapter 7; factors affecting acquaintance potential are discussed in chapters 3 and 6. While we see some of these dimensions as important, others appear less central to inter*group* contact. For example a situation of high acquaintance potential with a high-status individual who disconfirms the outgroup stereotype may easily be perceived as one of interpersonal contact, with little chance of generalizing attitude change to other outgroup members. New dimensions might also be incorporated into this stage, such as Ben-Ari and Amir's discussion in chapter 2 of whether contact takes place on ingroup, outgroup or neutral territory. It should also be noted that we have included sociolinguistic factors in this stage. These have been almost totally neglected in previous work on contact (see Giles and Wiemann, in preparation).

III   Stage three includes some of the factors that can be used to augment the effects of contact (see pages 22–28). It should be noted here how stages (e.g. III, V and VII) interact, so that co-operation resulting in failure could still be positively interpreted, providing participants did not blame the outgroup for this outcome (Worchel and Novell, 1980).

IV   Stage four represents the core of our intergroup approach, where contact bifurcates into interpersonal and intergroup varieties (see pages 13–16). Here it must be emphasized that contact between two individuals can be, and often is, intergroup contact, in that social categories are salient, there is self- and other-stereotyping and the target is seen as a typical outgroup member. However, further research could usefully incorporate into contact some of the variables (singly, and in combination) known to increase intergroup salience. For example contact could involve multiple members of in- and outgroups, there could be clear majorities and minorities, and so on (Brewer, 1979; Brewer and Miller, 1984). In this respect it is interesting to note the finding reported by Wagner and Machleit in chapter 3 that contact between German and Turkish children in Germany is mostly a confrontation of two groups, and that such leisure contact *is* positively associated with liking for Turks in general.

V   Stage five accords a central position to cognitive processes at work in interpersonal (see pages 2–6) and intergroup (see pages 28–32) contact. These processes will determine the nature of contact, how it is interpreted and whether any resultant attitude change is generalized.

VI   Stage six is concerned with whether contact is focused on similarities and/or differences (and with assuming that this can be done in an evaluatively neutral or unthreatening manner). Figure 1 incorporates our view (based on research) that a focus on similarities or differences may (but does not always) have quite different effects in interpersonal and intergroup encounters (see pages 13–16). Here we follow Stephan and Stephan (1984) in suggesting that contact should involve: (a) a focus on fundamental similarities (e.g. 'There's only one race, the human race') *and* valued differences (e.g. symbols of cultural, religious or ethnic pride); (b) the explosion of myths about intergroup differences. Thus we disagree here with Ben-Ari and Amir on this point who, in chapter 2, advise that potentially conflictual differences (such as politics) be avoided. Without wishing to minimize the difficulties and dangers of addressing such issues explicitly, we firmly believe that it is up to future research on intergroup contact to suggest when and how such differences must be confronted. Interestingly, Hofman (1985), writing of the same intergroup situation as Ben-Ari and Amir tends, like us, to come to a rather different conclusion.

VII, VIII and IX These last three stages underline that it is the interactants' perceptions of contact as positive or as negative that matter; that in turn these perceptions determine how the target outgroup member is viewed. However, the generalization of attitude change cannot be assumed and must be traced back to whether the contact is seen as interpersonal or intergroup in nature.

This book and policy implications

The above model grew out of, rather than preceded, the chapters in this book; hence we have taken the liberty of disagreeing with some of our contributors on specific points. The choice of such a broad range of cultural contexts reflects our view that the problems of intergroup contact and conflict, while displaying some uniformities, also reveal unique cultural characteristics (see also Hewstone, 1985). We have not attempted a truly cross-cultural perspective, in the sense that our aim has not been to compare the same specific type of behaviour across vastly different countries. Instead, we have asked all contributors to address the following three issues in their chapters:

1 An introduction to the non-social-psychological background of the context being considered – including historical, economic, political and legal aspects of intergroup relations – thus giving the reader an idea of the antecedents of conflict, the nature of groups and settings involved and the nature of conflict and discrimination.
2 A focus on key studies in the domain, centred on dimensions of contact and giving weight to the authors' own recent and current research.

3   A guide towards the policy implications of the presented work, including an honest assessment of the extent to which a social-psychological analysis is beneficial.

Before concluding, it is appropriate to discuss some of the policy issues raised by these chapters and the literature in general. First, of course, we must note that any such discussion necessarily raises questions of a socio-political nature. Thus, for example, while it is frequently and unquestioningly assumed in contact literature that the goal of intergroup harmony is welcome in itself, we can conceive of many circumstances where this might not be the case. For instance a slave society may to all intents and purposes be harmonious. But since it is based on unacceptable premises of exploitation and oppression it is not one that recommends itself to us as a desirable policy objective. Other less extreme instances of intergroup domination recorded throughout this book may also raise questions about the value of 'reconciliation' policies. However, given that the contact hypothesis has had a major influence on public policy in areas such as housing, schools and sport, it is appropriate to ask a number of critical questions about the value and future use of intergroup contact. Here discussion is restricted to two pertinent questions: what are the alternatives to contact? And, assuming one's goal is the reduction of intergroup discrimination, is positive contact under 'micro' conditions better than no contact at all?

One obvious alternative to contact is propaganda. It is still important to note Horowitz's (1936) view that, 'attitudes towards Negroes are now chiefly determined not by contact with Negroes, but by contact with the prevalent attitudes towards Negroes' (pp. 34–5). It is a view that would seem to argue for massive propaganda campaigns as well as, if not instead of, contact programmes. Much of the relevant work has recently been integrated by Stephan and Stephan (1984), revealing a mixed pattern of results. A major problem is still that those who wish to, will avoid or misrepresent propaganda aimed at improving intergroup relations. In addition, attitude change may be only temporary and biased in the direction of socially desirable responses. Alternatively, one might intervene to change social behaviour and let attitudes follow. A cognitive-dissonance interpretation of contact would suggest that individuals committed to contact with outgroup members may reduce their initial dissonance by interacting successfully with them (Sears and Allen, 1984). Further dissonance caused by this close contact with a negatively stereotyped outgroup may be reduced by viewing the outgroup, or at least the target member, more positively (see Ashmore, 1970; Brehm and Cohen, 1962).

Of all the contributors to this book, Reicher in chapter 9 eschews the contact hypothesis most strongly and argues for a more radical approach based on collective action (see also Foster and Finchilescu in chapter 7). Obviously, our own view of the importance of intergroup contact is more sanguine (although we applaud Reicher's call for changes in the wider, racist social structure). We suggest that intergroup contact can be boosted by both propaganda and behavioural outcomes (e.g. successful co-operation or the achievement of superordinate goals) that will themselves engender or predispose a change of attitudes in line with principles of cognitive dissonance. Neither propaganda nor dissonance-oriented interventions need be seen as alternatives to contact, because they are not mutually exclusive. Furthermore, because the inter*group* contact proposed here has never been tried, it would seem premature to discard the contact hypothesis as such.[14]

Returning to the second question, is any positive contact better than none? Consistent with our demands for intergroup contact, we believe researchers should be more explicit about their aims. Much of the research summarized in this book is positive, in the sense of charting an improvement in relations between individuals from opposing groups. We should not however claim too many prizes until and unless the contact experience has been successfully generalized both to other outgroup members and across other members of the ingroup. Take for example the Northern Ireland community holidays described in chapter 5. It seems clear that these holiday schemes, by exposing children to places, cultures and people they would never normally experience, are both enjoyable and beneficial experiences. We have no doubt too that many interpersonal friendships are formed which may transcend the religious divide. What is less clear is whether this experience can have any real and lasting impact on subsequent Catholic–Protestant relations. Thus, while we do not wish to rule out interpersonal contact programmes altogether – especially since, as Pettigrew (1971) has pointed out, prolonged isolation may reduce the likelihood of future intergroup contact – we caution practitioners to be modest in their expectations of such interventions. Thus, in policy terms, we urge the implementation of broader programmes of intergroup contact, but also acknowledge that some positive contact may be better than none at all.

CONCLUSION

In concluding this chapter, and looking ahead to the following ones, we are conscious of being faced with a vitally important area in social relations. Myrdal (1944) referred in a famous phrase to the 'American Dilemma', the contradiction that 'all men are created equal', but that inequality is evident and pervasive. Yet, as Westie (1964) argued, there is not only an American Dilemma, but a whole variety of Israeli, German, British and other dilemmas. This fact of pervasive inequalities between groups is the background to the contact hypothesis and indeed to any analysis of contact and conflict in intergroup encounters.

The message of this book is that intergroup contact can play a role in improving intergroup relations in society, but that the contact hypothesis as traditionally conceived is too narrow and limited. To create the conditions for truly successful intergroup contact, more radical social changes are a prerequisite. For example, following Triandis (1976), blacks and other oppressed groups must seek a share of power; members of majority groups secure in *their* identity must learn the value and integrity of *other* groups or cultures; economic programmes are required that will guarantee jobs to every capable citizen willing to work. These changes will not come easily and will have to be fought for on many fronts. It is our hope that this book will underline the valuable contribution that social psychology can make in bringing those transformations about.

ACKNOWLEDGEMENTS

The authors would like to thank Howard Giles and Michael Banton for their critical comments on an earlier version of this chapter. We are grateful to Addison-Wesley Publishing Co. Inc. for permission to reprint G. W. Allport's list of kinds of contact (from *The Nature of Prejudice*, pp. 262–3; copyright © 1979).

NOTES

1   While Allport was certainly not the first person to entertain the contact hypothesis (see Watson, 1947; Williams, 1947), it is his ideas which have unquestionably had the greatest impact on subsequent social psychological work. According to McClendon (1974), studies which have attempted to test the contact hypothesis date back to at least 1943 (Smith, 1943).

2   Throughout this chapter page numbers for quotations from Allport (1954) refer to the 1979 paperback edition.

3   The use of the word 'Negroes' appears in Allport's original list. Throughout this chapter the word is only used if used in the original publication (because this serves as a reminder of the wider context of black–white relations at the

time of the original study). Otherwise, the term black(s) is used to emphasize the importance of this label and self-referent as an index of a move towards a positive black identity (see Pettigrew, 1971, chapter 12). And, of course, we dissociate ourselves from his exclusive use of the male pronoun in the table.

4   In passing we can note that nowhere in these extracts is there any mention of Allport's concern with the 'typicality' of the contact experience (see extract from Allport). Neither is there any recognition of the importance Allport attached to contact being perceived in terms of intergroup relations.

5   Banton (1983) relates an extraordinary story told by a former secretary of the National Association for the Advancement of Coloured People who had visited US troops in Europe in 1944. One black sergeant had been invited to visit an English home: 'His hosts took care to put a cushion in any chair on which he was likely to sit. Two months later, when he was better acquainted with them, the sergeant learned that they had been advised by white American troops that it was dangerous to entertain Negroes but that, if they did so, they ought to keep in mind that all Negroes had tails which made it impossible for them to sit in the ordinary hard-bottomed chair without first becoming extremely uncomfortable, then excited and dangerous' (Banton, 1983, p. 549). Incredible as this story appears today, there are doubtless many equally ludicrous 'racial beliefs' in current circulation.

6   The importance of ingroup stereotypes was underlined by Lambert and Klineberg's (1967) finding, that children's stereotypes of their own nationality actually developed prior to their stereotypes of other nationalities.

7   Interestingly, Fishbein and Ajzen (1975), in talking about the contact hypothesis, make a similar point. In their view the contact hypothesis is an example of an inappropriate selection of target beliefs to be changed (i.e. trying to change attitudes towards groups as a whole by changing beliefs about particular members of the group).

8   In apparent contradiction are the results of Hamill, Wilson and Nisbett's (1980) study in which student subjects were provided with a description of a humane prison guard who was supposedly atypical of guards in general. This information led subjects to judge prison guards to be more humane than did a control group not provided with the exception to the rule. It should, however, be noted that this study is not clearly about inter*group* perceptions. One would like to have seen the effect of such atypical information on prisoners', rather than students', judgements of prison guards.

9   In our view, some of the interventions reported in chapters 2 and 5 (e.g. Benjamin, 1970; Doob and Foltz, 1973) are most *un*promising avenues for conflict reduction. Divorced as they often are from the rival groups' real concerns, they bear little relation to Sherif's notion of superordinate goals that have 'a compelling appeal for members of each group but that neither group can achieve without participation of the other' (Sherif, 1966a, p. 89).

10 Criticism of this research by Brown and Turner (1979) suggested that the

reduced discrimination might be due to the cognitive difficulties posed by the 'criss-cross' arrangements for the children who served as subjects.

11 To show that subjects had actually blamed the room more in this condition, an attributional dependent measure would be required; no such measure was reported.

12 Brewer and Miller's (1984) edited volume appeared as work for this book was underway. Rather than attempt to ignore this important development, we make explicit our points of agreement and of difference with respect to its theoretical perspective.

13 Note that this conclusion differs sharply from that advocated by Turner (1981) (see pages 21–22). Although Turner also advocates the abandonment of category divisions, this is to facilitate the development of a superordinate category identification. The interaction is therefore transformed from intergroup to *intra*group. However, it is still group-based interaction, which can clearly be distinguished from interpersonal interaction (see Brown and Turner, 1981).

14 In this respect we must disagree with Ben-Ari and Amir's claim in chapter 2 that empirical evidence supports an interpersonal rather than a category-based approach to contact. The research on category-based contact, in line with the present model, is yet to be done!

2 Contact between Arab and Jewish Youth in Israel: Reality and Potential

Rachel Ben-Ari and Yehuda Amir

The purpose of this chapter is to discuss and evaluate interethnic contact as a means of bringing young people from hostile nationalities in one country to live in mutual understanding and respect. The presentation will focus on Arab and Jewish youth living in Israel, with an emphasis on the unique characteristics of the intergroup relationship prevailing in that country.

The reasons for our choosing to focus on young people lie in the difficulty of producing changes in intergroup attitudes, perceptions and feelings when two ethnic or national groups are strongly alienated and divided along many lines, as in the case of Jews and Arabs in Israel. The assumption is that in such a case the possibilities for ethnic contact and change in the adult population are highly limited. For young people however avenues that are worth exploring may exist. Furthermore, positive ethnic changes that are produced at an early age provide a worthwhile personal and social investment for the future.

HISTORICAL BACKGROUND

We begin with a brief history of the intergroup relationship in Israel between the Jewish majority and the Arab minority. The establishment of the State of Israel in 1948 led to a dramatic change in the statuses of the Jewish and Arab populations. The Jews acquired a majority status, whereas the Arabs, who had constituted a significant majority under the pre-state British mandatory rule, became a minority under the Jewish rule. In addition to the continuing state of military and political conflict between Arabs and Jews, there were numerous other estranging factors, such as differences in language, in religion, in culture and geographical distance. Thus for instance 90 per cent of Arab Israelis reside in exclusively Arab towns or villages. Even the 10 per cent who do live in mixed cities occupy separate residential areas.

This situation of almost complete segregation in numerous areas of life where one group is dominated by the other provides fertile ground for the development of frustration and hostility on the part of the dominated group, and the evolution in each group of negative attitudes and stereotyping beliefs regarding the other (Blalock, 1982).

Surprisingly enough, both groups seemed to have accepted this situation of conflict. This acceptance stemmed, among other things, from the feeling shared by both groups that the existing intergroup situation was only a temporary one. The Arabs believed that sooner or later the Jewish State would cease to exist and they would regain their majority status. The Jews, on their part, believed that the 'problem' of the Arabs' presence in Israel would be solved either by the latter's emigration from Israel or by an extensive Jewish immigration that would reduce the Arab population to a negligible minority. Only recently, after more than 30 years of Israel's independence, does some change in the feelings of both sides on this issue appear to have taken place. This change is due primarily to the fact that neither the Jewish nor the Arab expectations have been fulfilled, and consequently both have come to realize that, one way or another, they will have to continue to live together in one country.

Two additional reasons for this change are the recent peace process between Israel and Egypt and the increased economic prosperity of the Arab population. These have led, on the one hand, to greater expectations for a solution of the political conflict and to social pressure for equality; on the other, to a growing feeling of frustration as a consequence of the continuing dominance of the Jewish majority over the Palestinians. In addition, the practice of a discriminatory ruler contradicts the self-image of the Jews (Zemach, 1980) and produces some pressure for change in certain strata of the Jewish population. All these factors have enhanced the readiness of both sides for intergroup acceptance and for the reduction of segregation by means of intergroup contacts (Benyamini, 1980; Hofman, 1972; Peled, 1980; Peled and Bar-Gal, 1983; Smooha, 1980a; Smooha and Peretz, 1982; Zemach, 1980). Yet at the same time, it was found that the most serious problem regarding their respective attitudes towards each other related to the very nature of the State. The Arabs reject the national consensus prevailing in the Jewish population regarding the existence of Israel as a Zionist state. This rejection, coupled with the support of the Palestinian ideology, probably underlies the perception of Israeli Arabs by some parts of the Jewish population as radical and disloyal to Israel.

An additional finding regarding mutual attitudes and perceptions indicates that neither the Jews nor the Arabs seem to be totally radical and stereotyped. In comparison with a small segment holding negative attitudes (14 per cent) and with a small segment with only positive attitudes (13 per cent), the majority of the Jewish public expresses both positive and negative feelings depending on the attitude domain assessed. Similar results were obtained from the Arab population. Thus, the mutual attitudes of the two sides comprise positive elements that could be strengthened in an attempt to attenuate negative attitudes and improve overall relations. It appears therefore that at present there exists a sound basis for establishing more positive relations between the Israeli Jews and Arabs providing an as yet unexploited potential for intergroup contact.

It must however be realized that despite the present existence of some favourable conditions, positive developments in Jewish–Arab relations will not take place spontaneously. Moreover, the decision to initiate the process of 'coexistence' must originate from the Jewish majority since they have the social and political power for bringing about the desired changes. In addition, Jews must recognize that their behaviour and their attitudes towards the Arab minority shape to a large degree the latter's reaction towards them. Smooha's (1980a) research demonstrates that the attitudes of Arabs towards Israeli institutions and public figures are not detached from the objective reality they encounter. For example, Smooha and Hofman (1976/77) found that only 25 per cent of the Arab respondents in 1974 felt more at home in Israel than they would do in an Arab country. Only 22 per cent thought that the young Arab had a future in Israel (Hofman, 1976). Another response to the prevailing reality is shown in Arab voting patterns. Rakah (a communist, anti-Zionist party) has steadily gained Arab votes: from 20 per cent in 1965, 37 per cent in 1973, to 49 per cent in 1977 (Smooha, 1980a). There has also been a sharp increase in the tendency of the Arab minority to identify itself as a segment of the large body of Palestinian people (Nakhleh, 1975). On the other hand, in the 1984 elections a Jewish–Arab party, whose proclaimed goal is coexistence in peace, entered the election race. The Arab members of this party have come to the conclusion that the solution of the conflict lies in co-operation rather than struggle, whereas the Jewish members are deeply concerned with the problems associated with the negative by-products of Jewish dominance and wish to alter the existing status quo.

To sum up, the general picture that emerges in both the Arab and the Jewish sectors seems to point to a growing readiness to change the status quo and to improve intergroup relations. If so, two questions arise: *what* to change and *how* to change.

WHAT TO CHANGE

The question of 'what' to change relates to the specific goals of the two groups, that is what do they want to achieve by the change. The answer to this question constitutes the prerequisite for addressing the question of 'how', which refers to the approaches, the techniques and the means for achieving these goals: the success of any programme for change is dependent upon a clear formulation of the aims involved. They could be quite different from each other, such as to learn about the other culture, to increase the readiness to accept the others socially, to develop a more positive emotional orientation, to change attitudes and perceptions, to integrate one group into another, etc. It is crucial that the different goals are clearly delineated, as they require the use of different methods in order to be achieved. Moreover, the relevance of certain goals and the probability of their attainment may not be the same for the different cultural and ethnic groups involved. Thus, when dealing with possible goals for Israeli Arabs and Jews, several important considerations should be taken into account:

1   Most programmes for intergroup or cross-cultural changes have been directed at the micro-level, that is, they concentrated on modifying individuals who moved from one society to another, without necessarily taking into consideration the situation at the macro-level, namely the relationship between the two societies.[1] In many cases, this treatment is adequate. However, the situation in Israel is different. The two societies under consideration are involved in a major historical, geographical and political conflict that stems from the claim of both groups for the same land. In such circumstances goals that can be achieved at the micro-level may be quite restricted and sometimes even impossible to achieve without some prior solution at the macro-level, that is limiting the social or political conflict.

2   In contrast to other cross-cultural programmes that focus on training representatives from one society in order to enable their functioning in another society, the Israeli project must address itself to *both* groups. However, the goals of the cross-cultural training and consequently the methods chosen to implement them may not be the same for the two groups. Thus, for instance, in a sensitivity training workshop with Jews and Arabs, Lakin, Lomeranz and Lieberman (1969) felt that the respective goals of the two groups in joining the workshop had been different – the Arabs seeking a platform for airing their grievances, and the Jews hoping for conciliation and understanding.

3   In the Jewish–Arab intergroup situation each side carries a 'load' of

negative feelings for the other. Consequently, any project that aims to change the existing state between the two groups must consider the fact that its recipients are not emotionally 'naïve'. In such a case it may be advisable for the planned cross-cultural training to start with a process of cross-cultural unlearning that will prepare the ground for the successful implementation of the programme.

4 Finally, let us consider the issue of motivation. Underlying any project aimed at fostering learning is an assumption of positive motivation on the part of the learner. Individuals participating in cross-cultural programmes are usually interested in their success because of some instrumental reasons. In this case it may be assumed that the emotional barriers and prejudices of the two groups greatly reduce their motivation or increase their fear of taking part in training. Under such conditions the design of a cross-cultural learning project must search for ways to cope with this problem.

In summary, it is clear that for Israeli Arabs and Jews the design of a project for cross-cultural change is quite complex and may be more difficult than comparable projects reported in the literature (Brislin and Pedersen, 1976).

Let us now return to the definition of the goals and specify those that are relevant to young people. As noted earlier, some of the goals may be identical for both groups, while others may be unique to each group. Two primary goals exist at the macro-level: (1) to educate young people to realize and accept the equality of rights of all citizens in a democratic society, particularly with regard to the majority–minority issue in Israel. This goal may be more relevant to young people from the majority group as those from the minority group probably already identify with it; (2) to attain social, political and economic equality, which is obviously more relevant to the minority group.

At the micro-level the general goal is to produce educational input towards co-operation for young people from two diverse cultures, who are likely to come into contact in various settings as adults. This goal may be operationally expressed by the following sub-goals, which apply to both groups:

to reduce the mutual alienation of Jewish and Arab pupils through mutual acquaintance;
to minimize stereotypes and prejudice;
to develop empathy towards the other group's members and/or culture;
to increase the amount of contacts between the two cultures.

For the Arabs there may be an additional goal, namely to learn to function more effectively in the Jewish society. Its basis relates to the fact that Israeli Arabs live in a country with a Jewish orientation and constantly interact with Jewish institutions and authorities. In order to function effectively, they must get acquainted with the Israeli *Jewish* society, its orientations, customs and needs.

One should also take into consideration that Jewish Israelis, as members of the majority group, are likely to be content with the achievement of their goals at the micro-level. In contrast the Arabs, as members of the minority group, may go further in their goal-definitions and will view the change on the micro-level as a means for attaining changes on the macro-level. However, such goals may elicit opposition amongst those Jews who may resist or fear a change in the status quo at the macro-level.

When coming to design a cross-cultural training programme it is also important to recognize the possible undesired aspects of change or resistance to it. In this particular case, any programme should take into account that *neither* side is interested in attaining social and cultural integration or in promoting intimate relations between members of the two groups. On the contrary, both sides favour strict cultural pluralism, and each group prefers to retain its cultural, social and national uniqueness, while maintaining a distinct group identity.

INTERGROUP CONTACT: A WAY TO CHANGE

Back in the 1940s and early 1950s there was a widespread belief that intergroup contact would inevitably lead to a change in the mutual attitudes of the interacting members and would improve their intergroup relations. This belief assumed that mere contact among individuals from diverse groups creates an opportunity for mutual acquaintances, enhances understanding and acceptance among the interacting group members and consequently reduces intergroup prejudice, conflict and tension. This belief has underlain decisions on national policy in the areas of housing, work and education, as well as various international programmes such as student exchanges, professional conferences, sports, etc. The foregoing assumptions are based in part on the empirical findings that have been summarized and reviewed by Allport (1954), Amir (1969, 1976), Cook (1962), and others. These reviews indeed lead to the conclusion that contact may change attitudes and relations between diverse ethnic groups. Furthermore, empirical findings suggest that other approaches trying to achieve this end have not proved successful (Ashmore, 1970).

In the field of intergroup relations Amir (1969, 1976) and Cook (1970) maintain that, while contact does lead to change in ethnic attitudes and relations, this change does not always occur in the desired direction. In order to achieve positive changes certain conditions must be present in situations of contact; other conditions may lead to negative results. This has been found in many areas of intergroup contact (Amir, 1969, 1976), as well as studies regarding Arab–Jewish relationships in Israel (Amir, 1979; Amir and Ben-Ari, 1985; Amir et al., 1982; Amir et al., 1980).

The more important conditions for positive change summarized by Amir and Cook are as follows.

1   Equal-status contact between the members of the interacting groups. As this is sometimes difficult to achieve in situations of contact between majority and minority groups, change may also be produced if important characteristics of the interacting minority members are different from and more positive than the stereotypes held by majority members with regard to these characteristics.
2   Intergroup co-operation in the pursuit of common goals. This kind of situation creates an interdependence between the groups and discourages competition between them.
3   Contact of an intimate rather than a casual nature, which allows the interacting members to get to know each other beyond the superficial level.
4   An 'authority' and/or social climate approving of and supporting the intergroup contact. Of particular relevance here is the support given to intergroup contact by the community, social institutions, friends and any 'relevant others'.
5   The initial intergroup attitudes are not extremely negative.

The theoretical rationale for some of the desirable contact conditions is based on cognitive explanations regarding the potential contact has for improving intergroup relations. This approach generally assumes that the development of stereotypes and attitudes stems from the absence of sufficient information and/or the existence of erroneous information held by one group about the other one, and that contact situations provide the opportunity for clarifying erroneous perceptions and for relearning by supplying new information. In other words, when during contact an individual discovers that the 'other' is not as dissimilar as has been assumed (Rokeach, 1960) or even holds similar attitudes (Byrne, 1969; Newcomb, 1961), he or she will tend to change negative attitudes or develop positive attitudes towards the 'other'. It appears thereore that contact, *per se*, may be a necessary but not sufficient condition for producing a positive change in attitudes and relations. In order for contact to be effective, it must occur under conditions of 'positive exposure'. Similarly, Cook (1978) stresses the importance of the 'acquaintance potential' in ethnic contact, by which enough information about members of the other group is revealed, facilitating their apprehension as individuals rather than as stereotyped group members.

There is some controversy over what constitutes the necessary focus of interaction for interethnic change to be produced. Brewer and Miller (1984) claim that in order to achieve this, the contact situation has to be *interpersonally* oriented, de-emphasizing group categories. Contrarily, Brown and Turner (1981) believe that only when the social categories of the groups are stressed and dealt with, can intergroup relations be changed. These two orientations also propose different predictions regarding the issue of generalization. Brewer and Miller assume that only when category-based information is reduced in contact and personalized information is promoted, may generalization to new situations occur. On the other hand, Brown and Turner believe that a generalization of the contact effect will take place only if the contact is based on categorical grounds. Ample theoretical basis is provided for both these orientations. Nevertheless, the empirical evidence regarding change in ethnic relations, including that in Arab–Jewish relations, seems to support the interpersonal emphasis in contact rather than the category-based one.*

CONTACT BETWEEN ARAB AND JEWISH YOUTH

Considering the complex relationship between Arabs and Jews in Israel, what opportunities are there for meaningful intergroup contact between members of the two groups? What are the outcomes when such contact does occur? In view of what has been said, it is clear that the opportunities for meaningful contact between Jews and Arabs are severely restricted. In addition, the conditions that characterize this intergroup situation have a number of features that would suggest that category-based social interaction is very probable.

Until recently, the Israeli educational system had totally disregarded the issue of Jewish–Arab relations. However, sporadic attempts on the part of schools or individual teachers to initiate meetings between their pupils and pupils of the other sector can now be seen. Such one-off meetings are usually the result of the goodwill and *ad hoc* planning of the organizing teachers and they are not counselled by specialists or professionals in the areas of Arab–Jewish relations or cross-cultural contact. The typical project of this kind includes a meeting between

*Editors' note: the editors differ from Ben-Ari and Amir, and Brewer and Miller on this point, see chapter 1.

Jewish and Arab pupils in the Arab school and a recriprocated meeting of both groups in the Jewish school. In most cases the pupils are not carefully prepared for the contact before the meetings, which are not structured and mainly include the young people making themselves acquainted with each other and individual or group talks. The effectiveness of such meetings has not been systematically assessed. However, on the basis of impressions and attitudes reported by students participating in some of the meetings, it is clear that also with this form of contact the results are not always positive, sometimes even strongly negative. Thus, for instance, among Jewish high school students who reported unpleasant contact experiences with Arabs, 67 per cent expressed hatred of most or all Arabs, as opposed to 37 per cent of those who had had no contact at all (Levy and Guttman, 1976). It is important to note that one possible reason for the failure of meetings of this kind is that they involve the discussion of the political conflict between the two national groups.

Universities constitute an additional setting for contact between Arab and Jewish young people. This setting is characterized by mutual negative attitudes. The national identity of the Arab students is crystallized and their political awareness is highly developed. They view themselves as belonging to the Arab nation and become increasingly alienated and hostile towards Israeli society. Furthermore, university contact does not usually involve the conditions listed above as necessary for producing a positive change. It is probably for these reasons that universities have frequently been scenes of clashes between Jewish and Arab students.

In recent years a new kind of contact has been gaining popularity. This development originated with the establishment of several organizations and institutes that are concerned with promoting Jewish–Arab relations. Detailed descriptions of several such organizations are provided by Rosen (1970) and Peled and Bar-Gal (1983).

All of these organizations share the general aim of encouraging coexistence in peace between Jews and Arabs, and their projects are based on meetings between Arabs and Jews. However, each organization acts as a separate unit and uses different techniques. Their meetings differ in intensity and duration, and the topics covered also vary. They may include cognitive contents such as the history of Jewish–Arab relations, the folklore and culture of the two peoples, and/or affective contents such as human relations training and other activities aimed at increasing intimacy. The political issue is addressed in some of the intergroup meetings and avoided in others.

Undoubtedly, the organizers of Arab–Jewish meetings of this kind invest considerable effort and goodwill in these activities. However, they do have serious limitations. First, they lack continuity and professional guidance. Second, they do not have institutional support and legitimization by the public and government agencies. Third, they are not specifically designed according to defined goals and some conceptual or theoretical orientation. Nevertheless, one type of intergroup contact that did show some positive changes in interethnic attitudes and perception and in mutual understanding was the sort made through encounter or sensitivity training groups (Benjamin, 1970; Bizman, 1978; Greenbaum and Abdul Razak, 1972; Gordon, 1980; Lakin et al., 1969; Smith, 1981).

The common feature of the more successful intergroup meetings is that they enabled the operation of some of the conditions recommended for effective contact. More specifically, these meetings focus on personal content that stresses the similarities between the participants and enables interaction on an equal-status basis. Most of them avoid the political-national issues that may cause tension and conflict between the group members. In addition, human relations seminars are of an intimate nature and encourage friendly relations.

CONCLUSIONS AND RECOMMENDATIONS

When the high percentage of Jews and Arabs who express a readiness for contact with each other, as found in various surveys, is compared with the low percentage who actually participate in contact, it becomes clear that the potential for Jewish–Arab contact in Israel has not been exploited. In view of the existing evidence that shows that contact may serve as a tool for reducing prejudice, enhancing tolerance and changing attitudes and stereotypes, this potential should not be neglected. However, it must be remembered that contact, by itself, is not sufficient. Some would undoubtedly argue that contact between Jews and Arabs should be considered as an end in itself, to be preferred to segregation. However, the negative outcomes of contact under undesirable conditions strongly support the position of Smooha (1980b) who objected to the unqualified belief in contact on the grounds that, under the conditions currently prevailing in Israel, increased contact in the various settings such as schools, housing and politics would only intensify conflict. According to Smooha, the separation of the two groups, while increasing alienation and hostility, also reduces opportunities for conflict. Smooha's conclusion is quite valid in cases where the establishment of contact under optimal conditions is impossible. However, as elaborated above, it is possible to plan and implement successful contacts that may yield more encouraging outcomes.

Major problems that generally emerge in contact situations of this kind as well as in the Arab–Jewish case are as follows.

1 There is no clear definition of goals that could provide a sound basis for planning the contact situation. In most cases they are stated as general, long-range and utopian declarations instead of short-term, operational and attainable aims. In addition, the expectations, concerning the goals, of the contact organizers and of the participants from the two groups do not always coincide. Consequently, unrealistic hopes often lead to disappointment and frustration. At any rate, contact may achieve results at the micro-level, but will not affect the macro-level; therefore, one should not expect changes in societal and political domains as a result of intergroup contact.

2 The absence of a clear *a priori* definition of goals raises problems regarding the choice of programmes to be included in contacts. The prevailing policy is 'the more, the better'. Consequently, contact organizers attempt to include a wide variety of cognitive, emotional and behavioural contents, by which they create contacts that include a large quantity of material, but of a highly superficial level. Such an input is likely to result in a limited and not very meaningful output.

3 A large proportion of contacts are one-shot events. It is hardly necessary to stress the theory that attitudes and relations are products of a long and continuous development, and that the belief that they can change in one meeting is, at best, naïve. However, this being the case, it is therefore necessary to plan long-term educational programmes for instilling stable attitudes and relations that begin at an early age.

4 In most cases, contact participants are neither prepared nor evaluated at an early stage. As was elaborated above, the initial attitude of the participants and their expectations play a central role in determining the outcome of contact. Therefore, appropriate preparation of the participants prior to their entering the contact situation is likely to increase the probability of obtaining positive results. The beneficial effects of early preparation were clearly demonstrated in a recent study that assessed the effects of contact between Israeli Jews and Egyptians (Amir and Ben-Ari, in press).

5 In most contacts insufficient attention is given to the establishment of optimal contact conditions and in some cases unfavourable conditions prevail. Reference to political and national conflict issues is disruptive in most cases, particularly at an early stage of the contact. It creates tension among the participants and gives rise to attacks and accusations on the one hand, and defensive reactions on the other. Because of the extremity

of the political differences between the groups, talks about a common denominator in the political realm are futile. Why emphasize the most basic difference between the two groups when we know that dissimilarity is a major cause of interpersonal rejection, whereas similarity is a potent source of attraction (Newcombe, 1961)? Furthermore, introduction of the Arab–Jewish conflict confronts the participants in a way that defines them as two antagonistic entities, thereby strengthening the tendency to consider members of the outgroup as undifferentiated particles in a unified social category, regardless of their individual differences. This will be reflected in a clear awareness of the ingroup-outgroup dichotomy; in the attribution to members of the outgroup of certain traits assumed to be common to the group as a whole; in value-judgements pertaining to these traits; in the emotional significance associated with these evaluations; and in other forms of behaviour associated with the ingroup-outgroup categorization.

As for those who argue that the political problems cannot be ignored, sufficient evidence exists to show that it is possible to establish relations between the Jewish majority and the Arab minority that are based on mutual respect and civil rights for all, even when there is a disagreement regarding the solution of political problems. Peled (1980) found that opinions regarding the overall issue of Israeli Jewish–Arab relations are not entirely generalized in the minds of respondents, that is expressions of conflict with respect to the international sphere are generally not correlated with those regarding the intergroup and interpersonal spheres. Zemach (1980) reported an absence of correlation between the Jews' perception of Arabs, which was mainly positive and the Jews' perception of Arabs' attitude toward Israel, which was mainly negative. Similarly, Levy and Guttman (1976) and Adar and Adler (1965) found no correlation among Jewish youth between interpersonal attitudes and attitudes in the political-national domains.

These findings support the notion that it is possible to deal with micro-interpersonal aspects of an intergroup conflict without addressing the macro-intergroup issues. This is, in fact, the source of hope for successful contact in this specific situation. One should realize that with regard to Arab–Jewish relations, action at the micro-level is feasible, whereas action at the macro-level is not under the control of social psychologists. Moreover, psychological methods and techniques may be fruitful when dealing with problems and conflicts that have evolved from a psychological origin. However, on the macro-level other factors, such as political, economic, religious and cultural ones may be the basis of the conflict, thereby restricting the effectiveness of the psychological tool to deal with its solution. This does not imply that the action at the micro-level is of no importance. On the contrary, beneficial influence in the interpersonal sphere of intergroup relations may be regarded as an end in itself, as both sides have to live together in one country even if they have not solved their political conflict. In addition, activities in this realm may serve as a salient social message that intergroup communication should be encouraged and promoted. Furthermore, it may be safely assumed that if intergroup relations at the micro-level deteriorate, this may create an atmosphere conducive to negative developments at the political macro-level. Likewise, if and when changes do occur in the macro-domain, the earlier changes at the micro-level will make an important contribution to the softening of the transfer from a state of segregation and hostility to a state of coexistence and peace. Thus, it is hoped that changes in the micro-sphere will facilitate the development of positive macro-processes.

Nevertheless, in spite of the enthusiasm often voiced by human relations workers who regard contact as a means of improving Jewish-Arab relations, it is necessary to be aware of the limitations of this tool in the Israeli situation. As noted earlier, the geographical distance between the two groups and the small size of the Arab minority hinder significant contacts between Jewish and Arab young people. If we add the problem of language (Jewish young people do not generally speak Arabic, and Arab young people cannot express themselves easily in Hebrew), the segregation in education and the resources necessary for organizing the meetings, it is clear that contact cannot fulfil all our hopes and expectations in the area of Arab–Jewish relations.

It is therefore necessary to search for alternative solutions. An obvious way is to recruit the existing educational system for developing new intergroup norms, values and attitudes. More specifically, a curriculum should be developed that is based more on the cognitive approach (Gudykunst, Hammer and Wiseman, 1977) and less on face-to-face interactions. An integrative programme including, in addition to cognitive contents, some intergroup contact that will emphasize the social and emotional aspects of interpersonal and intergroup relations may be even more effective. The cognitive section of such a programme may be built in a similar or a different fashion for the two ethnic groups of young people, as depends on the specific goals to be achieved for each of the groups and the corresponding optimal techniques to be used for their achievement. Mutual intergroup contact may serve as the concluding and integrative part of such a programme.

On the basis of the above considerations, educational programmes aimed at facilitating intergroup understanding and relations between the Arab and the Jewish youth are currently being developed. They are based primarily upon the cognitive approach, combined with a minimal number of intergroup meetings. The central effort is directed towards the development of relevant contents and suitable techniques for the implementation of the programme for the above-mentioned goals and different target populations. A general programme within the educational system, in addition to its wide scope, will also provide legitimization and institutional support for Arab–Jewish relations and thus may serve as a potent factor in the shaping of a peaceful coexistence between the Jewish and the Arab sectors of Israel.

NOTE

1   The distinction made here between *micro-* and *macro-*levels should not be confused with Tajfel's (1981) differentiation between *interpersonal* and *intergroup* aspects. Micro-processes relate to the individual, whereas macro-processes refer to social and political aspects of society. Tajfel's terms deal only with the individual and whether he or she acts as an individual or as a group member.

3 'Gastarbeiter' in the Federal Republic of Germany: Contact between Germans and Migrant Populations

Ulrich Wagner and Uwe Machleit

OVERVIEW

Since the economic boom in the mid-1950s foreign workers, mainly from mediterranean countries, have been employed in the Federal Republic of Germany (FRG); today there are more than 4.5 million foreigners living there. Our approach to 'contact and prejudice' refers to the relationship between Germans and these foreign inhabitants of the FRG, who in our opinion are wrongly called 'Gastarbeiter' (guest workers). We present first a short summary of our ideas about ethnic prejudice and how it may develop. An analysis of the present living conditions of the foreign workers, considering legal, economic and social factors, will follow in order to give an idea of the social environment in which prejudice develops, and in which contacts between Germans and foreigners take place. We shall then give a short survey of conditions hindering or promoting contact, followed by a presentation of the small quantity of work in this field that examines empirically the question of how prejudice between foreigners and Germans is affected by interethnic contact. Finally, we consider how these ideas might be made to play a more important role in the education of children and adults.

PREJUDICE

Ethnic prejudice is here considered to be a negative attitude towards a group of people who are defined in terms of ethnic or national characteristics. Traditionally attitudes and prejudices are considered to consist of three different components.

1 The *evaluative aspect* of prejudice represents the emotional reaction

of the prejudiced person towards the ethnic group in question. This evaluation is usually negative in the case of prejudice: 'I do not like Turkish people, they are not likeable!'

2   The *cognitive component* of prejudice is often called a *stereotype*. Ethnic stereotypes contain the 'knowledge' prejudiced persons think they have about an ethnic group, as evinced in such statements that for example start: 'All Turks are . . .'. It is especially evident with this cognitive component of prejudice that it may sometimes be difficult to distinguish between a 'normal' statement about an ethnic group and one that reflects ethnic prejudice. In order to reduce the complexity of our environment we often have to subsume different facts under one category and take them as being equal. Every 'normal' statement about a group contains expectations towards all members of that group, which necessarily entail a distortion of reality. A statement such as: 'The Turkish people are Muslims', could hardly, on its own, be considered a sign of prejudice, even though not all Turks are Muslims. Thus, in our opinion, all statements about groups are in effect stereotyping, that is they can only be distinguished by the degree to which they do stereotype. Some pragmatic criteria for differentiation were established by Schönbach et al. (1981, pp. 43 ff). A statement about a group becomes more clearly stereotyped if for example:

The group is described by only a few traits.
('The Turks are dirty and nothing else.')
The traits are attributed to all members of the group.
('All Turks are dirty.')
The differences between the outgroup and the respondent's own (national) group are clearly pronounced.
('All Turks are dirty. A German would never be that dirty.')

3   It is assumed that a *behavioural* or *conative component* of prejudice shows that negative emotions and opinions should be linked to discriminatory behaviour. A close relation between the affective and cognitive components of prejudice and overt discrimination will however only be noticed under certain circumstances. While we have defined prejudice as an attitude towards a *group* of people, discriminatory behaviour towards one single member of an ethnic group is only to be expected if ethnic group memberships are cognitively relevant for the people involved. Furthermore, most prejudiced people prefer to engage in those kinds of discrimination that can not be punished. One common type of discrimination that is largely tolerated is avoiding contact with members of ethnic minorities (see chapter 6).

Development of prejudice

In our opinion, ethnic prejudice is developed by a combination of specific social conditions and mechanisms of the human mind. The *impact of the social environment* can be elucidated by means of a few examples. First, a differentiation within a society between native and foreign people is not an *a priori*, given fact in itself; classification on the basis of whether the inhabitants of a country have blue or brown eyes could be as important or unimportant as a classification by national groups. Only by the different treatment of natives and foreigners within a society, for example by special laws and regulations, does the differentiation between natives and foreigners become evident and socially relevant to the individual. Furthermore, public and published opinion encourage prejudice towards certain ethnic groups by stressing the differences between these groups and the native population and by describing these differences in a negative way. At the same time they often deliver a qualitative reason for rejection by describing these negative features as if they were innate in members of the minority group. Alternatively, the foreigners are blamed for all problems within the country.

Social intercourse with foreigners may contribute to the development of prejudice in the individual members of society. This seems to be promoted by *psychological mechanisms*. As mentioned above, in order to reduce the complexity of their environment people often have to put a variety of facts in one category. Our system of information processing seems to be especially equipped for such categorization. Psychological research has shown that differences between categories are perceived as bigger than they really are, and that differences within one category tend to be neglected (Tajfel and Forgas, 1981). So this psychological mechanism will contribute to an overemphasis on externally ascribed differences. Thus, information processing reinforces the social and institutional way of dealing with foreigners.

Further research suggests that psychological mechanisms do not only support the emphasis on differences between ethnic groups, but also that discrimination and devaluation of strangers are reinforced by the functioning of psychological mechanisms. According to Tajfel's (1978a) social identity theory, people (at least those of the Western industrial countries) have learned to upgrade the status of the group they belong to at the expense of other groups, in order to improve their own social identity. Such a mechanism is perfectly consistent with ethnocentric forms of public opinion, which lay stress upon the superiority of one's own (ethnic) group as compared with others. Again, there is an interaction between social and psychological influences on prejudice.

In order to discuss the relation between German/foreign contacts and prejudice, we must keep in mind the actual living conditions of foreigners in the FRG. Interindividual contacts between Germans and foreigners may help the people involved to change their way of categorizing people by ethnic characteristics. It is however most probably the given social setting that determines whether or not these encounters turn out to be a positive or negative experience, and whether or not they diminish or intensify ethnic prejudice. Even positive contacts between foreigners and Germans will only have a minor impact on the reduction of prejudice, if these contacts remain exceptional in character and societal conditions do not change. Prejudice is a negative judgement of a group. If the social background remains unchanged, prejudice against a group and positive experience with single group members need not be an inconsistency: positive experience is just an exception to the rule.

FOREIGN WORKERS IN THE FRG: PAST AND PRESENT

History of migration

Employment of foreigners has a tradition in Germany. Even before the turn of the century foreign labour for industry and agriculture was called to Germany. There is for example a close connection between the development of the mining industry in the 'Ruhrgebiet' (an important industrial area between Duisburg and Dortmund) and the employment of workers from Eastern Europe. During the First World War, but even more during the Second World War, foreign civilians and prisoners of war were forced to work in Germany.

The employment of foreign workers in the FRG after the war started in the mid-1950s. Even though large numbers of Germans were deported or sought refuge from the East, the demand for labour in the expanding economy seemed to exceed the supply of German workers. In 1955 an agreement was made between the German and Italian governments concerning the recruitment and procurement of Italian workers. In 1960 recruitment treaties with Spain and Greece followed, in 1961 with Turkey, and between 1963 and 1968 further agreements were made with Morocco, Portugal, Tunisia, and Yugoslavia. As a rule, recruitment offices were established by the German authorities in these countries. Their main task was the medical selection of healthy potential workers. Often the selection was guided by the specific requirements of single employers; they needed foreign workers for jobs that no longer appealed to German employees.

In 1973, under the pressure of recession, a governmental resolution stopped further recruitment of foreign labour. Since then it has been practically impossible for inhabitants of countries not in the EEC to come to the FRG 'only' to find a job. Despite this resolution, effective since 1973, the number of foreigners in the FRG has increased during the last 10 years. One reason for the further increase was the deterioration of the economic situations in their home countries, which reduced the number of foreign workers prepared to go back. Indeed, there was a growing tendency for husbands or wives and children to be called to Germany. Thus, the number of foreigners increased from 4 to 4.7 million between 1973 and 1982. The number of foreign workers however decreased in the same period from 2.6 to 1.8 million (information from Statistisches Jahrbuch, 1983, p. 31). Foreigners in the FRG are therefore no longer only guest *workers*, but complete families. The majority (1.6 million people) are Turks;[1] there are approximately 600,000 Yugoslavians and more or less the same number of Italians (*Statistisches Jahrbuch*, 1983, p 68). By 1980 more than three-quarters of all adult foreigners had been living in the FRG for more than seven years (Mehrländer et al., 1982, pp. 539ff).

Politics and laws concerning foreigners in the FRG

The FRG has never considered itself an immigration country. The presence of foreigners has always been considered a temporary state of affairs. As a result the politicians responsible never developed a comprehensive so-called 'Ausländerpolitik' (policy concerning foreigners living in the FRG). Even the 'Bundesbeauftragter für Ausländerfragen' (authorized representative of the government for problems concerning foreigners in the FRG), Heinz Kühn, mentions in his report of 1979 (p. 2) that the prevailing development and the measures taken had been determined mainly by the priority given to labour market policy, by which socio-political problems were neglected. This indifferent and unplanned official policy, supported by increasing unemployment and a worsening economic situation, now seems to be drifting more and more towards rejection of foreigners in the FRG.

Present policy is revealed by the *legal status* of foreign citizens coming from outside the EEC. The current economic crisis means that old laws and regulations have a drastic impact on the lives of many foreign people, and in addition new measures have been introduced during the last years. Thus the legal status of many foreigners is quite insecure (acceptance of social assistance may lead to their expulsion). Children of foreign workers are only allowed to follow their parents to the FRG providing that they are not over sixteen; a lowering of this age limit to six years has been discussed by the federal government. Foreign spouses may only join their partners in the FRG after at least two to three years of marriage. Permission to work is granted after another four years of waiting. Foreigners are excluded from all political elections, irrespective of the length of time they have been in the FRG. In 1983 a law came into force that provides financial support for those unemployed foreigners who are willing to go back to their home countries. This could also be considered an act of rejection. (Concerning the political and legal situation of foreigners in other European countries see Schönbach et al., 1981, pp. 183ff.)

Living standards

A very small minority of the foreigners living in the FRG left their homes for political reasons. The majority expected an improvement in their personal economic situation, the price for which is having to accept unfavourable living conditions. Foreigners seem to be discriminated against in important daily matters, even in those fields where their legal status should be the same as that of Germans. For example the housing conditions of many foreigners are inadequate (Forschungsverbund, 1979, pp. 65ff), as high rents and the negative attitude of German landlords often prevent them from obtaining bigger and better-equipped apartments. Most of the foreigners in the FRG are employed as unskilled workers (Forschungsverbund, 1979, pp 63ff). Even if comparably qualified they have less chance of making a career than German employees (Forschungsverbund, 1979, pp. 122ff). The rate of jobless foreigners (12 per cent in 1982) is one and a half times higher than the total jobless rate (Bundesminister des Inneren, 1983, p. 12). The poor prospects for foreign children growing up in the FRG make the disadvantages quite evident. Most of the foreign pupils receive only the basic education prescribed by law; very few of them continue beyond this level (Statistisches Jahrbuch, 1983, p. 346); more than half of the foreigners who attend German schools do not complete their education (Forschungsverbund, 1979, pp. 60ff; Mehrländer et al., 1982, pp. 44ff). Unfortunately, there is not much empirically supported information about what the foreigners concerned think about their own situation. However, from individual cases studies and some empirical data (e.g. Mehrländer et al., 1982) there is evidence that they have to face living conditions that are becoming more and more oppressive.

German public and published opinion

Apart from the palpably unfavourable living conditions for foreigners in the FRG, there are clear signs of rejection to be noted in public and published opinion. Representative opinion polls among Germans have shown that negative attitudes have increased during the last years: foreigners are held responsible for high criminality rates, job shortages and housing problems (EMNID, 1982; cf. 'Der Spiegel', *18*, 1982). They are forced into the roles of scapegoats for social problems. A sizeable proportion of the Germans interviewed (66 per cent) said that foreigners should return to their native countries; half of them even demanded that this should apply to foreign children who were born in Germany. The majority reject the idea of bringing together foreign families in the FRG (INFAS, 1982). These opinions and demands, the so-called 'public opinion', correspond closely with the image of foreigners found in certain elements of the media, the 'published opinion' (cf. Delgado, 1972; Segal, 1981).

The largest group of foreigners in the FRG, those coming from Turkey, seems to come off worst in public and published opinion. Members of the other nationalities, such as Italians (Schönbach et al., 1981, pp 55ff) and Spaniards (Wagner, Hewstone and Machleit, in preparation) are judged in a comparatively favourable way by the German population (INFAS, 1982, pp. 7ff). Exact reasons for this have not yet been found. Possible reasons may be that the Turks are quite large in number and thus represent an imaginary menace, or that their way of life is rather different from that of the Germans. An advantage for Italians and Greeks may be that Italy and Greece are members of the European Community. Thus Italians, Greeks and Germans belong to a common 'European nation', in contrast to the 'strange' Turks.

In short, foreigners in the FRG presently have to live in circumstances that are marked by rejection and discrimination in many ways. At least in one of its meanings the neologism 'Ausländerfeindlichkeit' (hostility towards foreigners in the FRG) gives a description of discriminatory treatment by German society of foreign workers and their families. According to Hoffmann and Even's (1983) analysis in terms of the sociology of knowledge, this form of 'Ausländerfeindlichkeit' has even become one of the substantial and undoubted facts of German society. In discussing prejudice and contact between foreigners and Germans, as we do below, this social situation always has to be taken into consideration. 'Ausländerfeindlichkeit' contributes essentially to prejudice and the willingness of both foreigners and Germans to have contact with each other. If the public gets the impression that foreigners are only going to stay for a limited period of time, this has an impact on the kind of contact and its effects. Furthermore, within a society where the presence of foreigners is considered a nuisance, the circumstances in which contacts between foreigners and natives take place will often not be conducive to the reduction of individual ethnic prejudice. Finally, in the case of negatively experienced interethnic contacts that support the prejudices of the people involved, contact will even reinforce 'Ausländerfeindlichkeit' in German society.

CONTACTS

This discussion is divided into three parts. To begin with, we look at the actual conditions of contact between foreigners and Germans. The existing possibilities for contact between them have to be clarified before it is possible to analyse in a sensible way the connection between interethnic contact and the intensity of prejudice. The second part gives a summary of empirical studies carried out in the FRG and relates contact to the degree of prejudice. Finally, an excursion into pedagogics and adult education considers the possibilities for reducing ethnic prejudice by means of specifically organized contacts.

Opportunities for contacts between foreigners and Germans in the FRG

In 1982 more than 7 per cent of the population of the FRG was foreign. Given this figure there is a high statistical probability of interethnic contact. However, the number of foreigners in relation to the German population is not the only factor that influences the probability of contact; geographical distribution has also to be considered. The proportion of foreigners to Germans is higher in towns than in rural districts, and in the towns foreigners often live close together in ghetto-like conditions (Mehrländer et al., 1981, pp. 477ff). At the very beginning of their stay in the FRG the life in such a 'ghetto' may have offered them a feeling of security, but now it impedes contact with the native population (Esser, 1980, pp. 95ff; Forschungsverbund, 1979, pp. 210ff). At work the opportunities for contacts between foreigners and Germans are also quite restricted. Foreigners work mostly in low-status jobs that require minimal qualifications. These jobs do not attract Germans (Forschungsverbund, 1979, pp. 35ff), so that foreigners have few fellow workers who are German.

Effective contacts do not only consist of physical encounters – an intense personal contact needs real interaction. One basic requirement for such interactive contacts is the use of a common language. However, few Germans have knowledge of the languages that are spoken in the home countries of the foreign workers; foreigners also often have a poor knowledge of German (Forschungsverbund, 19791, p. 124; Bundesminister für Arbeit und Sozialordnung, 1980, pp. 106ff; Mehrländer et al., 1981, pp. 483ff, 498ff),[2] so that the opportunities for interactive contacts are already limited because of a very real language barrier. Empirically, there is a connection between the foreigners' increasing proficiency in German and the number of their German acquaintances (Forschungsverband, 1979, p. 216).

Contact and prejudice

Only a few German studies have examined the question of how the quality and the quantity of interethnic contact on the one hand and the level of mutual prejudice on the other hand are connected. In addition, the few empirical studies we know of concentrate on the German population and their prejudice. Despite these problems, we shall try to present a clear picture of what is known. Our presentation of the studies is based on the form of contact with which they deal (cf. Allport, 1954, pp. 262ff; Amir, 1976).

The majority of German studies concerning interethnic contacts and prejudice relate people's self-reported contact with foreigners to their level of prejudice. In this way indicators of *contact frequency* were defined in the studies by INFAS (1982, pp. 7ff), Schönbach et al. (1981, pp. 69ff), and Wagner et al. (in preparation). The INFAS study, being representative of the German population,. showed that with increased frequency of every-day contact with foreigners the interviewees' attitude towards foreigners became more positive. The studies by Schönbach et al. and Wagner et al. showed comparable results with schoolchildren. A causal interpretation of these correlations is rather difficult. Is the reduction of prejudice a result of frequent contacts, or is a low level of prejudice a precondition for contacts with foreigners? Unsöld (1978) considered two different contact measures in relation to children's opinions about foreigners: (a) German parents' statements of their children's frequency of contact with foreigners (pp. 247ff) and (b) teachers' reports of the intensity of contact in their classes (pp. 253ff). On the whole he too found more positive attitudes with increased contact frequency. Again there is the problem of causality: the correlation of contact frequency and indices of prejudice could in this case simply be a result of the fact that open-minded parents and teachers teach their children a positive attitude towards strangers, which includes guiding them towards contacts with foreigners.

Wenninger (1978, pp. 216ff) tried to derive *contact opportunities* from objective criteria. In accordance with the above-mentioned studies he was able to demonstrate that judgements about a foreign nation are more positive, the more members of this group there are among a respondent's fellow workers. Wagner et al. (in preparation) discovered indications of a comparable connection between the number of foreign pupils of a particular nationality in a class and the opinions of German pupils about this national group. A causal interpretation of these findings is relatively easy. The number of foreign associates at work or at school will hardly have been determined by the level of prejudice of the questioned people; most probably individual ethnic prejudice was influenced positively by contact. Corresponding to Malhotra's (1978) findings, the commonly accepted and published attitude towards foreigners or particular foreign groups may have been watered down by personal contacts with foreigners and foreign children. However, in contrast to the results of the studies by Wenninger and Wagner et al., Wagner (1983, pp. 177ff) was not able to demonstrate a relation between the number of Turkish pupils in school and other pupils' judgements of Turks. He noted a tendency towards an increasingly negative attitude as the proportion of Turkish pupils increased. These seemingly contradictory results can be clarified if we take into consideration that in all the studies mentioned so far only quantitative contact indices were related to prejudice values. Probably the effects of contact depend primarily on the quality of the encounters and their attendant circumstances. Presumably the interethnic contacts of those people questioned for the studies of Wenninger and Wagner et al. had taken place under very favourable conditions, whereas the pupils who took part in Wagner's study of 1983 had obviously had less encouraging experiences.

Some studies have tried to establish a relationship between the *quality of contact* experienced by the subjects and their level of prejudice. Following the results of INFAS (1982, pp. 7ff) and Wagner (1983, pp. 108ff), statements of liking are made more frequently if the interviewees report having had more positive contact with foreigners in the FRG. Subjects stating more unpleasant experiences give more unfavourable judgements about foreigners. The problem with a causal interpretation of these findings is again quite obvious. Did the positive experience with foreigners lead to an amelioration of society's generally negative picture of foreigners? Or can we assume that those people who already hold a positive attitude towards foreigners are much more inclined to call a contact positive than persons who originally held a negative attitude? Unsöld (1978) asked teachers to rate whether their pupils had had more positive or more negative experiences with foreigners. As expected, those pupils who seemed to have experienced negative contacts gave more negative statements about foreigners than those with more neutral experience with foreigners (pp. 257ff). Considering these results, it is more unlikely that the pupils' level of prejudice had a significant impact on the quality of the contacts as perceived by the teachers. More positive contact seems to have had a positive effect on prejudice. Other findings of Unsöld however lead to only a limited generalization of this conclusion. According to his analyses, the judgements of those pupils who had positive experiences are also more negative than of those pupils who had – according to their teachers – had more neutral contact with foreigners.

In a large-scale representative study dealing with the interrelation of interethnic contacts and prejudice, Bergius and his collaborators found increasingly negative attitudes towards Mediterranean nations by Germans who knew a larger number of foreigners in the FRG (Bergius et al., 1970). At first sight these results contradict those mentioned above, which had shown a decrease in the level of prejudice with increasing contact frequency. A more thorough analysis however explains this contradiction. The authors themselves proceed from the assumption that the effective variable in their studies is the *voluntariness* of the contacts. Correspondinbg to this hypothesis, they are able to prove with their data that – during the data-collection period in 1967 – contacts with foreign workers mainly took place at work, which implies that they were more or less involuntary and thus reinforced the rejection of foreigners (Winter and Klein, 1975).

One feature of the work by Bergius and his colleagues deserves mention. Among other things they compared the effect of contacts that took place in Germany with that of contacts with foreigners in their home country. From their knowledge about the socially defined background they are thus able to deduce different prognoses for such situations: a more negative effect was expected for contacts that took place in the FRG during the planning and the execution of the studies in the late 1960s, whereas contacts in the home countries of the foreigners promised a more favourable effect on the level of prejudice held by the German interviewees. The results of the study support the hypothesis. The procedure followed by Bergius and his collaborators can be taken as a standard for further analyses. Having knowledge of the actual situation in the FRG, predictions can be formulated concerning the effect of interethnic contacts in the neighbourhood, at work or at school, as well as during leisure time. We cannot expect interethnic contacts to reduce prejudice as long as there are tendencies towards rejection that have an impact on these important areas of every-day life (cf. Bundesminister für Arbeit und Sozialordnung, 1980, p. 260) and thus also affect the concrete contact situation.

Housing   In principle it can be assumed that contacts among people living together offer an opportunity to get to know strange cultures and customs. This may help the people involved to desist from classifying people on the basis of their nationality and to judge them from direct personal contacts instead. However, it is most probable that such an effect is strongly contingent upon the circumstances of the actual housing situation. In the FRG the commonly negative attitude towards foreigners often manifests itself in the allocation of flats to foreign families. As many landlords do not accept foreign families as tenants, a large number of them are compelled to live in derelict quarters earmarked for demolition. Thus, the settling of foreigners in these boroughs coincides with their delapidation, which is then falsely perceived as being 'caused by' the foreigners. In other cases, foreigners have to accept flats in huge, anonymous blocks where 'neighbourhood', from being a matter of community feeling, is reduced to mere physical proximity in poorly constructed accommodation. These reflections lead to the conclusion that interethnic contacts in the neighbourhood will hardly help reduce rejection if they take place under conditions such as those which at present characterize the FRG. The available, sparse data are consistent with this prognosis. An inquiry to the competent authorities of a small-sized town in the 'Ruhrgebiet' proved that the majority of the foreigners lived in public- or company-owned flats, which were limited to only a few boroughs where many of the inhabitants were foreigners. Most of these flats were huge blocks, some even situated in quarters that were to be demolished. When fourteen-year-old German pupils from the same town were questioned, they showed a stronger tendency to be prejudiced towards Turks when Turks lived in their neighbourhood (unpublished data by Wagner, 1983).

Work and school   Contacts at work or at school could also be considered to contribute to a more differentiated picture of the foreigners, and one which was less influenced by public opinion. At work however foreigners are often in lower-status positions than Germans, which means there are fewer chances for stereotyped ideas to be revised. Furthermore, the increasing economic difficulties and the growing number of unemployed has given support to the opinion that foreigners restrict job opportunities for Germans (cf. EMNID, 1982). Having foreign fellow workers might thus lead to a confirmation of such ideologically formed suspicion and to a deepening of individual ethnic prejudice. Empirical research gives support to both hypotheses. Winter and Klein (1975) found less liking for foreigners, if the Germans questioned had foreign colleagues. Other studies showed more favourable judgements about those nationalities with which questioned Germans had been in contact (Wenninger, 1978, pp. 216ff; Forschungsverbund, 1979, pp. 188ff). Presumably, the effect of work contacts on prejudice levels coincides with the deterioration of the economy and the employment situation. As data for the above-mentioned studies were collected in the period from 1967 to 1975, current prejudice levels, considering the present economic recession, can not easily be extrapolated from them.

With regard to school, teachers often report difficulties resulting from educating German and foreign pupils together (cf. Hopf, 1981). However, the degree of prejudice in German pupils should mainly depend on how they perceive their contacts with foreign classmates. But there is no relevant information available, other than the above-mentioned literature concerning the relation between the number of foreign classmates and ethnic prejudice of German pupils. Unsöld (1978, pp. 253ff) found that contacts in the school context seem to reduce negative ideas about the different ethnic groups the children came to know. Wagner (1983, pp. 177ff) did not find a significant difference between pupils who had interethnic contacts at school and those who had none (with the judgements tending to get more negative as the opportunities for contact increased).

Leisure time It can be presumed that private contacts between foreigners and Germans are by and large entered into on a voluntary basis. Contrary to the situations in the neighbourhood, at work or at school, interethnic contacts during leisure time should be avoidable – at least those over a longer period of time. Furthermore, the circumstances of leisure-time contacts between foreigners and Germans should as a rule be favourable and free of tendencies towards rejection. Therefore, it can be assumed that such contacts are accompanied by reduced ethnic prejudice. Empirical data of Wenninger (1978, pp. 221ff) confirm this assumption, as does one of the prejudice indices used by Winter and Klein (1975). Again the question of causality arises: if we consider the attendant circumstances of leisure-time contacts, it seems to make sense to presume that they lead to a reduction of interethnic prejudice. It is however also sensible to expect those persons having frequent leisure-time contacts with foreigners to hold a non-prejudiced attitude towards strangers already. We tend to accept causal influence from both directions. This would help to explain why people holding strong negative ethnic stereotypes keep their prejudice; they avoid contacts with members of different ethnic groups, because that could lead to positive experience contradictory to their own opinion.

Thus, one should expect a clear relation between contact and prejudice only for leisure-time contacts. Prognoses for the fields of work, school or the neighbourhood are less clear. Direct contacts with foreigners can lead to an individualization of ideologically determined prejudice, but conflicts occurring in the contact situation may give support to existing prejudice – even if the foreign partners in the interaction did not cause the conflict. In interviews with fourteen-year-old German pupils, Wagner et al. (in preparation) tried to relate the effect of contact with Turks in the neighbourhood, at school and during their free time to judgements about Turks. Each of these fields of contact was represented by various indicators. The data were evaluated in such a way that only the 'pure' connection between every single contact indicator and the prejudice value emerges: figure 3.1 shows the results. On the left are the variables of contact opportunities, that is whether or not the pupils had Turkish or foreign classmates and Turkish neighbours. These variables should determine the pupils' real uses of contact, arranged in the middle column of figure 3.1. On the right, is the measure of prejudice. Solid lines represent significant results; dotted lines marginally significant results. The numerical values illustrate the importance of the relations: positive values symbolize a positive relationship; negative values a negative relationship. As one can see from the figures, there is generally a significant relation between the number of leisure-time contacts with Turks and judgements about Turks. As expected, judgements are more favourable, the more the interviewees have contact in their free time. Contact opportunities have few direct influences on prejudice, and there are only small connections between contacts at work or at school and the level of prejudice (if the effect of leisure-time contacts is statistically controlled). These findings are in accordance with Unsöld's results (1978, pp. 249ff), which show that pupils who – according to their parents – only have contacts at school, give more negative judgements about foreigners than those pupils who have further contacts. In addition, figure 3.1 shows significant co-variations between the contact variables. The positive relation between the answers to the questions concerning Turkish neighbours and the number of informal talks indicates how the use of contacts is dependent on whether opportunities for such contacts exist at all.

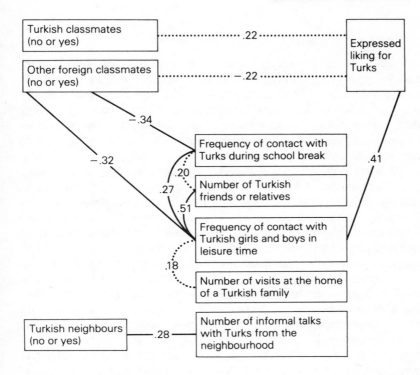

Figure 3.1 The effect of contact with Turks in relation to judgements about Turks. Significant (____p = .05; . . . .p = .10) results from a path analysis with different contact predictors and the criterion measure of expressed liking for Turks. Numbers for straight lines are beta coefficients, numbers for curved lines are partial correlation coefficients with the variables on the left partialled out (N = 60).
(From Wagner et al., in preparation)

Finally, the study by Wagner et al. (in preparation) gives an idea about how interaction between Turkish and German adolescents in the FRG actually proceeds. The pupils questioned stated that in most of the cases when they meet Turks, there are several Germans and Turks present. This means that these encounters are for the major part contacts between small groups that are definable by ethnic criteria. Meetings of a single German and a single Turk only happen sporadically. In no case did the German pupils report that they had ever had contact alone with a group of Turks. This illustrates how the majority/minority situation in society is reflected and experienced on a private level (for further details, see Wagner et al., in preparation).

Organization of contacts in the field of education

From the preceding text it should be evident that correlational connections between contact and prejudice variables are often not to be interpreted causally. However, it seems sensible to assume that contacts between members of different ethnic groups can reduce mutual rejection if they happen under favourable conditions. In this section we discuss this idea on the basis of contact programmes from pedagogics and adult education.

In the FRG a ten-year *school* attendance is prescribed by law, both for foreign and German children. The way education for foreign children is organized varies from state to state. In Bavaria the education of foreign and German children is completely segregated at present, which means the education of foreign children in national classes whenever it is possible. Many objections to this method can be put forward and the advantages it bears according to its advocates can be questioned (cf. Boos-Nünning, 1981). In Northrhine-Westfalia these national classes are, since 1982, only tolerated in exceptional cases. Foreign and German pupils should attend the same classes. When deciding in favour of this method, those responsible seem to have proceeded on the assumption that desegregation alone would be able to solve interethnic conflict and prejudice. However, in the US such a simple contact hypothesis has clearly proved a failure (cf. Cook, 1979). In our opinion the education of foreigners and Germans together offers hope, but it has to be adequately organized by means of pedagogic measures.

As early as 1954 Gordon Allport specified some preconditions for contact reducing prejudice. For example, the members of different ethnic groups should meet with equal status and should be aiming at the same superordinate goals. In the US, successful programmes for the desegregated education of white children and children of ethnic minorities were developed on this basis (cf. Aronson et al., 1978; DeVries, Edwards and Slavin, 1978; Slavin, 1977; see also chapter 4). The vast majority of German-language educational programmes dealing with the subject of 'foreigners' either concentrate on measures to optimize education only from the foreign pupils' perspective (e.g. Dickopp, 1982) or they are limited to the distribution of information concerning foreigners, primarily aimed at German children (cf. the review by Machleit and Wagner, 1983). Only very few give direct constructive help for the organization of interethnic contacts in the classroom (e.g. Meinhard, 1982; Pommerin, 1981; Stolz and Tjaden, 1980).

As a rule these suggestions are neither explicitly theoretically founded, nor are their effects evaluated. One exception is the work of Holfort (1982). His suggestions aim at improving contact between eight- to nine-year-old foreign and German school children by means of pedagogic games. He chose some children's games that promote communication (e.g. outdoor games, a telegramme game, a game by which they could learn some Turkish words from classmates, etc.). After having used this programme in eight lessons altogether, he found a positive change – however, only under particular circumstances. The German pupils' attitude towards their Turkish classmates had become more positive if the playgroups were balanced, which means they had to have equal numbers of Turkish and German children. It was not possible to prove any change of attitudes in groups where no contacts took place and only information was exchanged. Play contacts between German and Turkish pupils could even lead to a less favourable judgement about Turkish children, as in Holfort's study, if the groups were not balanced and the Turks were the minority – as is the rule at German schools. Should this last result be confirmed in further studies, it would of course have substantial consequences for the desired or recommended composition of the classes.

Especially in the field of education, the use of contact programmes for the reduction of prejudice seems to be quite efficient. We have already mentioned that the number of interethnic contacts a person has may be related to the liking this person feels for 'strange' ethnic groups, because persons holding a positive attitude will readily enter into contact, whereas strongly prejudiced people will be more likely to avoid such contact. This mechanism may lead to the result that it is those very people who most need the prejudice-reducing effect of positive interethnic contacts who avoid positive contacts. At school the opportunities for such avoidance guided by rejection are rather limited. As a rule it is quite complicated for parents to get their children into the primary school of their choice. Foreign classmates are not to be avoided and thus a favourable organization of such encounters at school may help to break the vicious circle of prejudice and avoidance of contact.

Measures of promoting and organizing interethnic contacts to be taken in *adult education* should be seen differently. It is generally on a voluntary basis that people utilize such education, which means that those people who from the start disapprove of interethnic contacts will hardly ever enrol for courses that promote it. In adult education contact-promoting programmes can be used to help overcome the tensions of unfamiliar contact situations and reduce mutual behavioural uncertainties. Wagner, Baumhold and Keuth (1983) have developed and brought about such a programme for adults. The participants in a family seminar of several days' duration worked in small mixed groups of foreign and German adults under the joint leadership of a foreigner and a German, one of each sex. Following the 'jigsaw-method' of Aronson et al. (1978) the groups were set tasks that could only be solved by the co-operation of all members. For the performance of a play, for example, one of the members designed the costumes, another one provided the text, the third was responsible for the decoration, etc. Furthermore, competitive games were organized between the small groups that could only be won by the complete group, not by a single person. This should lead to more solidarity within the group. For the same reason all necessary work was delegated to the small groups and not to individuals. For Wagner et al. this method was quite successful, because the relations between the participating foreigners and Germans seemed to have been improved. However, the participants of the seminar were volunteers, so were probably less prejudiced in advance. A strict empirical control is still to be executed to check the results and their generalizability more strongly.

SUMMARY

The majority of the studies discussed confirm that there is a positive relation between contact with foreigners and the level of ethnic prejudice. Can we thus conclude that the contact hypothesis was confirmed and that contact *alone* will lead to reduction of prejudice? We do not think so. Apart from a few exceptions the cited works did not allow us to determine which causal relation may lead to the correlation of contact and prejudice. It is as plausible to assume that contacts caused the change of prejudice as to hold the hypothesis that people frequently enter into voluntary contacts with foreigners only because they do not hold strong prejudices. From all studies mentioned, only Unsöld (1978), Wagner (1983), Wagner et al. (in preparation) and Wenninger (1978) determined contact in such a way that it is possible to interpret an empirically found relation of contact and prejudice with some certainty, in accordance with the contact hypothesis, as a causal relation. However, it is not only these findings that are equivocal. Wenninger and Wagner et al. found less prejudice if there were many foreigners working together with the interviewees or attending the same class, respectively. Wagner however, was not able to confirm this interrelation of contact opportunities and the level of ethnic prejudice. Unsöld reports a Ushaped relation between how positive the contacts at school were (teachers' judgements) and the level of ethnic prejudice of pupils.

The few available data are not contradictory to the contact hypothesis. They recommend however an extension of the perspective.

1   On the one hand, one should pay more attention to the attendant circumstances of contact. The effect on prejudice is presumably especially dependent on the circumstances under which the contact takes place. Positive results can only be expected under favourable conditions. There is of course a close relation between the quality of the circumstances to be considered and the way a society as a whole deals with minorities.

2   We also think it useful to pay more attention to the direction of causality contrary to the original contact hypothesis. With increasing prejudice, contacts will be avoided or negatively interpreted and taken as a confirmation of the negative attitude that is already held. The close relation between leisure-time contact and the level of ethnic prejudice can be considered as supporting these two additional assumptions. The high correlation could be attributed to the comparably favourable conditions that normally accompany leisure-time contacts. That means, first, that from these contacts one may expect a positive effect on interethnic prejudice – besides private contacts are relatively easy to avoid. This implies, second, that on the whole they are most probably experienced by those persons who are not very prejudiced anyway.

What implications result from this extended perspective? Despite the assumed feedback between contact and prejudice, we would not argue that well-organized contacts can not contribute to a reduction of ethnic prejudice. The use of contact programmes, for instance in schools, seems to be a sensible means of counteracting the development of prejudice and the tendency to avoid contact. If however the effect of contact is dependent on the attendant circumstances and the social setting, the use of such psychological techniques alone will hardly produce any mentionable change. Substantial change will also require wide-ranging political decisions concerning the way society in general deals with foreigners.

ACKNOWLEDGEMENTS

We are thankful to Anne Heynen, Stefan Hucke, Rudolf Schiffmann, and Harald Sporn as well as to the editors of this book for their helpful comments on an earlier draft of this paper.

NOTES

1   Not all people coming from Turkey would call themselves 'Turks'. If we confine ourselves to the term 'Turk' we do not mean the ethnic, but the national origin.
2   This lack of knowledge of German is also a result of the foreigners' living conditions. At work the communication possibilities with fellow workers are often restricted. Language courses are mostly unsuccessful (Mehrländer et al., 1981, pp. 491ff) because shift work makes regular attendance difficult. Finally, living in a 'ghetto' seems to obviate intensive efforts to learn German.

4   Black–White Contact in Desegregated Schools

Janet Ward Schofield

The history of black–white contact in the United States is long and complex. However, the last 30 years have seen changes in relations between blacks and whites of a magnitude virtually unparalleled in that long history (except for the period after the Civil War, which saw the end of slavery as a legal institution). In the last three decades major events affecting race relations include the rise of the civil rights movement; a number of major urban riots; the assassinations of Martin Luther King, Robert Kennedy and Malcolm X; and a series of new laws and Supreme Court decisions designed to do away with the legal barriers preventing the full economic, political and social participation of blacks in American life.

One of the most controversial of these changes in the law was the decision handed down in the *Brown* v. *Board of Education* case in 1954. In that decision the United States Supreme Court overturned the earlier doctrine, propounded in *Plessy* v. *Ferguson* in 1896, that 'separate but equal' public facilities for blacks and whites could be mandated by state law. Instead, it argued that such separation in the schools 'generates a feeling of inferiority [in black children] that may affect their hearts and minds in a way unlikely ever to be undone.' (347 US 483, at 494, 1954). Thus, enforced segregation by race was said to violate the equal protection clause of the United States Constitution (Read, 1975; Wisdom, 1975).

The *Brown* decision and later attempts to implement it raised a storm of controversy. In the South, which was the region of the country most clearly affected by *Brown* initially, anti-black organizations like the Ku Klux Klan and White Citizens' Councils suddenly flourished. However, some whites applauded the decision and indeed worked to bring it about. For example over 30 social scientists and educators, the large majority of them white, signed a lengthy statement that supported the plaintiff's position in that case. At the time of the 1954 decision and during the following two decades, many white liberals including quite a few social scientists believed that contact between blacks and whites would foster improved understanding and interracial harmony. This sense is reflected in the 1968 report of the National Advisory Commission on Civil Disorders, which urged that school desegregation be adopted as 'the priority education strategy', saying:

In this last summer's disorders we have the consequences of racial isolation at all levels, and of attitudes toward race, on both sides, produced by three centuries of myth, ignorance, and bias. It is indispensable that opportunities for interaction between the races be expanded. (p. 12)

However, as emphasized in chapter 1 of this book, contact between two previously separate and even hostile groups does not automatically have salutary effects. *The precise conditions of contact are crucial in determining what the outcome of that contact will be.* This chapter will argue that school desegregation in the United States has had a less positive effect than one might have hoped, because three problems that have plagued race relations in the US have affected both the *extent* and the *nature* of the contact that has occurred in desegregated schools. Implicit in this argument is the idea that there are ways to improve the outcomes of school desegregation. This topic will be covered explicitly, although briefly, at the end of the chapter.

SCHOOL DESEGREGATION AND 'THE AMERICAN DILEMMA'

Over 40 years ago the Swedish sociologist Gunner Myrdal (1944) described what he called the American Dilemma – the fact that the US, a society based on ideals of liberty, justice and equality, accepted, condoned and even heatedly defended attitudes and practices towards black Americans antithetical to such ideals. Myrdal wrote at a time when American blacks faced legal restrictions almost unthinkable today in the US, from the requirement of using separate 'colored' drinking fountains and rest-rooms to segregated units within the military (but see chapter 8). The legal basis for such discrimination was swept away in the great ferment of civil rights activity in the 1950s and 1960s. However, the abolition of the legal basis for the most obvious sorts of discrimination, sanctioned and enforced by the government, did not solve the American dilemma, as an examination of the situation regarding school desegregation will show.

Although the *Brown* decision judged segregated dual school systems illegal, there was no substantial amount of real change until almost 15 years later. Those 15 years were consumed by protracted legal battles, attempts to counter local resistance and efforts to evolve workable yet effective standards for implementation. Not until the late 1960s and the early 1970s, when the courts finally came to the end of their patience did the desegregation of schools occur on any large scale. Even recent statistics suggest that most black students are still attending schools in which the majority of the student body is non-white (Arrington, 1981). However, much progress has been made since the late 1960s. For example, the proportion of blacks in 90–100 per cent minority schools was cut almost in half between 1968 and 1980 (US Commission on Civil Rights, 1983).

Thus, although the push towards realizing the ideals of justice and equality, which form one horn of the American dilemma, culminated in a changed legal situation over 30 years ago, discriminatory habits and customs and prejudiced attitudes forestalled the implementation of the legally mandated change for nearly two decades. Not only that, such resistance has by no means disappeared today. Although the proportion of white Americans who, in public opinion polls, endorse desegregated schools rose from roughly 30 per cent in 1942 to almost 90 per cent in 1980 (Myers, 1983), a substantial amount of resistance continues, as evidenced by recent court battles in numerous cities such as Los Angeles and Chicago. So although on the one hand most white Americans now tend to accept school desegregation on an abstract, ideological level, old attitudes and habits persist, which both delay its implementation and lead some whites to take their children out of desegregated school systems (Rossell, 1978).

CONTINUING DILEMMAS IN DESEGREGATED SCHOOLS

The tendency toward resegregation

In spite of the continuing controversy about school desegregation, it is clear that desegregated schools are a fact of life for millions of American children, white and black. Thus, one might assume that such schools are a prime environment in which to learn about the effects of intergroup contact. Such an assumption however ignores an important fact about such schools, that many foster much less contact than one might expect. Just as the work by Taylor, Dubé and Bellerose (chapter 6) suggests that intergroup contact in Quebec is less than is generally assumed, so reseach on desegregated schools in the US has found a tendency towards resegregation that scholars and policy-makers did not adequately foresee (Gerard and Miller, 1975; National Institute of Education, 1977; Patchen, 1982; Schofield, 1982).

The resegregation of desegregated schools and school systems is a multi-faceted process; it has numerous causes as disparate as differential fertility rates between the black and white populations and whites' tendency to migrate from urban to suburban areas. However, this chapter will discuss just one important aspect of this process – factors diminishing the amount of contact between black and white students *within* schools with racially mixed student bodies. A number of common educational practices lead, often inadvertently, to partial or complete resegregation within desegregated schools. The most obvious and widespread of these are practices designed to reduce academic heterogenity within class-rooms. A whole host of social and economic factors contribute to the fact that black students in desegregated schools tend to perform less well, academically, than their white peers. Thus, schools that categorize students on the basis of standardized tests, grades or related criteria tend to have resegregated class-rooms.

The degree to which practices designed to minimize academic heterogenity can resegregate students is clearly illustrated by a study conducted by Schofield (1982) in a racially mixed middle school (grades 6–8). Over 80 per cent of those assigned to the academically accelerated stream in the eighth grade were white, just as over 80 per cent of those in the regular stream were black. In the sixth and seventh grades, which did not have formal streams, some teachers nonetheless grouped their students so that they had a 'fast' class, some 'average' classes and a 'slow' class. This practice led to considerable resegregation. For example, one black maths teacher had a fast class that was entirely white and a slow group that was entirely black except for one white boy. Teachers who taught more academically heterogeneous classes frequently divided children *within* each class into three or more groups. Again, it was not uncommon for the top group to be all white, or virtually so, and for the bottom group to be entirely or almost entirely black. Most teachers were aware that such grouping practices undercut the potential of their school to foster positive contact between black and white children, but saw this as a relatively unimportant sacrifice to be made in order to pursue the more important goal of teaching their subject matter as effectively as possible (Schofield and Sagar, 1979).

Although much resegregation stems from policies such as streaming or ability grouping, it is undeniable that students do often voluntarily resegregate themselves in a variety of situations, from eating lunch to participating in extra-curricular activities. For example, Collins (1979) studied a southern-state school in which whites dominated activities such as the student government, the yearbook, tennis and golf, whereas blacks populated the chorus and the basketball and football teams. The extent of such voluntary resegregation is sometimes surprising. For example, in one set of studies the seating patterns in the cafeteria of a school whose student body was almost precisely half black and half white were mapped for two years. On a typical day, when the seating positions of approximately 250 students during any particular lunch-period were recorded, fewer than 15 of them sat next to someone of the other race (Schofield, 1979; Schofield and Sagar, 1977). This was so in spite of the fact that there was little overt racial friction. Other studies have reported similarly marked cleavage by race (Cusick and Ayling, 1973; Gerard, Jackson and Connolley, 1975; Rogers et al., 1984).

Not only is there evidence that black and white children in desegregated schools often tend to avoid each other, such avoidance frequently occurs in just those types of situations that have the greatest potential for breaking down intergroup barriers. Theorists like Allport (1954), Cook (1969), and Brewer and Miller (1984) have argued that fairly close personal contact is more likely to create positive feelings than more distant contact, since the high 'acquaintance potential' of the former situation increases the opportunity for individuals to discover that they have similar interests, attitudes and the like. Yet, considerable research suggests that blacks and whites in the US are more willing to engage in fairly impersonal interactions than they are to engage in close personal ones (Bogardus, 1959; Cook, 1969; Triandis and Davis, 1965). This phenomenon is apparent in desegregated schools as well as in other arenas. In fact, there is experimental evidence demonstrating that the more personal the nature of a task-oriented academic interaction, the more white and black students tend to choose to work with peers of their own race. This is the case even when such a choice reduces the probability of earning desirable rewards for success at the task (Schofield and Snyder, 1980).

Fortunately there are ways in which teachers can work effectively with academically heterogeneous classes, as well as policies and practices that are generally successful in fostering voluntary contact and improving relations between black and white students (Cook, 1984; Johnson, Johnson and Maruyama, 1984; Rogers et al., 1984; Slavin, 1983; Stephan and Stephan, 1984). Some of these will be discussed at the end of this chapter. Unfortunately, the fact that it is possible to reduce resegregation does not mean that educators or parents will consider it a high-priority goal.

The emergence of new and subtle forms of racism

The tendency towards resegregation is one serious issue with which desegregated schools have to deal. However, it is not the only challenge they face. Pettigrew (1969) makes a very useful distinction between *desegregation*, the mere creation of a racially mixed institution and *integration*, desegregation under conditions likely to improve relations between members of previously segregated groups. He argues that desegregation is a necessary but not sufficient condition for integration, which requires equal status for, and co-operation between, members of all groups as well as normative support for positive intergroup relations. Thus, if they are to foster the development of positive intergroup relations, racially mixed schools need to find methods to combat the tendency to resegregate and, in addition, they must actively work to structure the nature of intergroup contact.

The legacy of the American dilemma remains to complicate this task. White attitudes have become increasingly liberal over time, and thus more consistent with egalitarian ideals (Campbell, 1971; Greeley and Sheatsley, 1971; Taylor, Sheatsley and Greeley, 1978). However, there is still a great deal of prejudice against blacks. Some of this prejudice is the 'old-fashioned' kind of obvious racism that Myrdal encountered when he studied the US in the 1940s. However, as such crude and obvious prejudice has become less socially acceptable, many whites have come to express their negative feelings towards blacks in other ways. For example, McConahay's work has suggested the emergence of 'modern' or 'symbolic racism', that is expressing through symbols or symbolic behaviour the feeling that blacks are violating cherished values or making illegitimate demands for changes in the racial status quo (McConahay, Hardee and Batts, 1982; McConahay and Hough, 1976). Obviously, if white teachers or students share such feelings it is hardly likely that they will initiate or be receptive to much personal or equal-status contact with blacks, even when conditions are favourable.

A different and even more subtle type of racism, which desegregated schools have to deal with, is the phenomenon which Gaertner and Dovidio (in press) have labelled 'aversive racism'. According to this research, many whites want to be unprejudiced and are careful to avoid actions that might threaten their self-concepts as unprejudiced, non-discriminating persons. However, such an orientation is often accompanied by unconscious negative feelings towards blacks. Gaertner and Dovidio argue that cognitive biases in information processing and the historically racist culture in the United States lead most white Americans to develop negative feelings towards blacks. Yet such feelings are in conflict with the traditional cultural values, which Myrdal described, favouring fairness and justice and thus cannot be acknowledged without producing high levels of guilt. This conflict forms the heart of aversive racism.

The significance of aversive racism for intergroup contact in desegregated schools is that individuals who believe themselves to be unprejudiced may nonetheless discriminate when they can explain their behaviour in ways that do not threaten their self-concepts. Specifically, Gaertner and Dovidio (1977; in press) argue that discriminatory behaviour does not challenge a liberal self-concept when non-racial rationales are available to justify the action. Unfortunately, the strong link between race and social class in the US means that socially acceptable rationales are available for much of the behaviour that ultimately works to the disadvantage of blacks. For example, black students are suspended and expelled from desegregated schools at a rate that is roughly double their proportion of the student population in such schools (National Institute of Education, 1977). Much of this difference is undoubtedly due to the disparity in the social-class backgrounds of the black and white children, since children from less affluent homes are suspended or expelled more frequently than others, even in segregated schools. However, the correlation between race and social class allows teachers, whose beliefs are less prejudiced than their feelings, to recommend disciplinary actions against black students without stopping to consider carefully whether race played a part in their decisions.

DISAGREEMENT OVER THE GOALS OF CONTACT: ASSIMILATION OR PLURALISM?

Desegregation as social-class assimilation

For many years the public schools have served the United States by helping to inculcate in immigrant children the values and ideals of WASP culture as well as by teaching them basic academic skills (Pratte, 1979).[1] Many Americans view school desegregation as a continuation of a similar process – a situation in which black children, the great majority of whom come from lower- or working-class backgrounds, are exposed to the same values, standards of behaviour and constructive peer influences as their more affluent white peers. This view of desegregation was most likely fostered by the widely publicized Coleman Report (Coleman et al., 1966), published just before the beginning of the big push to implement desegregation, which had been legally mandated more than a decade before. Based on a massive study, this report concluded that one of the most important factors influencing the academic achievements of pupils was the home background of their peers. It also concluded that the achievements of black children were more influenced by this factor than that of whites. Thus what Gerard and Miller (1975) have termed 'the

lateral transmission of values' hypothesis, which argues that desegregation helps black children by putting them in a milieu in which their peers
model positive attitudes towards academic achievement, became widespread.

The colour-blind perspective: a corollary of the assimilationist view
The emphasis on desegregation as a mechanism of class assimilation is in
tune with the widely held American democratic philosophy of which
Myrdal wrote – people should be judged by their behaviour as
individuals and not as members of particular social categories. This
emphasis leads logically to the adoption of the colour-blind perspective, a
viewpoint frequently found in desegregated schools (Schofield, in press;
Sagar and Schofield, 1984). This perspective encourages institutions and
the individuals within them to strive to ignore race completely in their
dealings with students. It can be illustrated by the words of a black
administrator in a desegregated middle school:

I really don't address myself to group differences when I am dealing with
youngsters . . . I try to treat youngsters . . . as youngsters and not as black,
white, green or yellow . . . Many of the black youngsters . . . have come from
communities where they had to put up certain defenses and these defenses are
the antithesis of the normal situation . . . like they find in school . . . I think that
many of the youngsters [from the] larger community have a more normal set of
values that people generally want to see, and therefore do not have [as] much
difficulty in coping with their school situation as do our black youngsters.
(Schofield, 1982, p. 50)

As a reaction to the invidious distinctions that have traditionally been
made in the US on the basis of race, the colour-blind perspective is
understandable and, from a social-policy standpoint, it seems laudable.
However, recent research suggests that it may foster, as a logical
consequence, other beliefs that can negatively influence the context in
which intergroup contact occurs in desegregated schools (Schofield,
1982; in press). For example in at least one school, the colour-blind
perspective fostered the development of a norm, almost strong enough to
be called a taboo, against even making overt references to race
(Schofield, 1982). This norm inhibited constructive problem solving in a
number of ways.

Furthermore, it is not a very great leap from the colour-blind
perspective, which says that race is a social category of no legitimate
relevance to one's behaviour and decisions, to a belief that individuals
should not or do not even *notice* each other's race. There is evidence
suggesting that the belief that race does not influence one's reactions and

that individuals tend not even to notice each other's race does not reflect reality. For example, there is clear evidence that in the US, at least, the physical appearance of others, including those characteristics that give clues about race, influences the individual's perception of them and their behaviour (Duncan, 1976; S. E. Taylor et al., 1978). Thus the contention that race is literally not noticed seems at odds with reality and is not an optimal basis for action.

The question of whether race, once noticed, makes a difference is more complicated and obviously more dependent on the particular individual. However, a wide variety of research suggests that the race of a person does influence one's reactions to that person. For example, Sagar and Schofield (1980) demonstrated that both white and black junior high school boys perceive certain actions differently, depending on the race of the individual performing that action. Specifically, when shown drawings of black children engaged in actions that could be interpreted either as playful or as mildly aggressive, such as poking another student, these boys, aged between twelve and thirteen, rated the behaviour as more mean and threatening and less playful and friendly than when those same actions were thought to be initiated by whites. Similar findings with a white college student sample have been reported by Duncan (1976).

Moving from the realm of perception to that of actual behaviour, Cohen (1980) has argued that in the US race operates as a diffuse status characteristic that cues certain expectations and sets in motion certain behaviour patterns. Specifically, her research demonstrates that even when the black and white students participating in an interaction are carefully matched on status-relevant variables, including social class, the white students tend to be both more active and more influential (Cohen, 1972).

The colour-blind perspective, with its assimilationist underpinnings, tends to lead administrators to the conclusion that the best approach to desegregation is to proceed with business as usual and to take no special notice of the fact that they are operating a racially mixed school. In this view, success can be judged by the extent to which the school's status quo is maintained. This perspective is well illustrated by a comment made by a staff member in a formerly all-white elementary school that Rist (1978, p. 83) studied during its first year of desegregation:

I don't think . . . that there should be any problems. Now if there were seventy-five or a hundred (black transfer students), it would be different. But I don't think twenty-eight will make any difference at all. *We probably won't know they are here.* This comment was greeted with nods of agreement from the other teachers. [Emphasis added]

The pluralist view of desegregation

The assimilationist approach to desegregation discussed above is far from unusual (Sagar and Schofield, 1984). However, it is in stark contrast to an approach, often advocated by members of minority groups, that places an emphasis on pluralism, rather than assimilation, as a guiding value (Glaser, 1954; Glaser and Moynihan, 1970; Rose, 1972; Steinfield, 1970). The assimilationist perspective tries to teach others to comply with the ways of the dominant majority. The pluralistic perspective recognizes cultural diversity and acknowledges the validity of subcultural values and communal identities. Advocates of the latter approach emphasize the importance of a multi-ethnic curriculum, an integrated faculty, and the like (Pratte, 1979). They are not likely to adopt a colour-blind stance, for their goal is to ensure that schools understand the special values and behaviour patterns of the various sub-groups they serve and adjust themselves to deal with all of them fairly and effectively. Thus, cultural pluralists would be more prone than assimilationists to see the differential suspension rates, mentioned earlier, as a problem and to call for an examination of disciplinary policies and practices to see if they do adequately consider subcultural values and behavioural styles.

There is reason to think that such an approach would be useful in desegregated schools. For example, Kochman (1981) has argued convincingly that black and white students utilize widely differing styles in class-room discussions and that misunderstanding the cultural context from which students come can lead peers and teachers to misinterpret involvement as belligerence. Differential suspension rates may be a function not only of the misinterpretation of interpersonal style but of conflicting social customs. The common prohibition against males wearing hats while in class is an obvious example. Although the rule fits well with Anglo-Saxon traditions, it does not reflect social customs in many poor, black, urban areas. Very much in the spirit of the pluralist tradition, Forehand and Ragosta (1976) recommend that administrators take a very careful look at those rules resulting in differential punishment rates for blacks and whites to see if they are both necessary and proper.

The pluralist perspective demands attention to the 'fit' between the expectations and requirements of the school environment and those of the home and community, emphasizing the school's responsibility to adjust to its students rather than the students' need to adjust to the school. No matter where one places the burden of adjustment, research suggests that the issue of fit is important. Heath (1982) for example in an interesting piece of ethnographic research, concludes that pre-school, white, middle-class children are asked the same sorts of questions at home that they will later be asked by their teachers in school. In contrast, she concludes that the types of questions asked in poor, black homes do not follow the same format.

Other research on this issue of fit raises the question of whether the very competitive atmosphere that typifies most American schools gives white, middle-class children an advantage over their Hispanic and, to a lesser extent, their black peers, who appear to have a somewhat more co-operative orientation (Kagan, 1977, 1979; Knight and Kagan, 1977).

These questions of fit are important for a number of reasons. First, outcomes like higher suspension rates or lower levels of achievement, as a result of non-corresponding expectations, are clearly significant both for the individuals involved and for society as a whole. This issue also influences less weighty but none the less important factors such as how comfortable students are likely to feel in the school, how they are perceived by their peers, and the like.

On the face of it then, especially given some of the problems stemming from the assimilationist/colour-blind perspective, a pluralistic atmosphere seems to provide positive conditions for contact. The value of all groups is affirmed and the school functions in a way that does not create or magnify differences in status between different groups of students. However, there are at least two issues that need to be addressed before one wholeheartedly endorses a simple pluralistic perspective. First, it is easy for schools to drift from value statements emphasizing pluralism to a situation in which a great deal of resegregation occurs and is accepted because it apparently reflects group loyalties or group-linked behavioural styles. For example, Collins and Noblit (1977) studied a southern-state school, whose black principal recognized and accepted race-related differences in taste and behavioural style in a way many schools do not. However, this acceptance of the importance of ingroup identities, with no countervailing efforts to ensure cross-group interaction, led to marked resegregation. Black students congregated in the recreational study halls in the school's annex whereas white students went to non-recreational study halls in the school's library. As one student put it, 'All the segregation in the city was put in one building' (p. 195).

Of course, a pluralistic perspective does not inevitably lead to resegregation. However, to the extent that this perspective does enhance the salience of racial or ethnic group membership, it has the potential to intensify social competition and rejection between groups. There is a considerable amount of theory and research suggesting that when individuals categorize others as members of a particular group they tend to perceive them in deindividuated and stereotyped ways and to react in a depersonalized manner (Brewer and Miller, 1984; Deschamps and Doise, 1978; Turner, 1978; 1981). Thus, schools adopting a pluralistic perspective, which tends to make group membership relatively salient, need to find ways of minimizing the potentially negative impact of this stance on intergroup relations. Research suggests a number of ways in which the salience of social categories can be reduced or the negative consequences of social categorization mitigated. For example, Deschamps and Doise (1978) have shown that the existence of cross-cutting categorical distinctions can mitigate the tendency towards ingroup bias. A very different type of study, conducted in a desegregated school, suggested a similar conclusion (Schofield and McGivern, 1979).

There is also a serious problem with a wholehearted endorsement of a rather simplistic type of pluralism that asserts that *all* group differences must be respected (Pratte, 1979). Some of these differences may pose serious handicaps to individual members of these different groups as they strive to make their way in the wider society. Take the issue of a co-operative compared to a competitive orientation discussed above. One can argue, as assimilationists do, that if children are going to succeed later in life in a very competitive society the school helps rather than hinders them by emphasizing competition, even if such an orientation initially clashes with that of the child. This is a serious and complex issue and basically beyond the scope of this paper. However, it is worth noting that there are ways in which schools can be sensitive to the diversity of their students without fostering dysfunctional behaviour patterns. For example, information from Heath's (1982) study of teachers' and parents' questioning styles, cited earlier, was used as the basis for an intervention effort with both students and teachers. Teachers were made aware of the differences in typical questioning styles and used this information as the basis for class discussions about different types of questions and how to approach them. Class exercises were then designed to give all children practice with all types of questions. Thus, diversity became a resource that was utilized to expand the repertoire of skills of all students as well as of their teachers.

IMPLICATIONS FOR POLICY AND PRACTICE

This chapter has suggested that the first hurdle faced by any attempt to improve intergroup relations through contact in desegregated schools is the problem of how to ensure that the desired contact actually occurs. When groups have a tradition of separation and hostility, merely encouraging or even requiring members of both groups to participate in a social institution does not guarantee much contact. A number of factors conspire to make this the case. At least some whites who would normally enroll in the public schools may enroll in private schools or may move to districts with small or non-existent minority group populations. The larger number will remain in a desegregated system but school policies, teacher practices and student preferences can all lead to resegregation.

There are a great many tools that can be utilized to ensure that this does not happen, or at least to minimize its extent (Cohen, 1980, 1984; Forehand and Rogasta, 1976; Hawley et al., 1983). A review of them all would hardly be appropriate here, but an example will be given to illustrate the possibilities that exist. First, since resegregation often occurs as schools strive to minimize academic heterogeneity within classes (in the belief that this will lead to more effective learning), it is important to point out that in most elementary and junior high schools such reorganization is not necessary. There are a number of class-room-tested methods for teaching heterogeneous classes that do not entail grouping according to academic ability. These methods increase the learning of the slower students while resulting in learning comparable to other methods for the middle level and more advanced students (Johnson and Johnson, 1982; Sharan, 1980; Slavin, 1983). Such methods tend to involve assigning students to work co-operatively in small interracial and academically heterogeneous work groups. Furthermore, most provide incentives for students to help each other and work together. Finally, most of them also try to find ways to minimize the impact, on each child's contribution to the group, of previous levels of academic achievement.

The second hurdle to be dealt with in trying to improve intergroup relations is, as this chapter has indicated, how to *integrate* desegregated schools – that is how one can realistically foster the *type* of contact that is likely to reduce hostility and foster amicable relations between members of the groups in question. This, of course, is the important but often ignored thrust of the work of Allport (1954), Pettigrew (1969), Cook (1969), and others working in the contact theory tradition.

One approach to this problem, often advocated by those concerned with achieving increasingly fair social policies and practices in the United States, is the adoption of a colour-blind approach. Ideally, such an approach leads individuals to focus exclusively on the attributes of others that are relevant to the situation at hand, such as their ability to perform a given job or to pay for given goods or services. This chapter suggests that although the colour-blind perspective has some merits, it is not a simple or complete solution to the problem of fostering positive relations or of achieving fair outcomes. Specifically, individuals and institutions rarely *are* completely colour-blind, as the work of researchers like Cohen, McConahay, and Gaertner and Dovidio demonstrates. To the extent individuals or institutions imagine that they are colour-blind, they may well ignore social processes that perpetuate differential outcomes for members of majority and minority groups. How one deals most appropriately with such subtle and even unconscious prejudice and discrimination will vary from situation to situation. However, an awareness of the problem is a prerequisite to constructive action. Such action is possible, as indicated by Cohen's research on ways to reduce or eliminate the tendency of whites to dominate interracial interactions merely because they are white (Cohen and Roper, 1972). A pluralistic approach to structuring contact situations appears to have some promise of creating truly equal status for members of different groups, although it too has numerous potential pitfalls.

In sum, this chapter has argued that the American dilemma is still with us, although in a somewhat new form. The legal barriers to blacks' full and equal participation in society, of which Myrdal wrote, have been removed. However, there is still considerable tension between the continuing reality of prejudice and racial isolation, and traditional values emphasizing equality, justice and fairness. Not surprisingly, this basic tension shapes, to a certain extent, social interactions in desegregated schools, even though such schools also hold real potential as a means for improving intergroup relations.

ACKNOWLEDGEMENT

The preparation of this paper was facilitated by a grant from the National Institute of Education (NIE) to the Learning Research and Development Center at the University of Pittsburgh. However, all opinions expressed herein are solely those of the author and no endorsement by NIE is implied or intended.

NOTE

1   WASP is an acronym commonly used in the US to stand for White Anglo-Saxon Protestant.

5 Catholic–Protestant Contact in Northern Ireland

Karen Trew

Northern Ireland is one of several locations that are internationally known for a specific reason: the level of violence and disorder that accompanies apparently insoluble intergroup divisions. The present cycle of violence in the region started in 1968. The pattern of overt conflict changes, and the level of violence fluctuates, but there appears to be no evidence that the Northern Ireland problem will be solved in the near future. One of the few beneficial outcomes of the conflict is that there is now a body of multidisciplinary research providing evidence on the nature and extent of intergroup relations in Northern Ireland. Most of the studies concentrate on group differences. However, the extent and nature of peaceful contacts between Protestants and Catholics have been examined in large-scale surveys as well as in in-depth participant-observation studies of mixed communities.

This chapter aims to bring together the sprawling multidisciplinary literature on intergroup contact between Protestants and Catholics. This evidence is assessed in terms of its relevance to understanding intergroup relations in Northern Ireland; its contribution to the interpretation of the nature of intergroup contact; and its potential as an agent of change. To provide some order to the discussion of these issues, research on the maintenance and impact of sustained intergroup contact is distinguished from studies that focused on short-term encounters between Protestants and Catholics in schemes designed to promote community harmony.

NORTHERN IRELAND: A SECTARIAN REGION

Northern Ireland is a small region with a population of some one and a half million. It is neither nation nor state; it is a political component of the United Kingdom and a geographical region of the island of Ireland. The ambiguity that surrounds Northern Ireland's status is the inevitable outcome of the decision by the British government to resolve the Irish problem by attempting to match territory with allegiance.

The Government of Ireland Act (1920) created a land border, which aimed to separate within Ireland two groups with divergent national aspirations. The wishes of the mainly Catholic majority, who wanted independence from Great Britain, were recognized by the establishment of what was to become the independent Republic of Ireland. It comprised 26 of the 32 counties of the island of Ireland. Six counties remained within the United Kingdom in response to the strongly expressed wishes of the Protestant Unionist minority. Although Protestants were in the minority on the island of Ireland, they were the majority in the north-eastern region, which consequently became known as Northern Ireland, or 'Ulster'. However, over a third of the population of this area were Catholics, who were mainly opposed to the continuation of the constitutional link between Great Britain and Ireland.

National identity remains as a major source of discord in Northern Ireland. The evidence of surveys (Moxon-Browne, 1983; Trew, 1983b) indicates that whereas most Catholics see themselves as Irish, most Protestants feel British. Politics in Northern Ireland was, and is, dominated by the constitutional issue. Questions of social and economic policy, the normal discourse of politics, are subordinated to fundamental questions about the legitimacy of the state and whether or not the citizen is willing to be directed by government. In this context the range of political options open to individuals is largely determined by whether they are Protestant or Catholic. There is a very narrow, non-sectarian middle ground, which has rarely attracted more than 15 per cent of the population's support at local and national elections, but political parties, with a few exceptions, aim to attract the votes of *either* Catholics *or* Protestants but not both.

The identification by Protestants living in Northern Ireland with Britain and Catholics' identification with Ireland extend beyond politics to embrace social and cultural divisions. The two groups identify themselves as belonging to two separate traditions that have coexisted in Ireland since the Ulster plantation in the early seventeenth century, when land confiscated from the native Irish Catholics was given to Protestant 'planters' from England and Scotland. Buchanan (1982) has indicated that initially the cultural gap between these colonists and the native Irish was not large. It was not until the nineteenth century, and the rise in nationalism, that the denominational labels became closely identified with two distinct cultural traditions, as Catholics, but not Protestants, embraced an Irish culture involving music, literature, language and sport.

Nowadays the cultural divisions between Protestants and Catholics are not accompanied by any difference in language or even significant linguistic variations (Milroy, 1981). Similarly, there are no obvious physical differences between the groups. An outsider would not be able to distinguish between a Protestant and a Catholic. Nevertheless, there is almost universal acceptance in Northern Ireland of the existence of subtle, cultural cues for religious ascription. It has been suggested (Burton, 1978; Cairns, 1980) that characteristics or details such as name, home address, facial features, accent and dress can be conceptualized as signs in a system that serves to emphasize the distinctiveness between Protestants and Catholics. Harris (1972) however points out that this system also helps to establish an appropriate frame of reference for interaction between individual Protestants and Catholics.

Although the conflict between Protestants and Catholics is not primarily based on theological differences, divergent religious values and doctrinal disputes cannot be ignored. It is therefore perhaps surprising to find that Protestant and Catholic clergy are in close accord on educational issues. They agree that children should be taught by teachers of their own denomination and attend schools with their co-religionists. As a result of this unanimity, sectarianism is most obviously institutionalized in Northern Ireland in a dual educational system. Within the compulsory school-attendance age range, the vast majority of Protestant children attend state-controlled schools, whereas all but a small minority of Catholic children attend schools managed by church authorities, although these are mainly funded by the state. The segregated school system in Northern Ireland reflects the divisions within the society. Its impact is seen to be important socially rather than educationally and relative standards of education between the two systems are not a contentious issue (Trew, in press).

In sum, many factors in the social fabric of Northern Ireland combine to suggest that there is a fault-line within the society, separating Catholics and Protestants politically, socially and culturally. Indeed, religious polarization exists to such an extent that almost every aspect of life – town, street, club, shop, individual – can be classified as either Protestant, Catholic or, occasionally, mixed. Clearly, the processes that divide the society contribute to the violent intergroup conflict that has been an intermittent feature of life in the region for at least two hundred years (Darby, 1976). At the same time, there are processes within the society that constrain these divisions so that the violence, the extent of which has varied over the years, is confined to specific locations and has not engulfed the whole society. As Leyton (1974) argues, the true enigma of Northern Ireland 'is not why so many have died: rather it is why so few have been killed' (p. 184). Voluntary segregation is one way in which overt conflict is minimized. The separate schools and social organizations maintained by Catholics and Protestants would seem to suggest that there is little contact between the two groups.

INTERGROUP CONTACT IN THE DAILY LIFE OF NORTHERN IRELAND

Many commentators, from inside as well as outside Northern Ireland, have assumed that there is virtually complete segregation between what is in practice two communities. Beattie (1979) for example argued that Northern Ireland has been deeply divided for a long time, with the two communities living, studying and playing apart. As with other widely shared opinions about the relationship between Protestants and Catholics, this viewpoint is based on incomplete information. Research reveals that although segregation is a feature of life in Northern Ireland, there is also considerable contact between Protestants and Catholics extending far beyond casual encounters between strangers, and opportunities for such contact occur in a wide range of settings.

Household surveys (e.g. Boal, 1982) indicate that although working-class inner city areas and new public housing estates in the cities tend to be segregated by religion, middle-class areas tend to be mixed. Similarly, detailed analysis (Poole, 1982, 1983) revealed that in terms of religious composition, housing in the vast majority of towns in Northern Ireland is also very mixed. Furthermore, although some sparsely populated rural areas can be characterized as predominantly Catholic or Protestant, in other areas Protestants and Catholics live interspersed in a patchwork pattern that was established in the seventeenth century.

The fact that some Protestants and Catholics live in mixed residential areas does not necessarily imply that they come into close contact socially or at work. The extent of intergroup contact among a representative sample of Protestants and Catholics was shown in a 1968 survey reported by Rose (1971). Identical questions were also incorporated into a 1978 survey (Moxon-Browne, 1983). It was therefore possible to establish whether the extended period of civil conflict, known euphemistically as 'the Troubles', had deepened divisions between Protestants and Catholics. In fact very few differences were found across the decade in the proportions of respondents who reported that friends, close relatives and workmates were of the same religion as themselves. An increased proportion did however report that their neighbours were co-religionists. Moxon-Browne concluded from the survey that the society had been 'crystallised rather than shaken by a decade of civil strife' (p. 129).

Both surveys indicated that Catholics saw themselves as having more contact with Protestants than vice versa. This would be expected given that Protestants are the majority in the region. Overall, Moxon-Browne found that some 60 per cent of Catholics and 75 per cent of Protestants reported that all or most of their friends and neighbours were co-religionists. However, only 36 per cent of Catholics and 52 per cent of Protestants reported that the people they worked with were mainly in the same religious group as themselves. In contrast, all but 6 per cent of Protestants and 15 per cent of Catholics indicated that their relatives were co-religionists.

It would seem that although there are Protestants and Catholics in Northern Ireland who mix only with co-religionists, there is a sizeable minority of the population who live and work in close contact with individuals who are members of the 'other' group. Detailed analysis of the nature of intergroup contact has mainly been confined to anthropological studies of mixed rural communities (Donnan and McFarlane, 1983). However, there have been a few studies that have evaluated the impact of long-term contact between Protestants and Catholics in the small minority of schools, which, for historical or educational reasons, have a fairly balanced intake of pupils from both groups.

Children with special educational needs, including the physically handicapped, the delicate and the 'maladjusted' attend non-denominational schools. There are also a small number of communities served by non-sectarian independent schools, which were originally established in the nineteenth century by the owners of textile mills to provide education for the children of their mill-workers. A review of a number of studies of children attending these schools, suggested to McWhirter (1983) that within the everyday context of school activities, denomination did not seem to be a relevant or legitimate element of social identity. Accordingly, it was not at all surprising that interpersonal friendships were found to have developed quite naturally across the traditional Northern Ireland sectarian divide.

The most detailed picture of intergroup contact in the daily life of a mixed community is provided by Harris (1972). In the 1950s she carried out prolonged and close observation of the social life of the people in an area she called Ballybeg. In this rural community in Northern Ireland, Protestants and Catholics lived interspersed on farms, which had often been handed down in families for several generations. Protestant and Catholic neighbours were intimately known to each other. Indeed, Harris found that there were stable, co-operative, mixed groups of Catholic and Protestant farmers, who shared equipment and worked closely together.

Nevertheless, although Catholics and Protestants lived peacefully together, they were separated into two very distinct social units. There was some friendly cross-linkage but basically most individuals in Ballybeg operated within a *de facto* sectarian social framework. Catholics and Protestants tended to mix socially with their relatives, all of whom tended to be co-religionists. Social organizations were closely associated with the church, and political, educational and recreational activities were sectarian. Indeed, Harris found that there was no non-sectarian meeting place in the whole district – even film shows took place in church halls! In these circumstances contacts between Protestants and Catholics were guided by shared norms of 'proper' behaviour towards neighbours, but were constrained by the awareness of group differences.

The result of the constraints on conversation were that although Protestants and Catholics, in some cases and in some contexts, had close and friendly contacts, for the most part they managed to remain in almost complete ignorance of each other's beliefs. It was for this reason that Harris argued that at the same time as there was decency and regard for neighbours of the 'other side', there was also the potential for intra-community violence. This potential she suggested 'was related to the readiness with which the people switched from a view of their neighbours based on a perception of reality in which each was an individual with a mixture of traits, good and bad, to a myth of good and evil, a myth of "our fellows" and "their fellows" ' (Harris, in press).

This pattern of behaviour, which involves a tolerance of prejudice and an accompanying distinction between 'you and me' and 'them and us' can be understood in terms of the theoretical separation between intergroup and interpersonal behaviour, which is central to current conceptions of social behaviour (e.g. Tajfel, 1981; Turner and Giles, 1981). Brown and Turner (1981) have convincingly established that the interpersonal-intergroup distinction does have an empirical reality. The evidence from Northern Ireland would clearly support this viewpoint.

In sum, it would seem that dimensions of contact such as degree of interdependence, co-operation, intimacy and status equivalence, although suggested as important in the traditional psychological conceptions of the impact of intergroup contact, do not account for the situation observed in the mixed communities in Northern Ireland. These dimensions may be important for the development of friendship between neighbours; they have very little relevance to the development of strategies that allow for the peaceful coexistence of members of groups divided on genuine and apparently irreconcilable differences in political goals and aspirations. In contrast, the findings from research on everyday contact between Protestants and Catholics exemplify the distinction between interpersonal and intergroup behaviour that is central to social identity theory. This is most clearly demonstrated in a scenario that received limited local attention in 1983. It involved the work-force of a factory in a provincial town in Northern Ireland. The workers were divided equally between Protestants and Catholics and apparently they worked amicably together until July 1983 when the Protestant workers erected the Union Jack in preparation for the Protestants' annual celebration on the 12th July. Catholic workers objected and the management removed the flag, but the next day it reappeared and the Catholics consequently went on strike. The management then closed the factory for an unscheduled fortnight's holiday! The flag that caused the trouble was removed at the end of July; the factory was re-opened after seven weeks and 80 per cent of the workers went back to work. Detailed reports of this dispute appeared in the local papers (e.g. Johnston, 1983; Kane, 1983). One of the workers in the factory was asked to describe the last days when the plant was in operation. He is quoted as saying: 'It was as crazy as this. You'd have seen a Protestant and a Catholic sitting chatting away at tea break pretending there was nothing happening. Then there would be a meeting called and one would go away determined to keep the flag up and one would go the other way determined to get it down.' As another worker suggested: 'In many ways it's just like a mini-Northern Ireland . . . if you found the answer to that dispute you'd have found the answer to the Northern Ireland problem' (Johnston, 1983, p. 7).

SHORT-TERM INTERVENTIONS AND EVALUATIONS

Intergroup contact was the theme of one of the first publications written by psychologists about the Northern Ireland conflict. Doob and Foltz (1973, 1974) described a ten-day residential workshop, organized and funded by Americans, for Protestant and Catholic grass-roots leaders from Belfast. The minimal goal of this intervention was described as 'merely to provide a milieu in which persons of many persuasions, abilities and interests could learn in one another's presence something about how they personally and collectively operate when they work with their fellow citizens on projects that interest them' (Doob and Foltz, 1973, p. 493).

The workshop, which was described as 'a high-risk/high gain enterprise' (Doob and Foltz, 1974), followed an intervention design that combined Tavistock and National Training Laboratory group dynamics approaches. Contact between Protestants and Catholics therefore occurred under the stressful conditions associated with the Tavistock approach and its emphasis on confronting issues such as authority, power and leadership. Nine months after the workshop, only one of the 40 participants interviewed by Doob and Foltz (1974) claimed not to have felt some stress during the workshop. Several of those interviewed report short-term negative effects. They included one person who was 'disoriented' for a month and another who reported three months of being quarrelsome and peevish. In a critique of the two Doob and Foltz articles, the administrators on the project (Boehringer et al., 1974) conclude that it was not only ineffective in its own terms but harmful to many of the participants.

Contact between Protestants and Catholics, which was considered to be part of the learning experience provided by the workshop, was encouraged by forming small mixed groups. These groups were asked to devise projects that could be implemented after the workshop was completed. Support for these groups in the community was not provided. The follow-up interviews revealed that although some lines of communication remained between Protestants and Catholics who had attended the workshop, none of the groups were functioning nor had any of their plans been implemented. In a reply to their critics, Doob, Foltz and their co-workers (Alevy et al., 1974) acknowledged that the workshop would have benefited from better planning and a better follow-up. In these circumstances it is difficult to assess whether intergroup contact had any impact on intergroup attitudes. In one respect however the influence of the project extended far beyond any impact it could have had on the participants. Shortly after the workshop had taken place, its problems and the associated differences between participants were widely publicized in the local media. Clearly, such public debate and academic controversy did not provide an attractive context for further intervention by psychologists. This did not stop the development of programmes, but it did impede evaluation and assessment.

The controversy in Northern Ireland appeared not to have changed the views of Doob and Foltz and their co-workers. They continued to believe that short-term intergroup contact in an isolated setting and under appropriate conditions, does have a beneficial outcome. Such views are still upheld by some of those in Northern Ireland who aim at reconciliation. These workshops are not necessarily widely publicized nowadays, but many have been carried out since 1972 (e.g. McWhirter, 1985). Outsiders are not the only people who consider that intervention projects can have an impact in Northern Ireland. Lockwood (1982) noted that 'The contact thesis is presented on many fronts in Northern Ireland as if it could save the society from its own incipient violence . . . The contact thesis offers hope in a no-hope situation' (p. 187). This belief would seem to be the basis for the willingness of government and voluntary agencies to allocate considerable resources to schemes designed to bring Protestant and Catholic children together during community relations holidays.

Holiday schemes are aided by government grants if they conform to five minimum conditions. These are that the holiday group should be comprised of at least 10 Catholic and Protestant children from Northern Ireland, who are mixed, as far as possible, on a fifty-fifty basis. The holiday must last for at least five complete days and it must be properly planned under responsible leadership, with a programme of activities that takes into account the community relations objectives of the holiday scheme. The Department of Education (Northern Ireland) considers that given these basic conditions the community relations holidays are 'a practical means of facilitating the coming together of children and young people in circumstances that will contribute to increased understanding between the two traditions' (Department of Education circular, March 1983). In 1983, 112 holidays involving 3030 children were grant-aided.

At this stage, evidence is not available to establish whether or not these holidays do contribute to increased understanding. There have been no published evaluations describing either the nature of interaction between Protestants and Catholics attending such holidays or the impact of the events on children's attitudes and beliefs. Emerging results from an ongoing programme of research on a range of community holidays (e.g. Trew, 1985; Trew et al., 1984) suggest that friendship is not constrained by religious group membership. However, the duration of these holiday friendships has not been established. There are some schemes that provide regular follow-up activities enabling some children to maintain their holiday friendships – including those with children from a different religious group; other schemes do not involve follow-up activities. In these circumstances children who attend segregated schools and live in segregated neighbourhoods have few opportunities to continue their holiday friendships with those of the 'other' religion.

The organizers of children's holidays, in accordance with the norms of the society, seem to assume that harmonious relationships between Catholics and Protestants will develop most successfully if sectarian divisions are ignored. Any discussion of religious group differences and similarities is therefore discouraged. Indeed, after four weeks on one American holiday a few of the ten-year-olds did not realize that their friends were not of the same religion as themselves. There is no suggestion that mere exposure to the 'other' group under these conditions has a deleterious impact, but equally no evidence that positive changes have occurred in the individuals' intergroup attitudes and beliefs about the 'other' group.

There is however one study carried out in Northern Ireland that does strongly support the view that short-term exposure can have a positive effect on intergroup perceptions, even though the setting was not designed to promote community harmony. Lockhart and Elliott (1980) took advantage of the integration of Catholic and Protestant young offenders in a residential assessment centre to examine whether this experience would change perceptions of the other group at the end of the five-week assessment period. Their informal observations suggested that at a time when sectarian violence was at its height, boys from the residential ghettos of Belfast were making friends regardless of religion. Using the Repetory Grid technique, they found that on entry, although Protestant and Catholic boys construed 'boys like me' very similarly, they showed considerable difference in the way they construed the elements of 'Roman Catholic boy' and 'Protestant boy'. At the end of five weeks' close contact there was far closer identification with the 'other' group, and this was maintained five weeks after discharge. It seems that the boys, who for most of their school-days had probably mixed exclusively with co-religionists, did modify their perceptions of the 'other' group after a short-term period of contact. Whether the experience also modified their sectarian political beliefs is open to question.

In general, the research on short-term contact, in common with the research on intergroup contact in the community, indicates that religious denomination is not a barrier to personal friendship. However, the influence of such relationships on social understanding and beliefs about the other group has not been established. Furthermore, as the studies were not manipulative many other issues remain unresolved. At a most basic level, the results relating to the duration of contact and its outcomes are not consistent. Although Lockhart and Elliott (1980) found a change in the social perceptions of Protestant and Catholic boys following a period of five weeks' shared residence, Douglas (1983) found that seven years' attendance at an integrated primary school had little impact on the intergroup perceptions of first-year secondary school pupils. Their attitudes towards, and beliefs about, the other group were little different from those of their peers who lived in a comparable, residentially mixed locality, but had attended segregated schools.

These anomalous findings might be attributable to methodological factors, but at least two other explanations are equally tenable. First, social identity theory led Trew (1983a, 1983b) to insist on the flexible nature of denominational and national identities. It is assumed that these social identities are influenced by the situation in the community as well as the immediate environment. From this perspective reaction to the 'other' denominational group, whether in response to a questionnaire item or in terms of social behaviour, would be expected to be influenced not only by past experience and dispositional factors, but also by the situation. The young people who have attended an integrated primary school or a community holiday may feel very well disposed towards the other group, until some event heightens tension in the community and increases the salience of the Protestant-Catholic distinction.

A second, equally tenable explanation of these anomalous findings can be deduced from Rokeach's belief dissimilarity theory of prejudice and the associated rationale (Rokeach et al., 1960), in which intergroup contact is seen as an agent of change. According to this viewpoint, contact between members of two groups (under conditions that maximize the probability that shared values will be present and perceived) facilitates change, because belief dissimilarity is seen to be a misperception. It is suggested that attitudes towards the other group become more positive as individuals discover the similarities in belief between themselves and members of the other group. From this perspective, there are two reasons why sustained contact between Catholics and Protestants in Northern Ireland would not be expected to have an impact on the incompatible ideological differences dividing them. First, such divisive issues are not usually made explicit as Harris (1972) demonstrated. Second, if divisive issues are raised, in most instances discussion would reveal that the political divisions between Protestants and Catholics are not illusory.

In contrast, it can be suggested that short periods of contact between Catholics and Protestants, who have had no previous opportunity to meet and talk to anyone from the outgroup, will allow individuals to discover their similarities but not to delve into differences. In these circumstances intergroup contact can serve to dispel misperceptions about the beliefs of the other group and increase awareness of similarities. Fraser (1974) highlighted how little some children, from Belfast in particular, know about the other group. He noted that when Protestants and Catholics meet for the first time there can be 'a sense of surprise communicated by, say, a Protestant child who discovers how his counterpart likes the same food and drinks, enjoys, like him, playing in trees and water and getting in a mess, and that he has the same rows with his parents over the same things' (Fraser, 1974, p. 175).

Overall, there is surprisingly little objective evidence on the nature and outcomes of the range of projects that bring together Catholic and Protestant children in order to promote community harmony. In particular, systematic research would help to establish the relative efficacy of not only making group differences explicit but also actively encouraging the discussion of controversial issues. Those who have attempted to 'cure' the problems of Northern Ireland with interventions such as the Doob and Foltz workshop do not necessarily assume that contact alone will effect conflict resolution. Nevertheless, they do seem to be suggesting that good 'human relationships' will promote community harmony in Northern Ireland. This argument also led the psychologist, Heskin (1980) and the psychiatrist, Fraser (1979) to join other commentators in advocating the introduction of integrated schools.

Heskin (1980) considered that 'The present political circumstances . . . offer a context . . . in which an integrated system of education could begin to contribute to improved intergroup relations' (p. 152). Fraser (1979) had no doubts that '. . . total integration of children from primary school age upward would be the most potent single factor in breaking down community barriers and in restoring long-term peace' (p. 180). However, advocates of integrated schools ignore the basic fact that schools in Northern Ireland are segregated because of the desire of both groups for separate education. Indeed, the Catholic case for denominational schools is a principle based on the conviction that parents have the right to educate their children in the beliefs and practices of their faith. They also fail to take into account the evidence that provides little support for the view that education systems can, in isolation, influence social values engrained in the fabric of society.

Although major changes in the educational system are not officially supported, the Department of Education for Northern Ireland (DENI) pointed out, in a circular issued to all schools in June 1982, that it had a statutory responsibility for 'formulating and sponsoring policies for the improvement of community relations'. In the light of this responsibility it has promoted school-based development projects as well as funding activities such as community relations holidays. According to the circular, these schemes are designed to ensure that 'children do not grow up in ignorance, fear, or even hatred of those from whom they are educationally segregated.' The DENI projects are modest and they recognize the limitations of their efforts. However, in the past few years there have been major efforts to increase co-operation between 'Protestant' and 'Catholic' schools and to encourage joint activities between pupils of different denominations (Trew, in press). Although these schemes will not change the society, they may help to lower some of the barriers of ignorance within it.

To summarize, the evidence from small-scale studies, including direct intervention, suggests that on 'neutral' ground, or in appropriate institutional settings, even Protestants and Catholics who previously mixed only with their co-religionists will develop close personal friendships. The contact may also contribute to the moderation of gross misperceptions about the 'other' group and an appreciation of a shared cultural background. At the same time, there is no empirical evidence or theoretical rationale to suggest that contact *per se* will either influence salient political beliefs or have any impact on sectarianism in the society. As Tajfel (1982b) suggested, 'whenever the underlying structure of social divisions and power or status differentials is fairly resilient, it is not likely to be affected by piecemeal attempts at reform in selected situations of "contact" ' (p. 29).

CONCLUSIONS

This chapter has attempted to bring together research on peaceful contact between Protestants and Catholics. The literature is not extensive but inevitably not all of the available material has been cited in the brief overview. However, findings from all studies presented a consistent picture. In mixed religious groups, friendships are formed without reference to denominational differences. However, Catholics and Protestants seem to assume that in order to maintain such personal relationships discussions of divisive issues must be avoided.

It would seem that when groups are in contact, but divided from each other by mutually exclusive political goals, specific strategies have to be adopted in order to enable interpersonal co-operation and friendships to develop between individuals, without threatening group allegiance. These strategies are an intrinsic part of intergroup contact and must be taken into account in any attempt to understand what is involved in social interaction between group members. This type of process does not feature in theories of intergroup relations that depend on either personal qualities (e.g. degree of prejudice) or situational constraints (e.g. co-operative vs. competitive encounters) as explanatory concepts. In contrast, the pattern of interdenominational mixing in Northern Ireland clearly exemplifies the distinction between intergroup and interpersonal relationships, which is highlighted in social identity theory (e.g. Brown and Turner, 1981).

Denominational categorization pervades many aspects of life in Northern Ireland. Interpersonal contacts between Protestants and Catholics cannot be viewed in isolation from events within the wider community. These group loyalties can be underplayed but they cannot be ignored. Contacts between Protestants and Catholics may provide a basis for some individuals to reinterpret their perceptions of the other group and its characteristics, but it is difficult to envisage how such contacts could impinge on the basic fabric of the society. This does not mean that contact between Protestants and Catholics is not potentially beneficial for the society as well as the individual.

This chapter has concentrated on research into intergroup contact and social relationships in mixed communities. This evidence cannot be divorced from the totality of research into intergroup relations in Northern Ireland. From this perspective, analyses of the consequences of denominational segregation and exclusive sociability suggest that there may be benefits from promoting, at least limited, interdenominational contact. Social isolation does not only lead to ignorance about the other group; it can also result in the groups developing increasingly diverse values (Pettigrew, 1979a). Research in one of the tightly knit sectarian enclaves within Belfast provides a clear example of how a selective perception of events is endorsed and ratified in communities in which divergent views are not represented (Burton, 1978; Hunter, 1982). In these circumstances, violence can become condoned and legitimized if it is identified with the defence of the communities' political aspirations. Similarly, opportunities for reconciliation are reduced as the interpretations of events by Protestant and Catholic communities increasingly diverge.

It is difficult to establish the extent to which segregation or integration influences beliefs. Segregated and integrated communities differ along many dimensions. However, it would seem that while the contact between Protestants and Catholics may not have a direct impact on ideological differences, social isolation may provide an environment in which polarized opinions flourish. It can be suggested that without the relationships that interweave between, as well as within, the Protestant and Catholic communities, the gap between these groups might have been so wide that it would have been impossible to begin bridge-building activities.

6 Intergroup Contact in Quebec: Myth or Reality?

Donald M. Taylor, Lise Dubé and
Jeannette Bellerose

The focus of this chapter is contact between English- and French-speaking Canadians in the province of Quebec. The broader concern is with intergroup conflict and the role contact may play in exacerbating conflict or improving relations between groups. We propose to address the question of contact and conflict from a perspective that differs from the more traditional approaches. Social-psychological research from the Quebec context will be used to illustrate this complementary approach.

An admittedly over-simplified, but nevertheless useful, summary of traditional approaches to intergroup contact is: the more the contact between members of two groups resembles contact between members of the same group, the more the barriers of prejudice and discrimination are removed, with the result that there will generally be greater harmony between groups. Specifically, from the traditional perspective, harmony between members of different groups is enhanced to the extent that contact is one-to-one rather than one-to-many; the contact involves co-operative interdependence; contact is supported by authority, law or custom; and there is equality of status between group members (see Allport, 1954; Amir, 1969; Pettigrew, 1967).

The argument to be made in this chapter is that the issue of contact and conflict should be approached differently. The traditional approach assumes that relations between individual members of different groups are normally conflictual. Research is then directed at specifying the conditions of contact that can reduce this conflict. Our own position is different. We begin with the assumption that, at the interpersonal level, relations between members of different groups are for the most part amicable. Thus, the orienting question should be: what are the normal mechanisms by which harmony is maintained among individual members of different groups, when the groups they represent are in conflict with one another? A number of social-psychological processes operate, we believe, to permit interpersonal harmony in the face of group conflict, and the role of contact features prominently in our analysis.

THE INTERGROUP CONTEXT IN QUEBEC

Although unique in certain ways, the intergroup situation in Quebec has its parallel in many different contexts. Quebec is one of ten provinces in Canada. The English-speaking (anglophone) minority in Quebec has historically enjoyed a privileged position, despite the fact that 80 per cent of the population of Quebec lists French as its mother tongue. French-speaking Quebecers have traditionally faced not only economic disadvantages in Quebec, but also an imminent threat to their language and culture, arising out of their minority status in the context of English-language-dominated North America. The French-Canadian nationalism, which began in earnest in the 1960s culminated in 1976 with the election of the current Parti Québécois government, one of whose major election platforms was, and remains, the political separation of Quebec from the rest of Canada. The Parti Québécois government has taken a number of steps designed to protect and enhance French culture and language, most notably passing Bill 101, which declares French to be the only official language in Quebec (see Bourhis, 1984). The extremity of this legislation and its implications have resulted in a long-term state of tension (see Taylor and Dubé-Simard, 1984). Feelings of being under threat and insecurity have reached such a point that there has been a steady exodus of anglophones from the province of Quebec.

Montreal, the province's major metropolis, is the meeting ground for anglophone and francophone Quebecers. The city is depicted as one of North America's few, truly bilingual and bicultural cities. Despite the clear bias for intergroup conflict, Quebec in general, and Montreal in particular, is often held up as a model example of harmonious relations between different ethnolinguistic groups. Confrontation, violence and rioting are rarely, if ever, witnessed; indeed one would be hard pressed to find a noteworthy confrontation between anglophone and francophone Quebecers. Even the one act of terrorism in 1971, which involved the kidnapping of a British trade commissioner and the murder of a francophone cabinet minister, was not generally viewed as a confrontation between anglophones and francophones and certainly did not affect relations between individual members of the two groups. To what do we attribute this apparent harmony? Is it, as the traditional perspective might suggest, because of the frequent contact between anglophones and francophones? Is it because the contact tends to be among equals? Has intimate contact broken down the barriers of prejudice, stereotyping and discrimination?

CONCEPTUALIZING THE PROBLEM

Our analysis of these questions begins not with a focus on intergroup relations, but with everyday observations of individuals and their interaction. Everyone is aware of situations, whether concerning the family, work or recreation, where particular individuals must interact despite having a dislike for one another or, at least, despite being involved in a short-term feud. Often such individuals, because of physical proximity, cannot avoid each other and so to a large extent they interact in apparent harmony, despite the underlying conflict.

The same observations can be made of members of rival groups who share the same social environment. The point here is that the highly salient examples of intergroup violence in the world, which seem to dominate the news media, may well mask a more pervasive phenomenon: the countless interactions between individual members of conflicting groups that are carried out in apparent harmony. As just noted, intergroup violence in Quebec is rarely heard of and racial clashes in the United States and Britain for example may well be atypical. While the importance and horror of these occurrences cannot be overemphasized, it is also true that they can be misleading. The salience of such violence leaves us with the impression that they are the norm, whereas quite the opposite may be true. For example Cook (1979), in reviewing the desegregation experience in the United States, comments that while attention has focused on the violence associated with desegregation, the 'near miraculous orderliness' with which 82 per cent of the communities managed this process is forgotten.

It would seem that individuals, of necessity, have developed a variety of mechanisms for interacting effectively with others, despite underlying conflict. It is these processes that must be explored. Conflict presumably would surface when these usual mechanisms broke down. What are these mechanisms for maintaining harmony? Three hypotheses will be examined in this chapter. The first is that where intergroup interaction is apparently frequent and necessary, individuals nevertheless subtly bias their contact towards members of the ingroup such that intergroup contact is more illusory than real. The second hypothesis is that when intergroup contact does occur, the interactions are qualitatively different from those with ingroup members. Finally, when contact is frequent and intimate, individuals psychologically define themselves, the other person and the context in other than intergroup terms.

110   *Donald M. Taylor, Lise Dubé and Jeanette Bellerose*

THE ILLUSION OF INTERGROUP CONTACT

A scientific approach to the study of contact and its effects on intergroup relations naturally requires that intergroup attitudes be examined among those who have varying amounts of contact, but where all other variables are controlled. Often this involves contrasting two sub-groups of subjects from the same group who differ dramatically with respect to their contact with an outgroup. Alternatively, the design may call for a time-sequence study, in which subjects who have had little or no contact with another group suddenly find themselves in a situation of heightened contact with members of that outgroup.

Practically speaking, much of the research on contact has attempted to capitalize on realistic social situations where variations in contact occur naturally. So for example the landmark decision to desegregate schools in the United States represents such an opportunity for the study of contact; racially and ethnically mixed cities, states or nations also provide a natural laboratory for such study.

Crucial to these studies is whether or not the independent variable truly represents increased contact as opposed to *apparent* increase in contact. Desegregating schools certainly places whites and blacks in close proximity, but does it truly alter the extent and nature of intergroup contact? This is important since the ambiguity of results that have emerged in terms of whether the self-image of blacks is altered, their school performance improved and intergroup prejudice reduced, may be owing to a lack of any real change in contact, rather than an understanding of what effects contact has. A study by Schofield and Sagar (1977) raises precisely this issue. They examined the pattern of interaction between black and white students in a desegregated school, involving 1200 students aged ten to thirteen. The school authorities strongly supported a programme of activities designed to help students get to know one another. The results clearly indicated a strong predisposition for both black and white students to prefer, and to interact with, others of their own race.

An examination of interaction between anglophones and francophones in the province of Quebec, specifically the city of Montreal, is revealing in this context. As noted earlier Montreal is characterized as a bilingual and bicultural city where anglophones and francophones freely interact on a variety of levels. But what precisely is the extent of intergroup contact, and can it shed light on the apparent harmony that exists between the two groups? The first hint comes from a study by Simard and Taylor (1973) where, as a pilot study conducted prior to the actual experiment, francophone students from a French language university and anglophones from an English language university were asked to record information about their recent conversations. Of 1008 conversations recorded, 99.9 per cent were with ingroup members. The paucity of intergroup contact was striking. This finding is corroborated by demographic studies, which show that, in terms of residence, Montreal is one of the most segregated Canadian cities (see Joy, 1972, 1978; Lieberson, 1970).

A further study by Taylor, Meynard and Rheault (1977), which dealt with ethnic identity, indirectly reinforces the present theme of the exaggeration of intergroup contact. Francophone students from different universities in the province of Quebec were asked to rate the extent of their personal contact with anglophones. Rating were made on a nine-point scale where one indicated 'no contact', and nine denoted 'intimate contact'. Even those francophone students who attended an English language university indicated only modest contact ($M = 4.41$). Those attending three other French language institutions, as might be expected, had even less contact with anglophones ($M = 3.02$, 2.24, 1.78 respectively).

A more in-depth analysis of the processes involved in cross-cultural contact was conducted by Simard (1981). In part I of her study, anglophone and francophone Quebecers were asked about their experiences in forming friendships. All agreed it was a normal process, but members of both groups perceived that forming acquaintances occurs less often and with more difficulties with members of the other language group. In addition, all respondents required that acquaintances be similar to themselves. However, members of the other ethnolinguistic group were required to be even *more* similar, on a variety of dimensions, than those from the ingroup.

The novel aspect of the study occurred in part II, where participants were actually required to go out and form an acquaintance. Participants were asked to meet either a person from their own ethnolinguistic group or a person from the other group. They were to approach people naturally and were not permitted to explain to a potential acquaintance that they were taking part in an experiment. Finally, participants were required to obtain the name and telephone number of their acquaintances so that the investigator could corroborate the details of the encounter recorded by the subject.

The findings indicated that forming acquaintances is not as easy as participants indicated it to be in part I, when of course they were not aware that they would actually have to carry out the task. What is more relevant to the present discussion is that both anglophones and francophones succeeded more often in forming acquaintances with members of their own group than they did with members of the other group. The details of the strategies subjects used will be described later, but for the present it is important to have behavioural evidence regarding the lack of intergroup contact corroborated by a more personal and in-depth study of intergroup behaviour.

This behavioural approach formed the basis of a study by Bellerose and Taylor (1984), which examined intergroup interaction in a context that maximized the opportunities for interaction between anglophones and francophones. The setting was McGill University, an English language institution in a province where French is the official language. Francophone enrolment at McGill has been increasing to the extent that approximately one-quarter of the students are currently French speaking. Francophone students have a number of French language universities from which to select and hence those who come to McGill have actually opted for an English language university. This fact, coupled with the liberal attitudes usually associated with university students, suggests that if ever there was a social environment conducive to intergroup contact, it is among such anglophone and francophone students.

Samples of students from the two groups were asked to keep detailed daily records of every one of their interactions for a period of one week. Francophones constituted 24 per cent of the student body, anglophones 76 per cent. Thus, if contact is not influenced by group membership, there should have been comparable figures in terms of the students' pattern of interaction. However, of 1419 interactions recorded, franco-phones interacted with members of their own group 49.7 per cent of the time, significantly more than the expected 24 per cent. Similarly, of the 820 interactions reported by anglophones, 87.3 per cent were with members of their own group, again more than the expected 76 per cent.

The results of several studies then converge to suggest that intergroup contact may not be as prevalent as believed. Even in situations that are apparently conducive to contact, because of physical proximity and positive attitudes, there is less interaction than would be expected. This bias in favour of ingroup contact may explain a primary mechanism by which interpersonal conflict between competing groups can be avoided, that is simply reduce contact.

Does this mean that contact is subtly biased in favour of the ingroup as a mechanism for avoiding conflict? The present data do not allow for a conclusion about people's motivation. It may be that people just feel more comfortable with members of their own ethnolinguistic group. However, regardless of motivation, where contact is only an illusion, interpersonal confrontation is neatly avoided.

THE QUALITY OF INTERGROUP CONTACT

Biasing contact in favour of the ingroup is an important but nevertheless primitive mechanism for avoiding conflict. In the studies reporting this contact bias, there remains a smaller but substantial number from both groups who do have contact with members of the other group. An examination of the nature of this contact may provide further insights into how interpersonal harmony is maintained despite tension at the group level.

The study that explicitly addressed this issue was that of Bellerose and Taylor (1984). Francophone and anglophone students were asked to rate every interaction they had in terms of its intimacy, its importance and how agreeable it was. The ratings were made separately for every interaction at a time when it was still fresh in their minds. The same pattern emerged for both anglophone and francophone students. Interactions with ingroup members were significantly more intimate and important than they were with outgroup members. It would seem that when cross-cultural contact does take place it is at a more superficial level. What effect does this superficiality have on the harmony of intergroup encounters?

Respondents made ratings of how 'agreeable' each of their interactions was, with members of both groups. Both anglophones and francophones found their interactions with outgroup members as agreeable as those with members of the ingroup. At the same time interactions with outgroup members were judged to be relatively superficial. It is argued here that one mechanism for ensuring that cross-cultural contacts are harmonious is to limit them to relatively superficial encounters.

The Simard (1981) study, which involved forming an acquaintance, provides further evidence that when cross-cultural contact does occur, it may be qualitatively different from own-group contact. In part I of the study, francophone and anglophone participants were asked to rate how important it is for a potential acquaintance to be similar to them. The dimensions of similarity examined, included age, sex, occupation, social class, attitudes and personality traits. The results showed that every dimension of similarity is judged to be more important when applied to an outgroup member. So contact seems to be much more selective when it is with a member of the 'other' group and appears to be designed to enhance the probability that there will be compatibility.

A further way to enhance the probability that interactions will be harmonious is to avoid certain topics of conversation with members of an outgroup. Bellerose, Hafer and Taylor (1984) addressed this question by asking a sample of 50 adult anglophones about their interactions with francophones. Specifically, they were asked the extent to which they discuss topics such as work, world politics, Canadian politics, Quebec politics, entertainment, hobbies and personal problems with fellow workers and friends who are anglophone or francophone.

Participants in this study provided global and impressionistic ratings, rather than detailed accounts of their interactions as in the studies described earlier. Thus, the ratings in this study are much more subject to biases such as social desirability than those using the daily diary procedure. Nevertheless, there was a small but significant trend for anglophones in this study to discuss potentially sensitive topics more intimately with members of their own group than with outgroup members. Of particular interest was an unexpected finding that ran counter to the theme of this chapter. It was expected that Quebec politics, a sensitive intergroup issue, would be strictly avoided as a topic of conversation when anglophones were interacting with francophones.

Among the 50 anglophone participants, all had a close friend who was anglophone, and 35 participants also reported having a close friend who was francophone. Those who did have a francophone friend claimed they discussed Quebec politics *more* with this friend than they did with their anglophone friend. Clearly, a sensitive intergroup issue was not being avoided in interpersonal cross-group interactions.

How can this willingness to discuss a sensitive intergroup issue with someone of the other group be explained? Two concepts may be central, curiosity and friendship. First, an anglophone would know the political views of fellow anglophones, but would be most curious about a francophone's attitudes towards the Quebec government. What prevents discussion on the topic is its potentially conflictual nature. However, the anglophones in this study were asked about discussing Quebec politics with a francophone *friend*, not a casual acquaintance. So, the person respondents would have in mind would be well known to them, someone with whom they had already gone beyond the stage of 'reducing uncertainty' (see Berger and Calabrese, 1975); in short, someone they knew and trusted. With such a person, respondents would no doubt feel confident discussing even very sensitive issues, and their natural curiosity would make this topic far more interesting to discuss with their francophone friend than with any of their anglophone friends.

In general however there seems to be a superficial and selective quality to cross-group interaction, designed perhaps to ensure smooth inter-personal relations. Nonetheless, when the trust associated with friend-ship has already been established with a member of the other group, sensitive intergroup issues may be popular topics of discussion. In this sense the friend may serve the important function of a valuable source of information about the outgroup as a whole.

MECHANISMS INVOLVED IN INTIMATE CROSS-GROUP INTERACTION

Once the bias towards ingroup contact and the quality of cross-group contact, when it does occur, are taken into account, there still remain a number of cross-group interactions that may be frequent and intimate. Indeed, intergroup marriages, while not the norm, are nevertheless not uncommon. Thus, for intimate relationships, there must be important psychological processes operating, which guard against interpersonal contacts becoming repeated enactments of the tensions underlying the respective groups. What are these processes and is there any evidence that they are actually used? Since the issue has not been addressed in this form, direct evidence is scarce. Nevertheless, there exist a number of findings from the literature on intergroup relations in Quebec to at least encourage further research in this area.

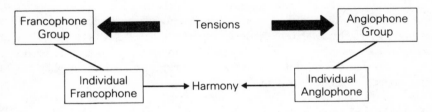

Figure 6.1 Schematic representation of interpersonal harmony in the context of intergroup tension

A schematic representation of the interaction pattern depicted in this chapter can allow us to visualize more clearly the possible psychological processes. From figure 6.1 there are two major categories of mechanisms that would allow individuals from competing groups to interact peacefully: (a) the denial by individuals of tensions between the two groups and (b) the dissociation of individuals from their respective groups.

Denial of tensions   At least two forms of denial must be distinguished. An individual may simply not acknowledge any tension between the groups. Such an individual might say 'everybody, and especially the media, is always looking for conflict between francophone and anglophone Quebecers. There really is no conflict and I wish everyone would stop trying to invent or instigate one.' A second form of denial would be to acknowledge tension but to not interpret the tension as a conflict between francophones and anglophones. So, the opinion that it is the government that francophones (anglophones) are against, not anglophones (francophones), exemplifies this. Either of these forms of denial would put interaction between individual members of the two groups in a co-operative context, and even a strong awareness of the ethnolinguistic identity of each interlocutor would not jeopardize the quality of contact between them.

Indirect evidence for the operation of this denial of group tension mechanism comes from a survey by Taylor et al. (1982). The study explored how anglophones interpret threats that allude directly or indirectly to intergroup relations in Quebec. The threats ranged from French-Canadian nationalism, discrimination against anglophones in the work setting and anglophones being forced to take French exams in order to qualify for jobs, to having to speak in French on the phone or having one's son or daughter marry a francophone. An analysis, with multidimensional-scaling, of anglophones' perceptions of these threats indicated that they did not interpret threats from a framework of intergroup relations. Even though the threats were clearly focused on relations between francophones and anglophones, there was little or no indication that the respondents perceived intergroup conflict *per se* as the root source of social threat in Quebec.

In two further studies (Taylor, Simard and Papineau, 1978; Taylor et al., 1982) anglophone and francophone managers were asked to judge the extent to which there were cultural differences in the way members of the two groups approached and executed their jobs. A substantial number of respondents from both groups claimed that there were no differences in orientation between anglophone and francophone managers. This may indicate a desire for some people to emphasize similarities between groups as a form of denial of potential tensions.

These studies do not directly confirm the hypothesis that, through denial of tensions between two groups, interpersonal harmony can be maintained in cross-cultural contact. At no point in these studies was any relationship established between individuals' perceptions of the relations between groups and their personal relationship with individual members of that group. What these studies do confirm is that not all Quebecers focus on or interpret as valid the ethnic tensions that, according to the media, various social scientists and many politicians, appear to dominate Quebec society.

Dissociation of individual from group   There are a number of ways to dissociate an individual from his or her group in the context of interaction; the most basic probably involves defining the relationship such that, in this case, one's own or the other person's ethnic identity is minimally salient. Focusing on individual traits, roles or other social identities effectively reduces the importance of a person's ethnic identity.

That individuals will, at different times, in different situations, place different emphasis on their group identity and their unique self-identity, has been described in some detail by Tajfel (1978a) and Brown and Turner (1981). The Bellerose and Taylor (1984) study, which examined the interaction patterns of anglophones and francophones at an English-speaking university, indirectly exemplifies this process. Participants were asked to review every interaction they had recorded for the week and to note those that made them aware of their ethnic identity. It was anticipated that francophone students would be especially aware of their ethnic identity as they met the challenge of adjusting to an English language institution for the first time. However, of the 1419 interactions reviewed, only 9.9 per cent made the participant aware of his or her identity as a French Quebecer. For anglophones, only 6 per cent of the 820 interactions reviewed involved their ethnic identity as English Quebecers. One interpretation of these findings is that both anglophones and francophones studiously avoided defining their interactions in ethnic group terms. In so doing, intergroup tensions would not intrude on the interaction, and instead the focus would be on other dimensions of self-identity, those perhaps that interlocutors had in common.

A second form of dissociation has already been noted in the literature associated with ethnic stereotypes. The dissociation involves perceiving an individual member of an ethnic group as different from 'typical' members of that group and has been labelled as 'fence mending' (Allport, 1954) or 'the exceptional case' (Pettigrew, 1979b). This process has been described in the context of how prejudiced individuals maintain their bigotry in the face of socially desirable behaviour on the part of individual outgroup members; they merely exclude the outgroup individual from the disliked group. As Pettigrew (1979) notes, 'This resolution can even lead to generous, if often patronizing, exaggeration of the positive qualities of this exceptional person in order to differentiate this "good" individual from the "bad" outgroup' (p. 307).

This form of dissociation, we believe, has more general application. It is not merely a mechanism for prejudiced individuals to deal with discrepant information. Rather, it may be a fundamental process whereby cross-group interaction can occur at the interpersonal level in the context of conflict between groups.

Suggestive evidence for the operation of this process in the Quebec context comes from the study by Simard (1981), where participants were required to make an acquaintance with a member of the other group. Surprisingly, in order to accomplish this, participants did not spend time in settings where large numbers of outgroup members congregated. Instead they remained within the confines of their own ethnic group while searching for the individual member of the other group. So for example anglophone students, instead of going to a French language university in the city, went to a neighbouring English language university, but in search of a potential francophone acquaintance. Moreover, participants judged that the other group members they did meet often engaged in cross-group interaction and were limited in their interactions with members of their own group.

What these data suggest is, that when intergroup contact occurs, it is not with individuals who are, or are perceived as, prototypical of their own group. As Simard (1981) notes 'typical members of one group were not necessarily meeting typical members of the other group' (p. 190).

CONCLUSION

In this chapter we have suggested mechanisms by which individuals from competing groups may approach intergroup contact in order to avoid conflict at the interpersonal level. While data on the avoidance of contact seem relatively clear, research on the quality of cross-group contact and the processes involved in intimate cross-group contact is only in the early stages.

What this chapter represents however is an approach that complements the traditional orientation to the study of intergroup contact. Instead cf emphasizing the necessary contact conditions for harmonious interaction to occur, we propose that most cross-group interactions at the personal level are, on the surface at least, harmonious. Addressing the issue from this perspective shifts the avenue of enquiry and leads to two questions. First, what are the normal mechanisms used by individuals to maintain interpersonal harmony in cross-group contact? The second question would be what causes the breakdown of these mechanisms such that the intergroup conflict does become actualized in a situation of one-to-one contact? Research on these questions is only just beginning, but it is hoped that by addressing issues in this complementary fashion, new insights into contact and intergroup relations can be gained.

7 Contact in a 'Non-Contact' Society: The Case of South Africa

Don Foster and Gillian Finchilescu

INTRODUCTION

Given that separatist assumptions lie at the heart of apartheid it is surprising that South African research has paid so little attention to questions flowing from the contact hypothesis. Perhaps it is because the standard criteria for optimal contact so rarely occur in this divided society. Nonetheless, liberal thinkers implicitly invoke some version of the contact hypothesis in discussing the possibilities of reform, as do some social researchers (Heaven, 1983; Lever, 1971). In the opposite direction, the policy of apartheid could be seen as providing an elaborate, Machiavellian and distasteful experiment for testing a negative version of the contact hypothesis.

In examining these issues in this chapter we first provide a general description of contact under apartheid; second, review some South African research related to the contact hypothesis; third, in giving results of a recent field study, we also look at theoretical questions, arguing that social identity theory may offer a better account of contact outcome than the traditional contact hypothesis. Our central argument is that in a deeply divided social structure, riven by a long history of conflict and power imbalance, *social identity* penetrates the personal sphere to such an extent that interpersonal contact *per se*, even under the most favourable conditions, is not likely to alter substantially established social relations.

It is also clear however that current policies of large-scale non-contact have contributed little to establishing harmonious group relations. Therefore black–white contact will be both desirable and necessary to transform the social order. In conclusion we suggest that mere contact is not enough. Change will emerge only through social action, involving black–white contact, which is centrally directed at transforming present power·relations constitutive of racist identities. This process will perhaps require theories beyond the present scope of either the contact hypothesis or social identity theory.

THE APARTHEID STATE

The central hypothesis of apartheid may best be stated by some of its principal architects. During the second reading of the Group Areas Bill in 1950, the Minister of the Interior explained that:

points of contact inevitably produce friction and friction generates heat which may lead to conflagration. It is our duty therefore to reduce these points of contact to the absolute minimum which public opinion is prepared to accept. The paramountcy of the white man and of western civilization in South Africa must be ensured in the interests of the material, cultural and spiritual development of all races. (cited in Kuper, Watts and Davies, 1958, p. 21)

Minister C. R. Swart (subsequently the first State President of the Republic in 1961) stated in connection with the Immorality Act in 1950 that:

Our point of departure in this matter is that we wish to separate the white and coloured populations as far as possible from each other in order that there may be no mingling of blood which would exacerbate our problems in the future. (authors' free translation from the Afrikaans; cited in Joubert, 1974, p. 75)

The guiding principle of apartheid may thus be presented in the form of a negative contact hypothesis: that if contact between blacks and whites could be reduced to the absolute minimum, conflict and racial problems would disappear, or would be reduced to a minimum, while simultaneously 'civilization' and 'peace' would be maintained.

Conflict between white and black was present almost from the beginning of contact between Dutch invader-settlers and indigenous Khoikhoi. Establishment of settlers on Khoikhoi grazing ground provoked the first war from 1658 to 1660 (Katzen, 1969). Yet it has been argued (MacCrone, 1937) that religious, not primarily racial, distinctions were responsible for the first ordering of group relations in the Cape. It was those in the category of heathen or non-baptized, rather than coloured, who were excluded from full acceptance in early Cape society. As a result of the baptism of freed slaves, mixed marriages did occur. Certainly the viability of intimate contact was such that by 1675 a sizeable number of children born in the colony were 'half-breeds'. The consequence was that by 1685 marriages between whites and full blacks were forbidden (Legassick, 1980). Although some doubts have been expressed regarding the accuracy of MacCrone's depiction of early settlement life − for example Legassick (1980) claims that racist ideas were 'there from the beginning' − it is clear enough that the relationship between contact and racism has a substantial history in South Africa. The roots of apartheid run deep.

While territorial segregation on the eastern frontier was not unknown during the first half of the nineteenth century, it was very largely in reponse to the threat of black urbanization and proletarianization during the late nineteenth and early twentieth centuries that segregationist policies took a firm hold (Rich, 1984). Following a strike in the mines by whites, the industrial colour bar was established in the 1911 Mines and Works Act. In 1913 the Natives Land Act drastically curtailed rural African landholding rights, and in 1923 the Natives (Urban Areas) Act established the principle that Africans were only to be in white-dominated urban areas to service the economic needs of whites.

The apartheid state formally dates from 1948 with the coming to power of Malan's National Party, and subsequent years have seen the extension of segregationist policies on an unprecedented scale. However, it would be an error to regard the contemporary situation as entirely an 'invention' of the National Party since 1948, as a considerable degree of continuity in racial policy has been demonstrated over the course of the twentieth century (Legassick, 1975). On the other hand there can be no doubt that the sheer *extent* of legislated segregation has increased enormously since 1948. The pre-Nationalist period from 1908 to 1948 saw the enactment of 49 laws seeking to regulate relations between racial groups. Between 1948 and 1960, 53 such laws were passed, with a further 98 laws from 1961 to 1971 (cited in Randall, 1971, p. 29). It has been suggested that the number of such laws has increased as crude 'baasskap' (white mastership) has declined (Savage, 1975, p. 297).

Unquestionably, as Savage (1975) has argued, apartheid legislation has attempted to formalize behaviour in a wide range of interethnic contact situations, in a general effort to 'stabilize' intergroup relations. From a social-psychological point of view it will be useful to examine some of these laws in order to grasp the context of forms and types of contact in South Africa.

Recent social-psychological analysis of intergroup behaviour has given a good deal of attention to the categorization of groups. In this respect the Population Registration Act of 1950, with its many subsequent amendments (see Horrell, 1978, pp. 16–19), must be regarded as pivotal. In effect this classifies all people as either White, Coloured, Asian or African, while provisions are made for the further categorization of Africans into various ethnic subdivisions. It is no exaggeration to claim that the total pattern of every person's life is circumscribed by his or her classification. No matter that the laws themselves are woefully lacking in uniformity of definition, lack any scientific basis and are contradicted by other legislation (Suzman, 1960):[1] the political effects are both real and powerful. There are very few South Africans who entirely escape thinking almost 'instinctively' in terms of these categories, however much they abhor and intellectually reject the social genesis of these groupings.

Following in the wake of this central Act is a formidable battery of laws, regulations, proclamations and judicial interpretations that prescribe behaviour in a vast array of potentially interracial situations, such as wedding, bedding, dining, entertaining, learning, praying, playing, defecating, voting, resisting, fighting, working; that is the medley of actions and activities that constitute a person's life. Even plain conversation may, under certain circumstances, contravene the Internal Security Act.

Recognizing that the regulation of interaction is a complex matter, two approaches to setting out the restrictions on contact in South Africa will be used. First, the approach of van den Berghe (1971), which proposes three forms of segregation, and second, an approach examining segregation in terms of institutional spheres.

Van den Berghe, in differentiating between three kinds, or degrees, of segregation, first describes *micro-segregation*, widely known as 'petty-apartheid'. This involves the prohibition of social contact in countless everyday locations, such as public transport, waiting rooms, beaches, sporting facilities, toilets, offers, restaurants, theatres, conferences, meetings and so on. Particularly noteworthy at this micro-level of contact are the notorious Acts prohibiting sexual intimacy across the colour bar: the Prohibition of Mixed Marriages Act of 1949 and the Immorality Acts of 1950 and 1957.

At this micro-level of contact, segregation has been somewhat relaxed in recent years. For example convictions under the Immorality Act averaged roughly 250 per year in the 1950s, about 470 per year in the 1960s, but numbered only 98 in 1980. (Data drawn from annual Survey of Race Relations in South Africa.) However, both the Mixed Marriages and Immorality Acts still remain on the statute books.[2] Partial relaxation of segregation has occurred in other micro-interactional settings, such as parks, public transport, theatres and so on, and certain observers have hailed such moves as signs of 'progress'. However, this process is highly uneven, and Adam (1971) has typified it well: it involves whites being flexible where it matters little, but resilient in areas where change could undermine their domination. Furthermore, while black–white contact may have increased – for example in the workplace – this has hardly altered the structure of these contacts.

The second kind, or degree, has been labelled *meso-segregation*. This aims for the residential separation of classified groups into racially homogeneous areas. The Group Areas Act of 1950, frequently amended and consolidated in subsequent years, is the key legislative machinery at this level. Apart from providing provisions for the proclamation of specified and controlled areas, this Act also imposed control over interracial property transactions. Of the estimated three and a half million people who have been relocated under all the legislative provisions since 1960, roughly three-quarters of a million people have been moved because of the terms of this Act; many of the planned removals have now been completed despite sustained resistance (Platzky and Walker, 1983). Meso-segregation is related to matters of military and police control (van den Berghe, 1971), particularly in the case of African 'townships', which are frequently sited outside white towns, facilitating military control measures, such as their sealing off at times of unrest. From the point of view of contact research, South Africa is clearly at an opposite end of the scale to North America, where action has been directed towards desegregating schools and residential areas (Hamilton and Bishop, 1976; Stephan, 1978). The segregation of organizational activities typical of neighbourhoods necessarily accompanies South African residential segregation: schooling, civic and voluntary associations, recreational societies and churches. This situation therefore precludes most activities satisfying the contact hypothesis criterion of 'co-operation in the achievement of a joint goal' (Cook, 1978, p. 97).

Macro-segregation, the third form of non-contact, is the grandiose apartheid scheme. The avowed ideal is to render all Africans (75 per cent of the total population) citizens of ten separate, ethnic 'homelands', which in totality constitute roughly 13 per cent of the nation's territory. The stated principle is that each African ethnic group constitutes an embryo 'nation', and that these 'nations' are thus to be granted full 'independent' status. At the time of writing, four such homelands have been granted 'independence': Transkei, Ciskei, Venda and Bophuthatswana. Many Africans will in fact remain in urban areas, as their labour is crucial. However, to facilitate the 'homelands' or 'bantustan' policy, approximately two and three-quarter million Africans have, since 1960, been moved and relocated in 'homelands'. As a consequence the percentage of the total African population living in the 'homelands' has increased from just under 40 per cent to over 50 per cent between 1960 and 1980 (Platzky and Walker, 1983).

It cannot be assumed that separatism is a benign and mutually desired mode of parallel democracy or 'separate-but-equal development' as is sometimes claimed. The repressive apparatus of the South African state is considerable, and many forms of opposition to state policy are ruthlessly suppressed. Although marginally decreased during a climate of constitutional 'reform', censorship, bannings, detention and police harassment are still the order of the day. And on the matter of the constitutional 'reform' in 1984, it should be noted that Coloured people and Asians have been granted the franchise, but in separate chambers from whites, with representatives in the ratio of whites: four, Coloureds: two, Asians: one. Africans do not have the vote; at least, not in South Africa. For as non-citizens of South Africa, their political rights are to be exercised in the 'independent states' – which, incidentally, are recognized by no one apart from themselves and South Africa.

With segregationist conditions of the magnitude described above, it seems reasonable to dub South Africa the 'non-contact society' as expressed in our title. Yet, considering the population's racial composition of 86 per cent black (Africans, Asians and Coloureds), 14 per cent white, Pettigrew (1971, p. 175) is undoubtedly correct in suggesting that there is more interracial contact in South Africa than in the USA. Rapid industrialization has also drawn groups together, and the workplace has become the greatest single site of contact. In addition, the *de facto* black population in many white, residential areas is considerable, with many 'unseen' domestic workers and their families existing in 'white' areas. Thus, a significant degree of contact, particularly centred on economic relationships, does occur. The South African social formation is indeed riven with contradictions.

A second method of schematizing contact in South Africa is to examine patterns of interaction across different social institutions and organizations. While an unwritten rule in South African organizational hierarchies is that no black should be placed in a position of authority over whites, exceptions *are* to be found, for example in the English-speaking churches, the burgeoning trade unions, in underground or outlawed political organizations and in broad fronts of resistance, such as the recently constituted United Democratic Front. To a lesser degree a sprinkling of such cases may also be found in English-speaking universities and a few business organizations. Admittedly, such occurrences form a minority of instances in terms of the general pattern, but these arrangements are generally harmonious and successful, and are pointers to an alternative future for South African group relations.

In the area of organized sport, a tiny degree of relatively equal-status relationships may be found, but at the same time sport is a major focus of resistance to white dominance. Many blacks refuse to participate when the few opportunities they have to do so arise, on the grounds of substantial inequalities in schooling, facilities and even nutrition, all of which affect the potential sportsman or -woman. The justifiable general slogan is 'no normal sport in an abnormal society' (see Archer and Bouillon, 1982).

Black–white relations in the police and the military are paradoxical, for in these institutions blacks are in effect employed to maintain white domination. However, the role of blacks is a distinctly subordinate one. In these regimented, formal hierarchies, it is the whites who give the orders. In the military it has long been a principle of white domination not to arm blacks, yet blacks have been used in the forces alongside whites since the earliest times. During the Second World War, 37 per cent, by 1943, of the total South African field forces were black, but strict segregation still remained, and Grundy (1983) argues that little positive change in racial attitudes was effected. Since the mid-1970s, blacks have slowly been recruited again as military volunteers; only whites are formally conscripted. Nevertheless, despite the purported common goal, segregation remains the dominant pattern. According to Grundy, 'rather than breaking down racial barriers the South African defence forces are attempting to use racial and ethnic differences to maintain the political and economic regime' (1983, p. 278).

The economic sphere, as already suggested, constitutes the major arena of black–white contact, but the standard form of relationships is anything but conducive to reducing prejudiced attitudes. Although there have been changes in the colour bar, and job reservation has either been relaxed or flouted on an increasing scale, the major form of interaction remains that of white dominance and black subordination. Most white South African homes have black domestic workers, and the work relationship of white 'madams' and black 'maids' (Cock, 1980) is more or less prototypical of the exploitative nature of work relations in general.

Interpersonal contact in South Africa is thus clearly dominated by the political and economic context that is entirely shot through with separatist principles. One of the primary contradictions of South Africa, therefore one of the dynamics of change, is the complete necessity for interdependence, juxtaposed with the ruling class's insistence upon the practice of segregation. As Savage (1975, p. 296) has pointed out, South Africans, particularly whites and blacks, are too often 'contiguous yet utterly remote'.

SOME RESEARCH ON CONTACT RELATIONS

A useful starting point is to examine the grand apartheid hypothesis on a national scale and scrutinize its assumption that the reduction of contact leads to improvement in race relations. Government apologists may argue that the hypothesis is as yet untestable, as the apartheid grand plan has not yet been fully implemented. Yet, segregation *has* been massively advanced on all levels and it is justifiable to ask whether 36 years of apartheid policy have had beneficial effects upon relations between racial groups.

The answer to such a question is overwhelmingly negative. Events of the Soweto uprising, which led to nation-wide unrest during 1976 and 1977, provide only one measure of the state of race and class relations in South Africa. Others include the increase in black industrial action and organization, the militarization of South Africa and the increased actions of the military wing of the African National Congress, the rise in incidents of urban guerrilla action, and widespread school and bus boycotts. Not even the most ardent apartheid protagonists would depict South Africa as characterized by tranquil or harmonious race relations. Surveys of black opinion have shown substantial discontent and continuing support for banned political organizations and for leaders who are openly opposed to apartheid (Hanf, Weiland and Vierdag, 1981; Lodge, 1983; Schlemmer, 1976).

In turning to the substantive contact literature in South Africa, we note that in addition to studies on black-white interaction, research has also been conducted on relationships between English- and Afrikaans-speaking whites and on contact within black categories: Indian, Coloured and African. While these are additional features of the South African situation, there is no doubt that black–white relations constitute the central problem. Hence our examination of research is directed to studies of black–white contact.

We have already seen that apartheid ensures little in the way of personal or social contact between whites and blacks. Yet we have also argued that a considerable degree of contact does occur, particularly at work. What is the nature of such work-related conduct? Gordon (1977) provides an interesting account of a Namibian mine compound: a classic description of the master–servant relationship. Differences are made salient not only by colour, but also by the typical status identifiers, 'boss' for white and 'boy' for black. Interaction is framed by rigid rules of conduct – mining etiquette – which require blacks to be anonymous (many are known only by their number), humble, deferential, circumspect and yet accepting of their lot. If a black calls a white 'mister', he is censured for 'acting white' and if he asks too many questions he is branded an 'agitator'. These 'bad boy' definitions place blacks in jeopardy of dismissal. No challenge to white authority is tolerated, however oblique; thus much of the behaviour of blacks is governed by 'staying out of trouble'.

On the part of whites, supervisory ideology precludes any close relationships with blacks on the grounds that it would 'spoil' blacks. Second, blacks should not be asked too many questions as this could make them aware of their dissatisfactions. Third, whites are subject to intense peer pressure against personal relationships with blacks; a white who is too friendly is labelled a 'kaffir boetie' (brother, or friend, of blacks) and faces both ostracism and ridicule. As a result, whites typify black workers as indolent, irresponsible, primitive, dirty, impulsive and completely lacking in honesty, drive or ambition (Gordon, 1977, p. 68). In turn, blacks view whites as 'dishonest, ambitious, untrustworthy, fearsome and above all capricious and unpredictable' (p. 90). However, both groups recognize their economic interdependence and develop styles to cope with the required interaction.

Hahlo (1969), in a study of a South African bus company, characterized the relationship between lower-status manual workers and white supervisors as paternalistic and jokey: this is an institutionalized way of dealing with potential conflict. However, as Gordon points out in describing the same phenomenon, 'Blacks laugh not because they want to or feel like it, but because they cannot return a counter-curse, neither may they keep quiet' (1977, p. 121). When the black worker has a relatively high post, both Gordon and Hahlo recognize a second, 'sponsor–client' form of relation. Based on instrumental exchanges, this allows for a limited form of privileged friendship with mutual responsibilities. Since the sponsor–client interaction transcends typical boundaries it is highly vulnerable and risky. Blacks in this type of relationship are sometimes beaten up by fellow workers, and whites once discovered are rejected by their groups. Furthermore, Hahlo reports that these relationships are temporary and exist only at work.

From the above it is clear that work contacts are situated at the intergroup rather than interpersonal end of Tajfel's (1978b) continuum. Mutual knowledge of each other is minimal. Neither is this situation likely to be altered, since one of the key elements of black survival in a white industrial world lies in keeping whites as ignorant as possible about blacks (Alverson, 1970).

What happens in other forms of black–white contact? Recalling the apartheid hypothesis that contact will lead to conflict, one may ask whether research reveals this to be the case. Two studies (Russell, 1961; Watson, 1970) produced data to the contrary. Watson studied a white school in Cape Town in which about 40 per cent of pupils were 'passing for white'. Although difficulties were presented for the pass-whites in attempting social mobility in a society that, in effect, has a caste system, relationships were generally harmonious. Russell's excellent study of an interracial neighbourhood in Durban, prior to the effects of the Group Areas Act, similarly reports friendly and amicable relationships, and certainly no conflict.

Russell's main results showed the following. (a) Residential proximity was associated with increased contact between whites, Indians and Coloureds. (b) Contact in turn was also associated with a greater degree of friendly relationships; there were widespread beliefs in the neighbourhood that friendliness was both essential and desirable. (c) Answers to the question of whether contact would lead to the reduction of prejudice were rather more complex. No formal attitudinal scales were administered, but thorough interviews revealed certain patterns. Whites were far more favourable towards local blacks than blacks in general. Discrepancies were also found between behaviour towards blacks (positive) and stated attitudes that were less positive. These results together indicate that whites conform to reference-group norms that preclude positive expressions about blacks. Nevertheless, in comparison with general South African standards, both the attitudes and actions of these whites were considerably more positive. (In relation to these results see also the work of Pettigrew (1958) and Orpen (1975) who show that conformity to racist social norms provides a better explanation of race prejudice in South Africa than does the 'individualistic' theory of the authoritarian personality.)

Attitudes of Indians and Coloureds on the other hand were tolerant of and favourable towards whites, while their behaviour was more wary, watchful and tentative – a defence against rebuff. Patterns of visiting and borrowing support this picture. Whites visited and borrowed far more than did Indians and Coloureds. Whites were the recipients and Indians, in particular, the helpers, givers and lenders; again a mirror of the dominant social structure. Because of the pervasive nature of apartheid structure, it is doubtful whether interracial neighbourhood relations could ever fully be considered as equal-status contacts. Nevertheless, the results of Russell's study are surprisingly positive.

The pattern of black–white *attitudes* presents a less optimistic horizon for future peaceful coexistence. Investigations by MacCrone, Lever, Pettigrew, van den Berghe and others provide a consistent picture of prejudice and ethnocentrism on the part of whites, with Afrikaners more conservative, authoritarian and socially distanced than English speakers. Schlemmer (1976) found considerable differences in the attitudes of English speakers and Afrikaners towards certain racial issues. For example 53 per cent of English speakers, but only 18 per cent of Afrikaans speakers, agreed with allowing blacks into white residential areas. Regarding schooling, 69 per cent of the English speakers would permit blacks into white schools compared with only 19 per cent of Afrikaners. However, whites in general still show strong beliefs in black inferiority. In his nation-wide representative sample, Schlemmer found that 88 per cent of all whites endorsed the statement 'it will be many years before the Bantu reach the same level of civilization as whites', while only 18 per cent agreed that 'inherently the whites and the Bantu are equals.'

Conversely, less well-researched black attitudes, while also dominantly ethnocentric, show surprisingly positive attitudes towards English-speaking whites, but not towards Afrikaners (Lever, 1978; Mayer, 1975). In general, blacks appear to be less racist than whites and despite the lengthy period of exploitation and humiliation at the hands of whites, there appears to be still a remarkable degree of potential goodwill. Groenwald and de Kock (1979) in a sample of 500 Coloured men in the Western Cape, found that only 2.6 per cent desired no contact with whites, while 94 per cent claimed to have a white person whom they viewed as a friend. It should also be recalled that liberation organizations in South Africa have always proposed non-racial policies and the acceptance of whites in a future society, even if some of these organizations have adopted black separatist strategies *en route* to the goal (Biko, 1978).

Finally, a few recent quasi-experimental studies have examined the contact hypothesis for changes in prejudice among whites. In the most extensive of these, Mynhart (1982) tested 972 English-speaking white schoolgirls, from ten different Roman Catholic private schools, on several attitudinal measures. Some girls had institutional contact with other racial groups; some did not. Although contact conditions were favourable – it had strong institutional support and voluntary attendance, while the participants had equal status, similar socio-economic backgrounds and experience of at least a year of contact – girls in the contact group were found to be significantly more prejudiced towards Africans, Indians and Afrikaners that non-contact girls. Regarding attitudes towards Coloured people, contact and non-contact groups were similar. In short, contact appeared to have either deleterious or neutral effects on whites' attitudes towards blacks.

Apparently more positive outcomes were achieved by two other studies. Luiz and Krige (1981) conducted an extensive programme of contact involving equal-status Coloured and white schoolgirls (some of whom were from convent schools) engaged in co-operative tasks and were successful in changing whites' attitudes in a positive direction. Spangenberg and Nel (1983) compared the attitude scores of 95 white academics who had taught for a while at a Coloured university with those of a comparable group of 100 whites at an Afrikaans university. (The choice by whites to teach at a black university does not necessarily indicate *a priori* positive attitudes towards blacks.) On the overall social distance measure the contact group were found to be more positive. However, it is noteworthy that when Afrikaners in the sample were separated from English-speaking subjects, contact and non-contact groups differed on only one of the seven social distance subscales – the admission of Coloureds to the home as friends. On the other six subscales, contact and non-contact subjects did not differ significantly. This indicates that racial attitudes did not vary much between two groups of Afrikaner academics, despite favourable conditions of contact. English speakers were again found to be significantly less prejudiced.

While overall results of the last two studies tend to point in a positive direction, caution should be exercised in interpreting results. Viewed sociologically the groups in these two studies are vastly unrepresentative of South African people as a whole. Second, the research settings (universities and private schools) tend to be supportive of positive race attitudes and are unrepresentative of general situations. It should be remembered that in similar favourable settings Mynhart, with a far larger sample, found negative contact outcomes. Third, the fact that under such optimal conditions Afrikaner academics hardly differed from their non-contact colleagues and still retained reasonably strong prejudices, would seem to be grounds for pessimism, not optimism.

CONTACT AND SOUTH AFRICAN GROUP RELATIONS

As preceding pages have shown, existing contact between black and white South Africans generally takes the form of domination, with substantially unequal status and an absence of co-operative or common goals, which allows little opportunity for intimate or personalized relations. Furthermore, the state authorities actively perpetuate category distinctions and intervene in efforts to promote collectively organized alternatives. In terms of Tajfel's (1978b) distinction, contact across political categories in general is characterized by intergroup rather than interpersonal forms of interaction. Despite some variation in degree and kind of contact, social rather than personal identities determine most cross-category relations. In the wake of a lengthy history of institutionalized racism, it is not surprising that even the most progressive exceptions to the general pattern (cited earlier) fail to escape entirely the negative effects of the rigidly categorized and unequal social structure. Having reviewed some evidence from contact studies, an assessment of the traditional contact hypothesis as a strategy for change in South African intergroup relations may now be attempted. Before tackling this question directly however a brief theoretical examination of the contact hypothesis will be required.

There are at least three discernible standpoints regarding the explanation of change, or identification of processes responsible for change, via contact situations. Although there is some overlap between these standpoints, focus is directed here to differences in explanatory emphasis.

1 The first position represented by Cook (1978) and the Allport–Pettigrew theory (see McClendon, 1974) locates primary explanation for change (prejudice reduction) in processes of interpersonal attraction through the medium of belief and value congruence. Status equality, common goals, co-operative interdependence and normative support together constitute optimal conditions and provide opportunities for 'developing and discovering similarities of interests and values' (Pettigrew, 1971, p. 276). While Pettigrew is clearly aware of the complexity of changing racial attitudes and stresses a whole range of other requisite factors – institutional protection for minorities, changing institutional practices, legal changes and changing actions before attitudes – the primary explanatory emphasis lies at the interpersonal level. Other factors are viewed as necessary for setting optimal conditions for change in terms of belief congruence.

2 Sherif's (1966) functional stance lays emphasis upon task inter-dependence (not simply co-operation) aimed at superordinate goals not attainable by one group on its own. Successful attainment of goals may be an additional requirement for change in group relations to occur (McClendon, 1974). The psychological mechanism may involve a shift in group members' attention: from viewing each other, or the outgroup, as salient objects, to viewing the task as the salient object, thus facilitating a reduction in the salience of group identity markers.

3 In partial agreement with Sherif, the Tajfellian or 'social identity theory' position (Brown and Turner, 1981) claims to go further in emphasizing a distinction between interpersonal and inter-group beha-viours, and then argues that the latter cannot be explained adequately by the former. Task interdependence and goal attainment may contribute towards the alteration of social identities, but are not of themselves sufficient to do so. For example two groups may successfully attain a superordinate goal, but not alter their separate identities as groups. Such an outcome would still facilitate ingroup bias and favouritism. (For supportive evidence see Deschamps and Brown, 1983.) According to social identity theory, neither the first not the second standpoints provide

sufficient conditions in themselves for the reduction of *intergroup* hostility and concomitant negative attitudes.

An additional theoretical distinction, with respect to status equality, is pertinent to the South African situation. Following other researchers, McClendon (1974) and Riordan (1978) draw a distinction between status equality *within* the contact situation and status *outside* the situation. The first apparently refers to role relations within the contact situation and equal contribution to the task at hand, whereas the second refers to a social-structural sense of status. Theorists are not entirely in agreement regarding which conditions are necessary for prejudice reduction. Pettigrew et al. (1973) argue that the contact hypothesis places special emphasis on status equality within the contact encounter. McClendon (1974) claims that both are necessary. Riordan (1978) regards the concept of status equality as problematic and doubts whether within-situation equality conditions are ever satisfactorily met. In his view, status equality should be treated as a dependent rather than an independent variable.

This distinction is particularly germane to South Africa where socially structured status and power differentials assume such significant proportions. As Pettigrew has noted with reference to South Africa (1958, p. 40): 'In areas with historically embedded traditions of racial intolerance . . . sociological factors are unusually crucial and account for the heightened racial hostility.' Our position in this regard is that extra-contact, or social-structural, status permeates most contact settings in South Africa to such an extent that within-situation status equality is a most difficult condition to satisfy. Put in another way, black–white, face-to-face encounters in general are likely to involve intergroup rather than interpersonal behaviours, hence extra-contact status differentials are likely to remain highly salient, irrespective of within-situation conditions. Findings from the review of South African contact research lend support to this contention. Interpersonal contact even under relatively favourable conditions was generally insufficient to overcome socially structured identities. The dominant form of social relations penetrated the micro-contact setting, leaving modes of interpersonal conduct, social identities of participants and attitudinal structures only marginally altered.

A recent field study by Gillian Finchilescu illustrates some of the processes from the general perspective of social identity theory. One hundred and thirteen trainee nurses from four private hospitals in Natal took part in the study. Two of the hospitals conducted integrated nurse training programmes (contact condition, N = 56) and two did not (one black-only and one white-only hospital; non-contact condition, N = 57). This context was selected as nursing activity requires very real forms of co-operative contact and allows for both frequency and intimacy of contact. Within-situation status was similar in terms of qualification, job position and duties. Social-structural status identity, that is, the political category of subjects, constituted one of the independent variables. Dependent measures included ratings of the advantages of integrated training, salience of race in 'determining how nurses are treated in the hospital' and evaluations of hypothetical target nurses of different race groups (ratings of both in- and outgroups were required of each subject) in terms of 'personality' and 'work ability'.

It should be recalled that for Tajfel's theory, social identity and intergroup behaviour are products of large-scale relations between groups and are determined by two major factors – relative social status and perceived legitimacy/mutability/security of social category boundaries. In applying this theory to black–white contact in South Africa, one may expect some of the following outcomes. (a) Given the large status/power differences between blacks and whites and their perceptible differences regarding the legitimacy of the social order, contact is likely to have differential effects for high- and low-status groups. It is noteworthy in this respect that many traditional contact studies have been little concerned with outcomes for lower-status minority groups. (b) Contact may, in addition, increase rather than decrease the salience of race categorization, particularly for lower-status groups, because of processes of either defensiveness or positive assertiveness. The crux of the hypothesis is that the overwhelming psychological importance of race categorization in South Africa may override other positive factors operating in favourable contact conditions.

Results from Finchilescu's study showed the following. First, contact seemed to provide some positive outcomes, since support for integrated training was significantly greater in the contact condition, while contact subjects also reported a more positive ratio (advantages : disadvantages) in favour of integrated training. This suggests that contact was associated with attitudes conducive to favourable future interaction in the hospital setting. In a further positive outcome, white contact subjects rated both their own group and blacks more positively on personal attributes than did non-contact whites. Ingroup bias was thus reduced for whites.

Second, for lower-status (black) subjects however contact appeared to increase awareness of social identity. For whites, the 'salience of race' index was similarly low in both contact conditions. This would be expected from Tajfel's theory for those in a high-status and relatively secure intergroup position. On the other hand, black subjects in the contact condition rated race as more salient than did non-contact subjects. Within the contact condition, race salience was notably higher for African than for Indian subjects, reflecting the hierarchy of status operative among blacks in South Africa.

Furthermore, a difference was found between high- and low-status groups within the contact situation on the evaluative measures. High-status subjects rated both in- and outgroups similarly high on 'personality' and 'work ability' attributes, whereas low-status subjects displayed a marked ethnocentrism, rating whites significantly lower on both attributes than themselves.

Looking at results overall, the following conclusions may be suggested. First, contact under relatively favourable conditions for South Africa appeared to have some positive effects, particularly in improving attitudes to future integration, although caution should be expressed about generalizing this finding beyond the hospital situation. Second, beneficial effects were limited largely to white subjects; nevertheless, the relative lack of ingroup bias on the part of whites may be viewed as encouraging. Third, contact apparently has differential social status effects, increasing the salience of race categorization and failing to reduce ingroup favouritism among the lower-status black groups. In so far as boundary maintenance and category salience are key processes in defining behavioural interaction as intergroup rather than interpersonal, it is argued that the contact situation studied here has not been entirely successful in improving group relations. Finally, we would claim that results, while providing some support for the traditional contact hypothesis, provide even stronger support for the social identity theory position. The study is not without weaknesses and problems, but despite limitations there seems to be enough support for social identity theory to cast doubt upon the sufficiency of interpersonal contact to alter entrenched intergroup attitudes and behaviour in any substantial manner 'since the two domains are controlled by different psychological processes' (Brown and Turner, 1981, p. 60).

CONCLUSION

If the previous statement has merit, it requires us to suggest the processes by which intergroup relations may be improved. It should be made plain that our argument is *not* that black–white contact may not contribute to positive effects. On the contrary, there is no doubt that lack of contact has been used as a central strategy to maintain white dominance. Furthermore, a fully integrated society is unquestionably a cherished goal. The argument is rather that given the history and present nature of the South African problem, contact *per se* is not sufficient. In this regard we disagree with both Lever (1971) and Heaven (1983) who propose that contact is a central ingredient of change in South Africa. To be precise, disagreement is with the traditional version of the contact hypothesis used by these writers.

The dynamic of change for social identity theory centres around processes of social categorization and resultant ingroup-outgroup boundary distinctions. Genuine social change will require action directed towards the reduction of the processes of categorization and distinction themselves. Certainly intergroup contact may contribute to this intervention, but it must be contact of a certain sort. We mentioned earlier that there *are* a few notable exceptions to the dominant pattern of black-white relations in South Africa. Most important of these are the liberation movements and activist groups who oppose apartheid. A central strategy among these movements involves the direct counteraction of received group identities. Interpersonal behaviour in such contexts would not ignore the contemporary intergroup nature of interaction, but rather is likely to deal directly with it, consciously developing strategies to transcend and transform given social identities. In short, we suggest that black-white contact among such groups is typified by efforts to redefine socially structured identities. Current theories will probably need to be extended if they are to account adequately for such processes.

In attempting to restructure the received definitions of social categories, the typical picture of South African society alters slightly, but in important ways. Major intergroup conflict is thus perceived as being between those (blacks and few whites) who resist and struggle, and those (whites and few blacks, for it must be recalled that 'homeland' rulers are collaborators with apartheid) who wish to maintain the status quo. While of course recognizing that the struggle is largely a black-white one, it is important to realize that it is not *only* black against white, but also the worker against the capitalist and the democrat against the authoritarian. Social action that undoubtedly will transform the racist state is already under way. The task of change will involve collective action directed towards many areas – material and ideological. To re-establish human contact in the non-contact society will require collective black-white strategies directed centrally at the very processes of social categorization that constitute the destructive lack of contact.

ACKNOWLEDGEMENTS

Thanks are due to Professor Michael Savage of the University of Cape Town and to the editors of this book for helpful comments on an earlier draft. Gillian

Finchilescu wishes to thank the Human Sciences Research Council for financial assistance received from the Main Committee of the HSRC Investigation into Intergroup Relations. Views expressed here are those of the authors and should not be regarded as those of the Human Sciences Research Council.

NOTES

1   There is no adequate scientific basis for a theory of race classification and thus no method for testing 'racial' differences (see Montagu, 1964 and 1972). The very use of the term 'racial' in this paper is problematic, particularly as No Sizwe (1979) has shown that in South Africa group classification actually relies on a range of criteria such as ethnicity, language, religion or 'race', which in turn are variably applied to different groups. The term 'race' therefore is retained warily here only as referring to one type of reality construction in political and subjective terms.

2   During the 1985 parliamentary session, the first of the tri-cameral parliament, the government scrapped the Mixed Marriage Act as well as section 16 of the Immorality Act. The latter, forbidding sex across the colour line, was responsible for prosecutions of over 10,000 people in its 35-year history. The government has also proposed the repeal of legislation forbidding multi-racial membership of political parties.

8 Contact and Conflict in Industry

P. T. Allen

To many observers conflict often seems the central theme of industry, and industrial conflict the prime symptom of inequality in the capitalist system. Most observers, not just those who look to wide social and historical change in the Marxist tradition, see that this system, which must bring people together to function, in doing so generates inequalities and tensions that disrupt it temporarily in an expensive and wasteful manner, even if so far they have not actually split it apart.

Some would say simply that the basic conflict of interests within capitalism generates these problems and that they can only end when capitalism itself evolves into something entirely different, or is overthrown. None the less, whatever the long-term future of the capitalist system, the visible variation in relations in the economies of the Western world is, and has been historically, a problem for both explanation and practice alike.

Factors have been identified which exert systematic effects on the level of industrial dispute, and quite frequently, in the explanations for the variation in industrial relations that have been put forward, the structural features or organizational processes that sociologists and economists have identified have been combined with psychological factors. Variations in the quality of *contact* implicitly or explicitly underlie several such explanations.

This perspective has changed a little in recent years, with a gradual enunciation of the probable dimensions of psychological response in the arena of employment relations. Social psychology is making a contribution to research in this area, but, perhaps surprisingly, the field remains relatively obscure (for a review see Stephenson and Brotherton, 1979). Whatever the starting-point of an analysis of industrial relations, progress is only likely to be made if the fundamentally *social* character of these relations is recognized. A social-psychological intergroup perspective can illuminate the situation – and in the present case can point to the more useful of the questions to be asked.

It is the aim of this chapter therefore to bring the social-psychological perspective on contact to bear on the arena of industrial conflict, by reviewing the literature on this form of conflict in so far as this relates to the 'contact hypothesis'. Such an approach, of course, takes place in the context of an academic tradition that has not so far been directly related to the area of industrial behaviour. The contact hypothesis has its origins in the study of rather less structured situations involving the occurrence of discrimination and prejudice, for example in respect of ethnic relations. In its basic form the hypothesis argues that increased contact between actually or potentially disputing parties is a 'good thing' that leads to better understanding and hence to reduced conflict. However, this simple formulation is not typical of social-psychological treatments.

More detailed discussion of the tradition will be found elsewhere in this book, but for the purposes of the present chapter the main features of social-psychological treatments should be noted. Pettigrew (1971) for example recognized that contact could have contrary effects; that it enhanced existing processes and depended on the situation. The basic issue therefore concerns 'the types of situations in which contact leads to distrust and those in which it leads to trust'. In his formulation Pettigrew echoes the earlier work of Cook (1962) and, explicitly by reference, Allport (1954). Allport gave four main characteristics of the 'contact situation' leading to positive change: (a) equality of status; (b) shared goals; (c) co-operative interdependence; (d) socially authorized inter-action. However, it can be added that attitude change, if it does occur, may well be of intensity rather than direction (Amir, 1969).

The major part of this chapter comprises an examination of the adequacy of those approaches to industrial conflict that include aspects of the contact hypothesis. However, this examination will be prefaced by a brief discussion of contact and conflict, as these terms apply to the field of employment relations. It will be followed by the presentation of some novel evidence that shows how a social-psychological characterization of the complete, intergroup situation can uncover some of the processes at work. Finally, some conclusions will be drawn relating to the general value of contact theory in the study of employment relations.

CHARACTERIZING THE CONCEPTS

Conflict

Almost any activity in industry can be considered an expression of the basic conflict between employee and employer. Most summaries of activity refer to workers' behaviour and there are a number of classifications of forms of action (Knowles, 1952; Kerr, 1964). Lupton's (1983) classic text for prospective managers for example discusses structural (bureaucratic) conflict, conflict over scarces resources (money; power) and protests over conditions (job and work satisfaction). However, as the author notes, actual conflict is just as likely to be a combination of all three forms and in particular cases these assumptions may not hold. For example absenteeism may be the result of individual frustration or the expression of a generally disgruntled work-force that changes its usual, normative regulation of absence rates or it may even be the result of well-organized unofficial holidays, which do not disrupt working arrangements (Allen, 1982). Surprisingly, there have been no attempts to form composite indices of conflict based on a range of possible actions – possibly because much of the analysis of industrial conflict has relied on official statistics rather than on surveys. Those surveys that have covered a reasonable sample have in fact shown considerable discrepancies between published, government strike statistics and their own results (e.g. Brown, 1981) and have shown that threats of striking or other sanctions add considerably to the overall level of conflict (Parker, 1974).

The main features of industrial conflict, as treated in the industrial relations literature, may be briefly summarized. There is, overall, something of an emphasis on strikes and much work has therefore been done in identifying factors that relate to strike rates. Given the reliance on official sources, such factors tend to be those that are themselves officially recorded, for example size (employment level), or can be inferred directly, for example technology, or indirectly, for example bureaucracy. Explanations for the various identified effects are most often couched in 'economically rational' terms and employ indices of unionization, market shares and so on. Here our concern will be only with those accounts that are based on, or refer to, psychological elements.

Contact

Employment relations are relatively well defined and take place in a well-defined context. Within this context, relations across power and status dimensions are necessarily constrained by the nature of the enterprise. However, although the contrived nature of these relations is limited to the context of the firm, typical roles in industry contribute to social standing outside the firm; the principal criterion of socio-economic class being occupational status. Explaining variation in relations across organizations need not evoke this social or cultural aspect, since it can be assumed to be relatively constant. However, claims that the situation is otherwise will be discussed below.

Two dimensions can effectively characterize most approaches to industrial behaviour in terms of the relationship between contact and conflict. Recognizing the contrived, bureaucratic nature of employment relations is best achieved in terms of a formal-informal dichotomy and, as a parallel to that, recognizing the essentially unequal but systematic distribution of power and skills is best done by reference to an individual-group categorization.

The latter distinction is complicated by the nature of the group. Whereas 'management' is perhaps more easily seen as an homogenous category, workers may confront that management or, indeed, one another as members of work-groups, occupational groups, unions or a class (Walker, 1979). Conflict, when it occurs, may derive from perceptions and events that have their origin in any such category, for example disputes over the payment of rates agreed for a whole trade.

Further distinctions can usefully be made in reference to contact; not only does the nature of a group vary, but individuals may act within a group or as agents of it in an intergroup context. The other questions concerning contact that are relevant to this discussion are: the extent to which there is a need for contact and the examination of those factors that affect opportunities for contact. The former question is a main feature of those theories that rely on postulated psychological needs underlying problems at work, whereas the latter, often in conjunction with the first, appears in accounts of behaviour that follow the (psychological) consequences of bureaucracy and/or technology on work patterns.

EXPLANATIONS OF BEHAVIOUR IN INDUSTRY

Behaviour in industry has attracted the attention of several academic disciplines, and spawned its own in the shape of industrial relations. A central concern for many approaches has been industrial conflict; its structural antecedants, its history and its links with organized labour and social unrest. Psychology has a long and extensive tradition of research in industry, but, heavily biased towards an individual orientation, its main concerns have been with selection, work and job satisfaction and motivation. Social psychologists however, being more concerned with collective actions, have begun to interest themselves in disputes and especially in negotiation and bargaining processes (Morley and

Stephenson, 1977; Warr, 1973). Industrial conflict nevertheless remains a strangely under-researched area for social psychology (Bain and Clegg, 1974), and there is considerable irony in this, since it is psychological, and especially social-psychological, 'explanations' that frequently appear in the sociological, economic and industrial relations literature concerning industrial conflict. So much is this the case in fact that some disgruntled sociologists have urged a return to genuinely sociological accounts (Curran and Stanworth, 1979).

However, what mainly characterizes such 'explanations' is that they are merely assertions and, more often than not, have built-in assumptions of psychological needs. It can be seen that there are two main types of approach bearing on the issue of contact and conflict in industry. The first of these looks to the deprivation of interpersonal activity as a source of dissatisfaction in work and hence to non-co-operation and dispute. The second covers the social and physical isolation of work-forces and the effect of differential exposure to managerial ideology. Very broadly, it can be said that the kinds of effects are seen as associated with the affective or informational consequences of contact, although naturally these need not be separated in practice.

Intragroup contact

The first important form of contact to be considered is the relatively informal contact between workers at their place of work. The distinction 'at work' is made since, below, the implications of wider networks will be brought into the discussion. Clearly, many factors can affect the possibilities for this intragroup contact, the most notable being the size of the workplace and the nature of technology. However, it is the consequences of interpersonal contact among peers that form a plank in most accounts of conflict driven by dissatisfaction. There is a long academic tradition, dating from the period when managers were first being urged to take serious note of employees' feelings and attitudes (e.g. Drucker, 1955), to account for trouble in terms of notions like morale or (global) satisfaction. Although the main point of arguing for a 'human relations' approach was the improvement of *production*, writers at the time had noticed the increase of poor relations associated with larger size of organization for example and had attributed this to the increasing formality of relations with management (e.g. Revans, 1956). None the less, it is interpersonal interaction that is thought to be the basis of good morale (Talacchi, 1960) and, more precisely, communication with and attraction to other members of the organization (Indik, 1965).

Underlying the thinking attached to these findings is the idea that people have expressive needs, which can be met by interpersonal contact at work or frustrated by organizations that constrain it. Notwithstanding the relative failure of need-satisfaction theories dependent on universal motivations such as Herzberg's (1966; for summary of evidence see Jabes, 1978), there remains the problem of variation, for example with size, which seems to indicate some affective changes linked to structural factors. Despite the apparent need for an organization-based explanation of such variation, one of the most influential sorts of approach made by sociologists locates the source of much of this variation outside the organization. The forms of contact available in organizations are seen as a consequence of the social setting and/or are chosen by employees as a result of socialization processes external to the organization.

Both organizational and social factors appear in the explanation of the 'size effect' offered by Ingham (1967). Noting the increase in industrial disputes with larger-scale organizations, Ingham identified bureaucracy as the element most associated with change linked to size and pointed to its effects on the formality of relations. However, Ingham also argues for the importance of extra-organizational factors; workers' 'orientations' to work, structured by expectations and experience. Differential contact is a feature of this approach in two respects: workers seek different amounts of contact and are exposed to contact with different groups.

Ingham offers what is essentially a cognitive account of workers' behaviour – based on their orientations or definitions of the situation; but although the meaning of their occupational situation might differ for people in the ways he suggests, the situations themselves differ in ways other than the simple orientations approach recognizes. Workers postulated to have a 'positive expressive' orientation seek expressive rewards by greater friendly contact at work and are supposed to concentrate in smaller firms. In such firms however there is likely to be greater contact with the *employer*. Those who are seen as having 'negative expressive' orientations collect in larger firms and are said to define the occupational situation as one of conflict. However, although such workers are less likely to have contact with the employer, they are more likely in many circumstances to enjoy considerable contact with peers. Therefore, in firms composed of large numbers of such like-minded people, it is likely that strong solidarity would evolve. Thus, on the one hand the approach ignores the positive benefits of work-group membership in even the largest firms, while on the other it accepts the stereotype of the friendly family firm.

Psychologists would seem to have had considerably more success in accounting for these sorts of process (see Kiesler, 1978), but, despite its weaknesses, Ingham's sociological approach does something that is rare in psychology – it attempts to locate actions in specific instances to a wider social framework, through the worker's previous experience and the community setting of the organization, to the organization of industry and the historical development of capitalism. It fails for several reasons, not least because the 'independent' source of orientations is, partly, previous work experience, and this surely begs the question to a degree. What remains is the general social background of employees in typical forms of industry.

Explanations of conflict that rely on notions of informal contact at work must carefully stipulate the probable meaning of that contact. In fact, part of Ingham's account can be reinterpreted as a restatement of the simplest contact-conflict hypothesis – that informal contact with the 'enemy' reduces the tension, so industrial relations in small firms are 'better'. On the other hand, the account ignores the probability that it is contact between equals that may foster solidarity in a context of formal intergroup communication, thus making industrial relations in larger firms tougher. This confusion over the roles of intra- versus intergroup contact reflects the complexity of the actual situation, but there is some experimental evidence that ingroup characteristics can affect outgroup discrimination (Allen and Wilder, 1975). We may ask however what role *control* plays in these two situations. Employers and managers must exert control. Can it be therefore that in small firms control is effective in suppressing trouble just because it is direct and ever-present, while the remote control of larger firms opens the way for employees to organize effectively and gain some power for themselves? An example may help answer this question.

When the quantity or quality of intragroup contact reaches certain levels, especially when intergroup contact is minimized, a work-group can provide considerable expressive rewards. If working arrangements permit it, such work-groups can also obtain semi-autonomous status. Although the latter situation might be seen as a further enhancement of affective rewards, reflecting the lack of direct supervision, it is also a source of instrumental benefit. As the famous Hawthorne findings showed, under these conditions workers begin to control their output for their own purposes (Roy, 1952, 1954).

In the author's (Allen, 1981) study of dockworkers it became clear that the isolated work-groups were a source of strong instrumental reward, rather than merely the providers of a positive affective climate. These workers were very isolated from management and, indeed, from close supervision; their working arrangements gave them considerable auto- nomy in working patterns. This situation had led to a number of rule- bending operations designed to enhance the 'effort bargain' in their favour. For example an organized 'absence culture' operated, producing statistically regular fluctuations in absenteeism, which, following the literature, might well be interpreted as evidence of a dissatisfied work-force but which, in this case, was primarily and more positively a source of satisfaction to the employees.

Both official 'sides' disapproved of this and similar activities – the shop stewards and other union officers disliked such practices because they undermined their own authority when pressing for better conditions. There was pressure from various commercial interests for a more concentrated work-force, giving direct control to the employer and greatly increasing management–worker contact. Managers in the techno-logically advanced firms certainly believed that direct employment of their own small work-forces, rather than the hiring of labour from the relatively remote Docks Authority, would create a more committed worker, who would perceive the superordinate goal of company profit. Such moves were opposed by most employees of course, precisely because their greatest source of satisfaction was the very low level of supervision and managerial contact. The functional reality of the work-wage bargain was not perceived in the same way by managers and workers. Seeing things from the other side's point of view, though possible, would have implied a real and immediate loss for the employees.

As these last statements indicate, the industrial setting hinges on value judgements. It could be argued for example that the workers' long-term interest would lie in co-operating with management so that, as profits increase, a better paid work-force would be possible. Such at least might be seen as a likely view of that management. In fact, it merely illustrates the ideology inherent in the situation. Recognition that an objective definition of the situation must include a treatment of the ideological element recalls the second sort of approach mentioned above: that concerned with the origin and maintenance of particular beliefs in the intergroup situation and their relation to contact both in and out of work. One aspect of Ingham's account of variation associated with size had to do with factors external to the organization and not, in turn, individual factors so much as social processes. This is actually part of a long tradition of direct attempts to explain action in industry by reference to social and social-psychological factors; a strong element of which is the presence or lack of outgroup contact.

Intergroup contact and isolation

Probably the classic example of this approach, which helped form the basis of an academic tradition especially prominent in the late 1960s, is the work of Kerr and Siegel (1954). What these authors attempted to do was conduct an international comparison of the propensity to strike across several sorts of industry. Their ranking of strike-days-lost, compared with the employment level of each industry, revealed that certain industries appeared to have higher rates of striking than others. Industries such as mining and dockwork showed the highest levels of activity, while others, such as agriculture, showed the lowest rates across a set of data from 11 countries.

The explanation that Kerr and Siegel advanced from their findings centred on their notion of the 'isolated mass' and on the psychological characteristics of the work-force typically employed in such industries. The direct psychological aspect of their explanation constituted a minor part of the explanation and warrants little attention. The picture they propose of physically hard jobs attracting tough, *macho* workers, who are more ready to strike, is perhaps best seen as the kind of popular stereotype that can find its way into even the most serious examination of society. The main part of their explanation however traced the supposed social-psychological consequences of the physical conditions and isolation typical of the highly strike-prone industries they had identified. The work-force, exposed to similar conditions and lacking contact with the rest of society, forms a 'largely homogeneous, undifferentiated mass'. The result of the lack of contact between this mass and its employers is the increased likelihood that grievance will not be mediated and hence will result more often in strikes.

Although in some respects this may seem a clumsy and simplistic explanation, it has become a classic in the industrial relations literature, largely because it constitutes an attempt to locate the origin of differential industrial behaviour in social factors that have their origin in the wider social context of employment. For Kerr and Siegel physical isolation provides the most obvious and important factor, but, in line with their imprecise approach, the authors also include a variant of 'social isolation' in reference to dockworkers. In the same year an unrelated study (University of Liverpool, 1954) suggested that the low social status of dockers, that is the attitudes of society at large, produced social isolation and the solidarity of the work-force that facilitated the mass walk-outs so typical of relations in that industry. In other words, both this study and the Kerr and Siegel approach deploy social psychology, particularly versions that deal with the group, to explain workers' behaviour, but significantly it is the nature of intergroup relations between workers, or workers and society, that takes pride of place in these accounts. Even the term strike-proneness focuses attention on the *employees'* actions and thus enhances the tendency to neglect the dynamic nature of the relations between workers and *employers*. The implicit ideological assumption is clear – it is as if management, as a group, never changes and is everywhere the same. In fact cogent criticism of the whole Kerr and Siegel research has been produced (Edwards, 1977), questioning both the methodology and the results, but also, more importantly, pointing out that the explanation has never really been tested as a set of hypotheses, despite having been widely accepted in the literature – almost as established fact.

The same sort of assumption surfaces in later accounts. One clear aspect of the Kerr and Siegel example is that social factors involving differential contact can affect individual behaviour. As noted above, the constrained nature of employment relations implies that explanations need not evoke variation in the wider social context, but in several versions this is the approach adopted. Lockwood's (1966) categorization of manual workers' self-perceived class position, and their related orientations to work, draws on both the sources just discussed to provide the characteristics of its 'proletarian' (strike-prone) types, who are relatively isolated *as a group* and opposes this to 'deferential' types (much less strike-prone) who may be isolated as *individuals* but have 'direct association' with their employer. Parkin (1971), in his influential essay on political order, takes up Lockwood's classification and adds that the face-to-face contact between deferentials and employers reinforces the symbols of class and status consequently accepted by those employees. Thus the contact hypothesis appears in the following form: the isolated work-force engages in more conflict than the individual who, though isolated from similar-status colleagues, has greater contact with the employer and enjoys relations that are typically less formal. In the latter case, fuller ideological acceptance of the managerial role is implied.

In fact both suggested types of worker tend to disappear under empirical scrutiny (Bulmer, 1975; Allen, 1984) and, in any event, fail in application in two main ways. First, such vague classifications – largely hypothetical and defined by a huge set of social influences – fail to account for much of the visible variation in industrial action. Second, and perhaps of more importance, most such classifications or typologies of *workers* ignore the fact that industrial control is largely vested with owners or managers who may also vary in their typical approaches, but who, crucially, enter into an intergroup relationship with their work-force that is dynamic and essentially competitive.

The pre-defined and constrained nature of this relationship will clearly dominate the patterns of activity that result – but the nature of this relationship is unlikely to vary sufficiently to account for the wider variation in activity that is observed. It is from the economic, historical, technical and structural factors that most explanations must be expected to come, but, recognizing the intergroup nature of the relationship, social-psychological processes may also be expected to play a part. The latter are evoked in the examples described above, though in a less than systematic way.

THE SOCIAL PSYCHOLOGY OF EMPLOYMENT RELATIONS

Many such social-psychological processes may be at work in the industrial context. For example Brown (1978) illuminates relations between work groups in one factory in dispute over payment differentials by reference to social-comparison processes. However, as Brown notes, the 'fundamental dichotomy' is between workers and employers. Even where other disputes may arise, this fundamental conflict will underlie the choices taken about action, which in most cases will have implications for group positions *vis à vis* this conflict. Thus, the central question must be: what effects might contact exert on this intergroup confrontation?

If the thrust of the above criticism is taken into account, this question demands that we answer first how the intergroup situation in the firm can be characterized *as a whole*. We should avoid assumptions that overt behaviours on one side are *caused* by that side, or even by the opposition acting alone. Furthermore, noting the inevitability that perceptions of the sides and of the situation will systematically vary, reliance can only be placed on measures that can take account of this variation, and we should attempt to develop and maintain therefore a *social* explanation of events (cf. Batstone, Boraston and Frenkel, 1978). The importance of such an approach is that it rules out individual variations (predispositions, personalities, etc.) as viable accounts of industrial action and focuses on the joint generation and sustaining of interpretive frameworks in the dynamic intergroup history of the firm.

The assumptions of such an approach are straightforward: they are that behaviour in the firm is the result of interaction between the sides over the course of time, and that the situation is not only perceived by both sides in ways reflecting their positions, but that mutual perceptions of one another contribute to a tradition of interpretation in the firm that helps pre-define situations and determine outcomes.

There is in fact good evidence that firms are characterized by specific patterns of interpretation in this way – that the sides' perceptions of one another are systematically related. In research into the attitudes and perceptions of employees in firms from several industries, it has been possible to show how it is beliefs about the opposition, on each side, that reveal the nature of the firm's industrial relations climate (Allen, 1983; Allen and Stephenson, 1983). In a substantial survey both shop-floor employees and higher line management, along with shop stewards and supervisors, were asked to complete attitude instruments concerning the roles of management and trades unions (see Stephenson et al., 1983). All respondents were also asked to complete these instruments again, this time as they thought might be typical of a member of the opposition. It is these latter completions, the attributed attitudes of each side, that begin to expose the climate of interpretation in the firm. At the group level, that is to say, considering the work-side versus the management within each firm, there proves to be no relationship between the sides with respect to 'own' attitudes. Attributions however are strongly related. Even more interesting is the comparison of attribution errors: where each side's attributions are measured against the actual views of the target group. These errors are strongly related and show how *both* sides err systematically. What happens is that both sides tend to see the opposition either as nearer to or further from their own side – at least in terms of attitudes towards the roles of either management or unions. Since, in some cases, both sides are fairly accurate in their assessments, Allen and Stephenson suggest that there are three basic climates of intergroup understanding: group assimilation, where the sides wrongly attribute attitudes close to their own side; group differentiation, where the sides conventionally stereotype; and accuracy, where both sides have a fairly realistic grasp of the other's views.

There is also reason to believe that behavioural outcomes are related to the form and degree of this misinterpretation that is typical in the firm. Allen and Stephenson (1985) report the results of a further study of the industrial organizations examined in their earlier survey. After an elapsed period of in all cases at least three years, additional data were collected from the firms, concentrating on relatively objective measures of behaviour recorded over a representative period – the preceding two years. Six forms of action initiated by both sides, for example disciplinary dismissals as well as strikes, were combined into a single index of 'friction'. This overall index correlated significantly with the previously measured climate of intergroup understanding in that higher frequencies of friction were associated with group differentiation, whereas group assimilation suppressed the incidence of 'friction' to lower levels.

How then might differential contact play a role in this situation? Returning to the classification of contact along a dimension of formality-informality it might be expected that informal contact would promote some indulgent interpretations and formal contact militate against this. However, hard evidence for the frequency and form of contact is rare. It is more usual in field studies to encounter structural information, on levels of procedure for example or on size. As discussed above, small size had been thought to facilitate informal contact – that is to say between employee and employer – as much as between peers. Certainly Allen and Stephenson report that size has a strong effect. The smaller firms they studied were characterized by an indulgent atmosphere of group assimilation. In other words, in such firms the management tended to think that the work-force was more pro-management than it was; the work-force in turn believed that the management was rather more pro-union than it was. The reality, what the sides *actually* thought was however no different in any of the firms examined. The basic competition for power and resources was everywhere viewed in approximately the same way – but in smaller firms both sides were prepared to believe that their particular opposition was less like the conventional stereotype. In larger firms the sides believed their opponents were more like the stereotype. The former situation, where the 'positive' (or 'quieter' perhaps, in industrial relations terms) effects of contact might be thought to operate most strongly, is nevertheless potentially unstable.

The fact that employment relations always have at least a minimum of formal, contractual definition, are subject to external market forces, and in any event are controlled in the main by only one of the sides, means that informally generated goodwill is likely to be possible only within a narrow range. Allen and Stephenson's findings also suggest that in general indulgent atmospheres, however they may be produced, are characterized by the misperception of the *opposition*. Thus, if there is greater contact in smaller firms, and if that contact is of an informal nature, then what it seems to produce is an atmosphere of mutual and indulgent misperceptions – the sides cannot really afford to misperceive the basic conflict of interests, but they are prepared to, or led to believe that their opponents are closer to their own position than they really are. The difference between 'reality' (what the sides believe) and indulgence (what the sides are prepared to believe about one another) may well help the conduct of routine industrial relations business, but in other circumstances this very difference may contribute to a drastic deterioration in relations.

Probably the most famous example of such an atmosphere and its breakup is reported by Gouldner (1965). Relations in the small plant studied by Gouldner demonstrated an 'indulgency pattern', which partly reflected informal neighbourliness. Attempts to introduce more formal technical methods precipitated a breakdown of relations and a wildcat strike. In other words, management, responding to the exigencies of industrial competition, inaugurated change and misjudged the probable reaction of the work-force because relations had always been friendly. Each move by each side illustrated the falseness of that sort of assumption and rapidly led to the breakdown of the wildcat strike.

THE ROLE OF CONTACT

Two main sorts of approach which include elements of contact have been illustrated. In the first opportunities for informal contact between employees, and between employees and employer, both in and out of work, are taken to provide expressive rewards and thus lead to a less troubled environment. In the second, relative isolation, coupled with formality in relations, is seen as leading to a less co-operative atmosphere and the hardening of ideological stance. The two qualities of contact involved here are the affective and the informational, but of course these are hardly likely to be separate in practice: information received from people with whom we have informal relations is likely to be perceived rather differently from that received via formal channels.

A great deal of attention has been paid to varieties of the 'size effect' in the literature – and it is the possible role of contact that has been seen to underlie some explanations of it in the sort of terms outlined above. Small firms are generally characterized as friendly places to work, having relatively informal relations and, in some versions, having work-forces who share, or accept, managerial values or ideology. However, a thorough social-psychological approach has thrown up a somewhat different interpretation of the situation.

There is in fact little or no evidence in the literature to support the view that workers actually do share the outlook of their employers in small as opposed to large firms. In the work on intergroup understanding, reported above, the actual views of both workers and managers varied little from size to size: the sides differed in outlook by much the same degree regardless of the size of firm. It was the joint atmosphere of misconception that changed with size and reflected subsequent frictional behaviours. The important point here is that the information received *on both sides*, one about the other, is clearly not producing an objective appraisal of the situation – except in a minority of cases. In the 'friendly small firm' both sides indulge their misconceptions about the opposition, while reserving their own views along much the same lines as their counterparts in quite different industries.

We can possibly answer some questions and raise yet others with this intergroup perspective. The direct evidence on informal contact at work is insufficient. Nevertheless, even assuming greater contact of such a nature in small firms, we can say that the effect is not on the basic outlook of the parties, but on their readiness to think differently about the stance of the opposition. It is precisely the attitudes about their respective roles and position, the elements of their 'ideology', that are misconstrued in the ways described. As the example from Gouldner amply illustrates, the real conflict of interest can rapidly puncture this inflated set of beliefs in a way that would seem unlikely if a genuine acceptance of the managerial ideology had been present. To the extent that contact theory has typically related to personal characteristics, rather than specific roles, it would seem unlikely to be able to say much about employment relations. Such relations tend to be well defined and constrained and, recalling Allport's classification, involve: unequal status; ideologically disputed goals; and regulated interaction. However, the ubiquitous 'size effect' argues for at least the possibility that variation in contact does affect industrial relations and not just, as we have shown, in strength, but in the direction of attributed attitudes. It is clear that we must warn social psychologists of the possibility that greater trust, to use Pettigrew's term, may not be founded on basic attitude change. Furthermore, we can note the implication that, where a form of interaction remains basically unchanging, increases in contact may lead to more accurate information and hence to a breakdown of such trust!

What we must ask about contact in the industrial setting therefore is how it generates these indulgent atmospheres, assuming that it does so, even when the basic situation remains objectively the same – and basic attitudes do not change. Furthermore, we can now see that the earnest attempts to impart information – or the complaints about the lack of it – probably miss the essential facts. Industrial peace, rarely permanent, is a product of the willingness to believe the best about the intentions of the opposition. It cannot however survive the exigencies of competition and, for the most part, both sides know this and enshrine it in their own fundamental outlook.

9 Contact, Action and Racialization: Some British Evidence

S. Reicher

INTRODUCTION

Since the 1950s the question of 'race' has come to assume a central position in British politics. Indeed one of the main issues (in some constituencies, *the* central issue) of general elections during the 1960s and 1970s concerned the right of entry of 'coloured' people into Britain. The pace was set by the words and actions of various right-wing figures. The best-known of these was Enoch Powell's 'rivers of blood' speech. Powell predicted that continuing 'coloured' immigration would inevitably result in violent racial conflict as indigenous 'whites' came to feel that their way of life was under threat. His solution was an immediate and complete ban on such immigration. His speech was structured around a crucial assumption that the experience of interaction with a culturally and 'racially' distinct group will result in an increase in racial prejudice.

While Powell represented an extreme position, and his speech was denounced by leading figures in both Labour and Conservative parties, the condemnation related more to the conclusions than the premises. Indeed, the major assumption was imported wholesale into mainstream politics, although it was seemingly tempered by a corollary. The argument was that if an increase in prejudice results from the influx of an 'alien' group, then one can only reduce prejudice by making the two groups more similar. Roy Hattersley, the Labour MP, epigrammatically summarized this thinking in the words: 'without integration limitation is inexcusable, without limitation integration is impossible.'

The terms of this political debate relate directly to the so-called 'contact hypothesis', for in both cases the concern is with the effects of interracial contact upon relations between the races. Thus, Bagley and Verma (1979) introduce their discussion on contact by saying: 'suppose that individuals have some attitudes towards an ethnic group . . . then, through migration of various kinds, contact is made with the ethnic group in question. What then happens to the inter-ethnic attitudes?' (p. 128). Of course 'contact theory' started from the opposite assumption to that of the political community. Cook (1962) and Pettigrew (1971) argue that interracial interaction will produce the conditions for interpersonal friendships and hence lead to a general reduction in prejudice. However, right from the start, it was clear that not just any form of contact would reduce prejudice. Consequently, the conditions under which contact occurs became a focus of research. Over time a series of such conditions, crucial to a successful outcome, was enumerated. These included equal status for the minority group member, intimacy, pleasant and rewarding interactions, the development of common goals and elite support for intergroup contact. Conversely, where contact is involuntary and unpleasant, where individuals are frustrated and where groups have cultural standards that are objectionable to each other, interaction will tend to increase prejudice (Bagley and Verma, 1979).

This proliferation of findings was worrying in two senses. First, on the practical level, it suggested that contact in the British context would be most unlikely to have favourable consequences. 'Coloured' migrants were mostly unskilled labourers competing with the indigenous work-force on the housing and labour markets. Additionally, for Asians if not for West Indians, their cultural traditions were highly distinctive. All these were conditions for increased prejudice through contact. Yet, and here a second, conceptual problem arose, it was impossible to predict exactly what might happen. The effects of a multiplicity of variables had to be borne in mind. Their simple effects were not fully understood, their interactions even less so. As a consequence reviewers were left to conclude, impotently, that 'personal contact with the ethnic minorities in question has complex effects. Such contact can both heighten or decrease prejudice according to the kinds of contact' (Bagley and Verma, 1979, p. 157).

Perhaps the most trenchant critique of the contact literature is that of Brown and Turner (1981). They argue that any incoherence is the result of the theoretical individualism of contact research. While this research is concerned with changing relationships between groups, the processes to which it refers are concerned with relationships between individuals. In particular, theorists have dealt with the antecedents of interpersonal attraction. Based on a presumed correspondence between similarity and attraction, the underlying rationales guiding contact researchers have been to increase similarity between individuals belonging to different groups and, through increasing attraction, to decrease prejudice. In this way, contact theory may be seen to echo Roy Hattersley's appeal to combine limitation with integration. Yet the assumption that underpins this line of argument is that interpersonal relationships underlie in intergroup relationships. It is precisely this assumption that Brown and Turner contest. They argue for a complete discontinuity between the interpersonal and the intergroup. It is perfectly possible to like a number of blacks as individuals but to remain hostile to blacks as a group. Indeed it is a commonplace of racist discourse to preface remarks with 'Some of my best friends are . . .'.

The aim of this chapter is to extend the logic of this critique. Brown and Turner propose that analyses of racism must be at the intergroup level. Yet it is important to note that their conception of race, as with other groups, is as a social category. In this they are in agreement with Montagu (1964). Montagu argues that the idea of race, in the sense of people divided into naturally distinct categories, is a social myth. This is not to deny the existence of clear genotypical and phenotypical differences between individuals. However, these differences are continuous and therefore the erection of boundaries in order to create racial categories is, biologically, completely arbitrary. None of the racial typologies that exist have any valid physical or genetic basis. There is no *a priori* reason why people should be divided into races: it is only as a result of social processes that they become racially labelled.

Before it is possile to consider racial prejudice it is necessary that first racial categories are available and second that they are applied in a given context. Hence there are two questions that logically precede intergroup considerations. The first concerns the processes through which the categories of race come to be constructed. The second relates to the way in which, given the construction of race categories, these come to be used in order to structure particular situations. The importance of these questions is that they lead to a radical departure from the terrain occupied by contact theory and the political mainstream.

The one crucial point on which theorists and politicians concurred was the presupposition of the existence and relevance of racial categories. The politicians saw the migrants in terms of race; the theorists asked about the effects of contact between races on attitudes and reactions to other races. Nevertheless the question remains. Why were many disparate peoples of West Indian, of African and sometimes even of African and Asian origin combined in a single racial category? Why were migrants categorized according to race instead of language or class or simply as migrant labour? The answer is not self-evident, and to restrict enquiry to the point where race is already in widespread use is to ignore the critical point in the formation of modern British racism, namely the way in which people and social phenomena come to be conceptualized in terms of race. Moreover, it is not simply that 'race' is presupposed, but that its continued existence is taken as given. Hence the possibility that racial categories may disappear from social usage is excluded. The preconditions for prejudice, if not prejudice itself, are seen as eternal.

Contact theorists may object that they accept the theoretical possibility of eradicating the use of race, but limit themselves to those cases where there is usage. Yet this argument has two weaknesses. First, to limit one's universe of enquiry to a racial domain is to submerge the provisional nature of race within one's discourse. Simply to acknowledge the plausibility of a non-racial universe without exploring it does not change the fact that all one's systems and explanations take race as given and thus unproblematic. Thus, one concedes to what Miles and Phizacklea (1984) refer to as the 'common sense of race relations'; that is the acceptance that different racial populations exist naturally. Whether or not difference necessarily entails discrimination, history and social psychology concur in showing that it is a very short step from one to the other.

The second point is that presupposing the existence of racial categories may often become a self-fulfilling prophecy. This is certainly the case with, and the motivation behind, much political rhetoric. When Enoch Powell, and others on the right, purported to describe a 'race problem', they were rather seeking to define a social process in terms of race. It was only through their actions, and the consequences of these actions, that black people were seen as a problem and causative of unemployment, poor housing and racist violence. Although contact theorists reject the negative evaluations of the racist right, their procedures frequently have in common the act of producing rather than simply measuring 'race'. That is to say that, in so far as it· is assumed that people will be categorized in terms of race, contact methodologies are insensitive to the way in which they render race salient and therefore elicit racist responses.

In order to substantiate these criticisms of the contact hypothesis, I shall examine the nature of contemporary British racism. In the next section I will show how the key to an understanding lies in the social construction of race over the last 30 years. In the third section I will consider how contact research has dealt with racial discrimination with the aim of demonstrating that it has served more to legitimize racial categories than to elucidate its dynamics. In the fourth and final section I shall outline an alternative approach and discuss the implications for a successful anti-racist practice.

THE CONSTRUCTION OF RACE IN BRITAIN SINCE THE 1950s

The first Africans in England arrived, with Roman legions, before the English. Since then there has been a continuous history of African settlement and hence to delineate a 'starting-point' will be necessarily arbitrary. The major influx occurred in the years following 1945. On the one hand, Britain experienced a labour shortage; according to a 1949 Royal Commission on population, 144,000 migrants were needed annually. Since Europe could not provide such a number, the Commonwealth was looked to as a source – the 1948 Nationality Act defining all Commonwealth citizens as British citizens with rights of entry into Britain and the right to work there. On the other hand, various factors precipitated emigration from the British Commonwealth. High unemployment in the West Indies was coupled, in 1952, with a block on entry to the United States. So, from 1951 to 1961, the number of West Indians in Wales for example grew from 15,300 to 171,800. Similarly, the partition of India from Pakistan displaced many people, especially Sikhs, who emigrated to Britain in the 1950s as soon as land claims had been settled.

Three important points need to be made about this immigration from the West Indies, India and Pakistan during the 1950s. First, the migrants came in response to a need for labour. Their aim was to make money and then return home; therefore there was no incentive to come to Britain unless jobs were there. Thus, Peach (1958) has shown that the figures for influx match the needs of the labour market in the absence of any immigration controls. The point therefore is that these migrants were, uniformly, members of the working class in Britain. Second, they nevertheless occupied a distinct position within the working class. The jobs to which they were recruited were those offering poor conditions or unsocial hours, to which neither indigenous labour nor workers brought by the various European schemes were attracted. Thus, black workers came to be over-concentrated in unskilled and semi-skilled manual jobs and in shift work – a situation, which, once established, was perpetrated by processes of discrimination (cf. Phizacklea and Miles, 1980). Third, despite the rapid increase in the work-force, of which the West Indians and 'Asians' were a major proportion, there was no accompanying expansion of facilities. In particular no new housing went with the new jobs. As a result the migrants were overcrowded into decaying older houses in the inner city, out of which the more favoured indigenous work-force had moved.

This background is crucial when one examines the emergence of racist arguments, which in the 1980s, are the common currency of British political discourse. A number of MPs on the right wing of the Conservative party began to talk of a 'colour problem'. On the one hand, they claimed, West Indians and, to a lesser extent, Asians were undesirables; unemployed, unskilled, carriers of disease and criminals. On the other, they talked of a threat to the 'British way of life' from alien cultures. They prophesied that as more 'coloured' aliens came to Britain the indigenous whites would respond defensively, with increased prejudice. Racial conflict would be an inevitable consequence. The only solution would be to call a halt on immigration, yet while they ostensibly meant all immigration, it was clear that their focus was on 'coloured' immigrants alone.

In the 1950s however it was not yet generally accepted that the problems that existed were those of race or race relations. It was argued by many in the Labour party and the Labour movement that migrants should not be seen in terms of race, but rather in terms of their class. What tensions existed between them and the indigenous population arose out of overcrowding and competition for scarce resources. The fault lay with employers who wanted a new work-force, but were not prepared to provide for their housing, education and health. This class definition of the problem stood solidly opposed to the incipient racialization of British public affairs. Confirmation of the class perspective relied upon a strategy to extract increased housing and public services from the capitalists. In the absence of such a strategy all the inhabitants of the 'inner city' could see were conditions deteriorating as the influx of migrants increased. A racialized perspective could be used to make sense of their experience. Thus, talk of a racial problem proved popular to sections of the working class and the Labour movement. Some working men's clubs operated a colour bar; the general secretaries of the National Union of Railwaymen and the Transport and General Workers' Union joined with the right-wing Tories in calling for immigration control.

At this point it is necessary to outline the dialectical relationship between 'elite' statements of racialization and the public support they receive. As in the case of their successors, the racist MPs of the 1950s denied the charge of racism – in the immediate wake of the Nazi holocaust it was politically essential to do so. Indeed, they maintained that they were concerned to lower prejudice. For this position to be coherent it had to be claimed that racial discrimination would inevitably result from a black influx. Thus, in voicing the need for (black) immigration controls, an MP claims only to be voicing the natural fears of his or her constituents. These statements are therefore built upon a necessary contradiction. While they are prescriptive, in that they define things in terms of race and hence seek to impose a racialized view of the world, they can only effectively do so in so far as they are seen as reflecting pre-existing views. Therein also resides their legitimacy. For their audience, on the other hand, it is the elite statements themselves that fulfil a legitimating function. First of all they identify 'black people' as 'the problem'. Second, they sanitize racist action as the expression of 'natural fears'. The consequence is a facilitation of such action. Moreover, 'white' racism is likely to be met by 'black' resistance. The resultant conflict is then used by the elite as confirmation of their viewpoint and to increase the clamour for discriminatory legislation.

Thus, the parliamentary talk of the early 1950s about the 'black problem' bore fruit in the so-called 'Notting Hill race riots' of 1958. The origins of these events is unclear. What is known is that, following a fight between West Indian migrants and indigenous residents on 23 August, on a number of occasions until 2 September, crowds formed to attack West Indian people and their property. Instead of being described as racialism, the very designation of the attacks as 'race-riots' posed the problem as if it were one of conflict between communities rather than the violence of one section of the community against another. On a national scale the media confirmed that Britain now had a 'colour problem'. The consequence was to relaunch the call for immigration control, both inside parliament and out. In the 1959 general election a number of new racist MPs were elected; groups like the Birmingham Immigration Control Association were formed. Together they formed a powerful lobby for legislation. The growing threat of such legislation led to a large increase in migration from the West Indies and the Indian subcontinent. People, in most cases, wanted to join their families before the door was shut. This was used by the racists to claim support for their predictions and finally their lobby proved irresistible. The Commonwealth Immigrants Act of 1962 replaced free entry for Commonwealth citizens with a limited voucher system.

This act was claimed to be a piece of 'colour-blind' legislation; simply matching the amount of immigration to the availability of jobs. Yet, as has been shown, no legislation was necessary to achieve this end. Moreover the Act did not cover Irish citizens who were free to enter at will. Thus, the argument that the legislation was needed to rationalize influx is inadequate. The real motivation is shown by the context in which the Act was born. It was intended as a sop to the racist lobby by putting a halt to 'coloured immigration'.

The advent of immigration controls placed the racialization of English society on to a qualitatively new plane. In the first place, the very existence of such an Act enshrines in law the belief that black people are a problem. If they must be kept out there must be something unpalatable about them such that they cannot be let into Britain. However, legislation also brings into being a set of practices that give practical reality to racial categorizations and that confirm the exclusion of black people. For instance, the artificial panic over 'illegal immigrants' created during the 1950s and 1970s led to a situation in which all those of African and Asian descent were seen as possible wrongdoers and were virtually forced into carrying identification. Similarly, recent legislation excluding foreigners from free medical treatment has led to situations in which black people have had to show passports to gain hospital admission.

Hence the 1962 Act marked the start of a process by which race came to structure the ways in which official and semi-official agencies operated and in which people's lives were lived. That is to say that race was given material as well as ideological confirmation. Yet, in 1962, the legislation, passed by a Conservative administration, was opposed by the Labour opposition who branded it as racialist and promised its repeal. The history since then has been one in which the notion of a 'race problem' and the associated calls for limitation and control have grown to embrace the entire parliamentary political spectrum and grown ever more extreme.

More Acts, in 1965, 1968, 1971 and 1975, by both Labour and Tory governments, extended and tightened the 1962 Act, making its racial basis ever more apparent. Since 1971 legislation has been based on the concept of 'patriality'. Patrials, those with a parent or grandparent of UK citizenship or who were born, naturalized or registered in the UK, could enter and settle; non-patrials could not. Patrials were from countries such as Canada, Australia, New Zealand – in effect they were whites. As one Tory MP said of non-patrials, they are those 'born with black or brown faces' (Miles and Phizacklea, 1984). So by 1971 racism was respectable enough to be brought into the open. Of course, along with the limitation came the Race Relations Acts, which supposedly outlawed racial discrimination. First, however, neither the 1965 nor 1975 Acts had real teeth. Second, there is an obvious contradiction in defining black people as a problem and then arguing against treating them as such. It is impossible to reinforce a racialized perspective and then wish away its effects with race relations legislation – even if that legislation was effective, which it was not.

The story of British racism after the Second World War began with the 1948 Nationality Act, which sought to facilitate migration to Britain from the entire Commonwealth. By the 1970s the concept of patriality made 'black' or 'New Commonwealth' citizens at once undesired and second class. To overcome this contradiction the Nationality Act of 1981 changed the definition of citizenship to one based on patriality. Those who had been *de facto* second-class citizens now had it confirmed *de jure*. Thus, in the 1980s, things have come full circle. Not only entry into Britain but the very concept of 'Britishness' is now defined by reference to racial categories. Moreover, the official practices that give material confirmation to ideologies of race no longer relate simply to influx, but now control every aspect of the life of black people in Britain.

CONTACT THEORY AND BRITISH RACISM

It is wrong to see contact theory as a homogenous body of work, for it encapsulates a series of different hypotheses; some see contact decreasing prejudice, others see it as increasing prejudice, yet others predict a complex or curvilinear function (Elkin and Panning, 1975; Lyon, 1970; Studlar, 1977). Different indices of contact are used and different measures of prejudice are taken. Sometimes they even fail to match, as when Schaeffer (1973) considers the effect of proximity to West Indians, Indians or Pakistanis upon prejudice against 'coloureds'. Yet, if one clear conclusion can be made, it is that there is no simple relationship either between contact and prejudice or between simple contextual variables (unemployment, housing shortage, political response, etc.) and prejudice (Bagley and Verma, 1979; Schaeffer, 1973; Studlar, 1977). Studlar also fails to detect any general regional differences in prejudice: this is not to say that the level of prejudice is constant across the whole country; indeed there are large differences between specific places. Little et al. (1977) show Bradford to have almost double the level of prejudice displayed in Lambeth, despite similar racial compositions. Thus, the point is that no simple variable can account for such differences.

A similar picture emerges from contact studies carried out in the school context. While a number of investigations seem to point to an increase in prejudice as the concentration of minority group members increases (Kawwa, 1968; Schaeffer, 1973), Pushkin and Venness (1973) obtained more complex results. They compared an area of low concentration with two areas of high concentration (Tottenham and Willesden, both in London). What was striking was the wide difference in prejudice between the areas of similar concentration. This they put down to differences in relations between adult majority and minority communities. Similarly, Davey (1983) shows no clear increase in ethnocentrism associated with racial composition. What he does show however is an increased bias in sociometric choice. What is particularly interesting is the relationship between friendship choice and prejudice. According to the attraction theory underlying the classic work on contact, choosing a 'coloured' friend should dramatically decrease one's level of prejudice against 'coloured' people in general. Yet Kawwa's (1968) data show no such relationship. Those individuals with black friends showed no less prejudice than those who do not choose blacks as their friends.

This finding confirms the argument that the interpersonal consequences of contact have no significance for general changes in racial prejudice. Thus, the generalizability of many contact findings must be put in doubt. For instance Bagley (1972) shows that partners in 'mixed' marriages lose their prejudice against their partner and, in Britain, in so far as one in seven black people who get married marry white people, this will have major repercussions on general racism. Yet, to lose prejudice against one's spouse does not predict behaviour towards blacks in general. It may be objected that there is some evidence to associate acquaintance with blacks with lower levels of general prejudice (e.g. Schaeffer, 1973). Yet such studies only reveal another widespread problem with the contact literature. That is research mainly consists of levels of prejudice at a given moment in time being related to the level of a contextual variable. Thus, it is ahistorical, correlational and considers distal relationships. Consequently, it is impossible to discover directions of causality – does acquaintance decrease prejudice or do only those with low prejudice get acquainted – or even, do those with low prejudice more willingly represent themselves as having acquaintance with blacks? Moreover even if it were possible to show that prejudice decreases among those who get acquainted with blacks, it remains impossible to specify the psychological process. It may be that interpersonal attraction itself has no causative role, but that rather acquaintance itself is a consequence of common group membership, which is what affects perceptions of blacks.

Support for the 'group' position comes from a study by Elkin and Panning (1975) on 1,155 respondents from 40 neighbourhoods. They found that only for those individuals who identify with their neighbourhood does the local 'climate of opinion' affect their racial attitudes. Moreover, it is only among 'identifiers' that this relationship increases as the proportion of their social network living locally increases. In contrast, for those who identify with other types of group (such as political activists), neighbourhood opinions have a negligible significance. If racial prejudice is a function of identification with a social group, then two things follow. First, the nature of one's racial attitudes will depend on group norms, independently of contextual variables. Thus, one would expect considerable differences in prejudice for people in the same area, or similar areas, with identical patterns of contact, but who identify with groups holding different norms. As Horowitz and Horowitz (1937) argue, it is not contact with blacks but contact with an anti-black tradition that leads to prejudice. Thus Kawwa (1968) found that the few children displaying high prejudice in his low contact area came from highly prejudiced social backgrounds. It would also provide a means of explaining the large differences in prejudice found by Little et al. (1977) and Pushkin and Venness (1973) in areas of similar migrant concentration.

As well as synchronic differences one would also predict diachronic changes in prejudice related to changes in social norms. Indeed, such changes are found, and two critical dates seem to emerge, both of which mark increases in prejudice. They are 1962 (Schaefer, 1973) and 1968 (Kohler, 1973). These dates relate, respectively, to the first Immigration Act and to Powell's speech, with the furore surrounding it. Such events may be interpreted as precipitating negative racial norms. On the other hand, as argued in the previous section, they may be seen as affecting the nature of categorization, rather than the norms associated with pre-given categories. This leads on to the second point.

If prejudice is related to social categorization, then it is dependent upon using race to categorize both oneself and others. Research into the use of categorization shows clearly that one can use different types of category both in order to identify oneself and to identify others (Tajfel, 1982a; Turner, 1982). Hence, in contexts where race is overshadowed by other identities there should be a reduction in prejudice. Thus for instance Schaeffer (1973) shows that people who work with migrants show less prejudice. This may be because work identities are structured around one's relationship to production (workers *v.* management) rather than around race. Yet if this argument is to hold, given that most migrants are working class, one would expect work experience to lead to a greater reduction in prejudice among workers, for whom migrants are ingroup members, than among management, for whom migrants remain distinctive in so far as they are almost all outgroup members. Schaeffer's results support this prediction. He shows that, for middle-class respondents, work experience with West Indians or Asians has no effect on level of prejudice, while for working-class respondents there is a significant decrease.

There is however a major problem in examining changes in the use of racial categories through the contact literature. The theoretical aspect of this problem has already been mentioned. It concerns the fact that contact research presupposes both the pre-existence and the continued existence of race; consequently it fails to address, explicitly, questions about changes in the use of race. Any relevant data must be gleaned from unintentional and unremarked results. Yet, even this is unsatisfactory, for there is a second aspect to the problem. The theoretical assumption has important effects on methodology. The key point is that, in so far as the use of racial categories is taken for granted, studies are blind to the ways in which they themselves may impose such categories.

Conventional procedures impose race in at least one of two main ways. The first of these relates to the independent variable: that of contact. This is assessed through such questions as 'What is the proximity of coloured neighbours?' (cf. Bagley and Verma, 1979). Yet this question also suggests the relevance of seeing neighbours in terms of their colour. Thus what is supposedly an index of contact functions as a manipulation of the salience of racial categories. Not all traditional studies are subject to this objection. In many cases the racial categorization is inferred by the researcher rather than imposed on respondents. Some studies contrast areas or schools of high and low 'coloured' immigrant population (e.g. Davey, 1983; Studlar, 1979); others analyse sociometric choices so as to discover those people who interact intimately with 'non-whites' (e.g. Kawwa, 1968). However, when it comes to the dependent measure the psychological literature is consistent in rendering race salient. Respondents are tested on various 'prejudice' or 'racism' scales, which measure their attitudes to 'black' or 'coloured' or 'West Indian' or 'Asian' people. Thus, they are forced to use 'racial' or 'ethnic' categories.

The effects of this imposed racialization will be complex and depend upon an important distinction between two types of items embedded in the various prejudice scales. On the one hand, there are general attitudes towards the racial group. These may either measure stereotyped perceptions (they live like animals – they are dirty) or intentions to discriminate (black people should not be given council houses). In these cases the evocation of race will lead to negative racial stereotypes, which Billig (1978) shows to have a long history in British culture, and furthermore the delineation of an outgroup will facilitate the expression of generalized as well as specifically ideological processes of intergroup discrimination (Tajfel, 1978a).

On the other hand, there are questions that ask whether racial groups are seen as the cause of other problems. For instance Kawwa (1968) asks, along with the general attitude questions, whether 'black people take our jobs' and whether 'we cannot get jobs because of them'. It may be argued that such items allow subjects to reject the relevance of race; yet they are embedded in a context, which continuously makes race salient, which highlights negative stereotypic traits and which, even in asking whether race explains other social questions, uses a bipolar scale in which race is the only explanation that is offered. In a context where the relevance of race is so clearly stressed, it is hardly surprising that it is used, as the only available resource, to explain social reality.

The assumptions and methods of contact research therefore lead not only to the expression of prejudice, but also to the perception of social problems in terms of race. These are precisely the key elements in the construction of racism in Britain since 1945. The reason for this correspondence is simple: just as political utterances that were pased as a reaction to racial problems actually defined race as a problem, similarly, that which appears to be explanatory or descriptive in contact theory in actual fact prescribes racial categories.

To put it slightly differently, contact research reproduces the central facet of what has been called 'the new racism' (Barker, 1981). That is the way in which the use of race is taken for granted and hence 'race' is naturalized. Apart from the clear political problems that this gives rise to, it also leads to a crippling internal contradiction. The contact paradigm seeks to address the general problem of the articulation of received ideology and experience on the expression of 'common sense' racism. Yet it disqualifies itself from the task in so far as it accepts and imposes the corner-stone of that common sense: racialization. It cannot solve the problem because it is part of the problem.

This argument is not intended to deny the importance of an understanding of the relationship between ideology and action in determining racism. Indeed, it is a question of the utmost importance both in the specific area and for a general understanding of human psychological processes. However, such an enquiry must not assume the use of race and must be sensitive to changes in racialization. This means, first of all, that one must rephrase the specific research question. Instead of asking about the effects of contact with blacks upon racial prejudice, which presupposes the categorization of migrants in terms of race, one must ask about the effects of experience upon racialization. Second, one must change the research methodology. Instead of supplying categories, it is necessary to analyse the categories that the subjects themselves use. This last condition is not as straightforward as it might seem.

Davey (1983) presented photographs to schoolchildren and asked them to divide them into groups. At first sight this may seem to fulfil the above criteria. Children are left free to choose their own categories. Indeed, Davey obtained interesting results, which showed the different ways race was used as a category. White children often differentiate by race over sex in schools with a high density of migrants. Yet, despite the fact that this method is an improvement on those of traditional studies, there is still a problem in getting respondents to categorize people on the basis of still photographs. This is because the total emphasis is put on physical features, and thus there will be a predisposition to use racial and sexual categories, which are the archetypes for justifying the physical categorization of humanity. Such a method ignores that many alternative forms of categorization, for instance class, depend on what people do rather than, principally, how they look. The only way to guard against such implicit bias is to start off by examining the ordinary language explanations of 'naturally' occurring events. The problem with such an approach lies in the complexity of analysis. Instead of simply applying quantitative techniques to limited response categories, it is necessary to use qualitative analyses in order to establish the categorical structure prior to statistical analysis. However, such an approach is perfectly feasible and indeed it does not exclude a quantitative approach. Thus, Phizacklea and Miles (1980) have analysed, from a sociological perspective, the extent of the racialized category system. By simply asking for explanations of issues concerning housing and employment they were able to assess the incidence of accounts stressing race and to analyse statistically the effects of independent variables upon the deployment of such explanations.

Phizacklea and Miles's results complement those of Schaeffer (1973). In comparing a 'residential' and a 'factory' sample, they show the latter to use far less racialized explanations of such things as the housing shortage. They also display less general racism. They argue that work experience engenders a feeling of class disadvantage, while residential experience is one of personal battles against a council seen to favour blacks: ' "Us" are disadvantaged workers in the factory and the disadvantaged English outside the factory gates' (1980, p. 220). Sparks (1980) supports this argument through an historical analysis of fascism. He shows that such movements, whose politics revolved around race, consistently failed to mobilize people at the workplace, which is structured around class. Instead they organized through 'street' politics. However, there remains a problem of generalization. To what extent does work experience change the use of racial categories outside the workplace? The research of Minard (1952) would seem to indicate that the answer is very little. He showed that while black and white mineworkers showed little prejudice while underground, above ground they displayed high levels of discrimination. Thus, to the extent that contexts are differentially structured, we may expect different uses of categories and consequently contradictory behaviours. Work experience would only have a general effect where it led to a restructuring of community life – perhaps in the context of a strike, where a working-class community needs to organize along class lines in order to ensure solidarity.

The general point that emerges from this research is that the consequences of experience upon racialization will depend upon the structure of that experience. If it is structured around race, then racial categories will be made salient and the conditions for racism will exist, if not, other categories will be used to organize cognition and action. Thus, while there is a general difference between work and residence, there are exceptions. Husbands (1979) has shown that where conflicts at the workplace are organized around race, through the introduction of migrant labour on lower rates of pay and with worse conditions for identical jobs, then racist behaviour increases. Conversely Ward (1979) analyses a campaign for rehousing in the Moss Side area of Manchester. In so far as all residents had common interests in opposition to the town hall, there was no racial divide and a decrease in racist behaviour.

The implications of this argument are that the difference between individuals with and without experience of migrants will not be one of *outcome* (the consequences of their having, or not having, experience), but rather one of *process* (the social practices that determined their experience). If the consequences of experience depend on the social practices that structure that experience, then those without experience will be more dependent on received ideology. Thus, Hartmann and Husband (1970) show that in areas of minimal migrant population, children get most of their ideas on race from the media, whereas in areas of high concentration, ideas derive from the nature of conflict over housing or employment. The corollary of this is that anti-racist education should be far more effective in areas of low than in those of high concentration – and indeed Bagley and Verma (1978) show this to be the case.

The different roles of ideology and experience in different contexts are not meant to suggest a division between the two. Indeed, they have been shown to be integrally connected in the construction of British racism. Racist ideology combined with a lack of class-based political action allowed the passage of the 1962 Immigration Act, which at once legitimated the racial coding of migrants and produced the social practices through which that code would be given experiential reality. Yet, just as the historical study reveals a changed dynamic once these practices were introduced, so there is a difference between areas of the country where these practices have effect and those where they do not. However, whatever the area, an opposition to racism must combine educational and practical elements. To conclude, the logic of this chapter points to a number of necessary elements to such an opposition, which can be briefly outlined.

FROM CONTACT TO COLLECTIVE ACTION

This chapter has been based on the argument that, in order to understand racism, one must start by analysing how racial categories came to be constructed and used. It has been argued that contact theory cannot carry out this analysis because it is part of the process of construction. Instead, it has been proposed that the use of race depends first on ideology and second on practices that organize experience around a racial dimension. In other words, racial ideologies are accepted when they help make sense of one's experience. The important point about this is that, in so far as they have this functional aspect, such categories cannot simply be attacked through education. They will only be replaced when another set of categories can be shown to make better sense of one's experience. This entails not only an alternative on the level of ideology, but also an attack on those concrete features that divide people according to race. In other words, racism will not be overcome through individual acts, which leave the racist structure of British society intact, but only through action to change the nature of that society. It will not change by contact but by collective action.

It is not only the outcome of collective action that is important, but its process. That is to say, independently of whether that action is successful in its challenge to racist practices, participation itself is likely to entail a change of perspective. Thus, Reicher (1984) has analysed the consequences of participation in the St Pauls 'riots' of April 1980. In so far as blacks and whites acted together against those agencies that they perceived as denying than 'the right to lead a free life' – principally the police – they ceased seeing each other as enemies and instead saw a common enemy. Instead of categories of 'black' and 'white' they adopted a common category of 'members of the oppressed St Pauls community' as against 'oppressive agencies'. The consequence was, at least temporarily, an expressed decrease in prejudice amongst participants.

It is customary to finish pieces on contact by issuing policy recommendations. Only two recommendations can be made here. The first indeed relates to policy. It is that all British Immigration Acts since 1962 and the 1982 nationality law be repealed – for it is this legislation that underlies the legitimacy of racial categories, as well as the official practices that treat people according to race. The second recommendation cannot be formulated in terms of policy. It is that the fight against racism depends on an alternative analysis of disadvantage and inequality in our society and in the struggle to overcome it. It is not enough to bemoan and deplore racial prejudice, it is necessary to destroy the social structures that produce it.

10   The Intergroup Contact Hypothesis Reconsidered

Thomas F. Pettigrew

INTRODUCTION

Social-psychological theory fails to live up to the discipline's ambitions.
Whether we regard this situation as a 'crisis', a scientific shortcoming or
just an embarrassment, social psychologists are in general agreement that
our models and even our approach to theory are in need of major
reassessment.*

Most social-psychological 'theories' are actually frameworks or general
perspectives, not theories in the full sense of being testable propositions
capable of being empirically falsified (Popper, 1959). In recent decades
these frameworks have emphasized cognitive factors and slighted
emotional ones. They typically stress similarity (mechanical solidarity)
and ignore the socially binding significance of differences (organic
solidarity) – Durkheim's other side of social life. They are largely static
rather than dynamic. As such, they tend to emphasize isolated, rather
than cumulative, effects – a reflection of the widespread use of non-
longitudinal research designs. Social-psychological theories also tend to
assume universality even though their tests rarely sample a wide range of
times, situations and cultures. Indeed, they are routinely conceptualized
and demonstrated in Western, and especially North American, cultural
terms.[1]

A more fundamental weakness is the absence of generic theory in
social psychology. The field provides to date only narrow- to middle-
range theories. It has yet to follow Karl Popper's 'principle of
preference': choose 'a theory with the greater informative content . . .

*Editors' note: We had originally invited Tom Pettigrew to write a brief commentary on
the contents of this book. However, as he put it, his ambitions got the better of him, for
which we are most grateful. He has produced what is, in our view, a substantial theoretical
reassessment of the field, but although he skilfully integrates many points from the
foregoing chapters into his analysis, it is not a commentary in the usual sense of the word.

even before it has been tested, [to] a theory with little content' (Miller, 1985, p. 112). This bold strategy of theory construction not only holds out greater hope for major advances, but it addresses the widely recognized problem of the near-impossibility of falsifying much of social-psychological theory. Bold theories, as Popper emphasizes, permit more challenging tests, for they are more likely to be falsified. Even if they are falsified, Popper believes that we may well uncover more 'new and unexpected facts and problems' in the falsification of bold theories than in the testing of theories with little content (Miller, 1985, p. 112). In stark contrast to the principle of preference, social-psychological ideas seem to be pursued as if in ever-narrowing, spiralling coils that increasingly specify the mediating processes of one particular and limited phenomenon. Harold Kelley speaks for many in the field when he writes:

The topics in social psychology read more like a Sears and Roebuck catalogue than like a novel. They provide a listing of items of possible interest to the reader rather than a story with a plot, development of characters, and so on. Our work is more like that of mining engineers, who find a vein of valuable material and dig it out, and not like the work of geologists, who identify various features of the earth, describe their interrelations, and explain their origins. These are ways of saying that we do not know the total list of the phenomena we are studying (what will be the popular motive next year?) and we do not know the interrelations among the various ones we have studied so far (what is their priority of hierarchical order, their underlying genotypic structure?). (Kelley, 1983, pp. 8–9)

While there is wide consensus on the existence of the problem, there is considerably less agreement as to its diagnosis and remedy. Given the interstitial nature of social psychology, between the micro-level of the individual and the various macro-levels of collective forms, it is apparent that the search for Kelley's 'underlying genotypic structure' must focus greater attention upon the *situation*. Experimental social psychology has for three decades been demonstrating in the laboratory the critical significance of the situation. This emphasis marks yet another convergence of the various branches of social psychology, for symbolic interactionists and other sociologically oriented social psychologists have long focused on the situation as a critical determinant of social behaviour. Yet, it took the dramatic findings of vivid experiments – from Asch on conformity followed by Milgram on obedience and Zimbardo on prisons – to establish situational factors as a potentially unifying focus for the field. None the less, progress has been slow over the past generation. Social psychology has yet to produce an effective taxonomy of situations or even establish their chief dimensions. Nor has the field made many significant advances in isolating the mediating processes between individuals and situations.

Two directions are possible, indeed both together are needed: *bottom-up* analyses that begin at the micro-level and link with salient features of situations and higher structures and *top-down* analyses that begin at the macro-levels (situational, institutional or societal) and link with individual characteristics.[2] Kelley (1983) for example attacks the problem with a bottom-up approach. He proposes that human tendencies (e.g. motives, needs) 'have their origins in the structures of situations that people commonly confront' (Kelley, p. 9). Within a functionalist framework, he emphasizes how individuals select, adapt to, modify, and even shape and transform situations. Rather than simply aiming to predict individual behaviour as such, Kelley (1983, p. 28) sets 'the additional goal of understanding the patterning and distribution of [human] tendencies, both as they exist over time and situations for any one of us, and as they are distributed over people and history'. Towards this end, Kelley's approach employs individual tendencies to analyse situations.

By contrast, the contact hypothesis exemplifies the top-down approach when it specifies the situational conditions that shape individual tendencies differentially. Moreover, its various forms, from Williams's (1947) and Allport's (1954) classic statements to the present, have focused on truly structural features of situations rather than 'pseudo-macro' variables that are mere aggregations of individual data.[3] Thus, Allport's (1954, chapter 16) emphasis on equal-status contact and the positive sanction of 'institutional supports' are both structural indicators that cannot be derived simply from the data of individuals in the situation. In this significant respect, the contact hypothesis is unusual among social-psychological theories; in its exclusive focus on face-to-face interaction, the hypothesis clearly anticipated the situational direction in which the discipline has moved since.

However, in other respects the contact hypothesis is similar to many other social-psychological formulations. It is at best a relatively static, middle-range theory of modest scope. It was derived to explain a particular and limited set of conflicting empirical findings in an applied area of interest – changes in intergroup attitudes as a function of intergroup contact under varying conditions. It focuses on similarity and mechanical solidarity with scant attention to differences and organic solidarity. Its specification more closely resembles a laundry list than a subset of corollaries of a single, more generic theory.[4] Finally, the contact hypothesis is very much a creature of its time and place: the late 1940s and early 1950s in the United States. Indeed, a major focus of this volume is to address and correct this temporal and cultural limitation directly. Thus, below is a brief review of the origins of the hypothesis.

THE ORIGINS OF THE CONTACT HYPOTHESIS

Many Americans recoiled from Nazi anti-Semitism of the 1930s and 1940s. This revulsion led to an extensive human relations movement in the United States following the Second World War. It worked diligently to combat intergroup prejudice in all its forms – racial, religious and ethnic. It attracted many prominent local and national figures – especially the political liberals of the day (in the current American, not the nineteenth-century-European, sense of the term). It took organizational form with such still-active groups as the National Conference of Christians and Jews. Additionally, as Allen notes in his chapter, the human relations movement extended into other intergroup domains including industrial relations. The movement rested on three basic, interconnecting assumptions:[5]

1 The fundamental problem of intergroup conflict is individual prejudice.
2 In turn, prejudice is an educational and psychological problem. Most prejudice simply reflects gross ignorance about outgroups. But for some, such as the dangerous 'Nazi-like' fringe, prejudice is a problem of bigoted individuals who externalize their inner turmoil through projection on to minority groups.
3 The effective remedy is education. Attitudes must be changed first, and then altered behaviour follows. Group stereotypes must be combated with 'Brotherhood Dinners', pamphlets and other informational means used to correct intergroup misconceptions.

Perhaps, the human relations movement helped to prepare white-American thinking for later events. Nevertheless, although well intentioned, the movement's operating assumptions doomed it to extremely limited success in the 1940s and 1950s. It is instructive to contrast these assumptions with the major conclusions that have arisen from social scientific research over the intervening decades. Tersely stated, the parallel contentions of modern analysis are:

1 Prejudice is an important, but not the fundamental, component in intergroup relations. Institutionalized discrimination is the core of the problem; prejudice both supports and is derived from these institutionally restrictive arrangements.
2 Prejudice is not simply 'a psychological problem.' The externalisation function, emphasized almost exclusively by the Human Relations Movement and the research on the authoritarian personality (Adorno et al., 1950) conducted during the same post-World War II era, is

only one of the personality functions served by prejudice. The cognitive aspects of prejudice and stereotypes, much better under-stood today than a third-of-a-century ago, reveal how 'human' prejudiced thinking is. Rather than the aberrant distortions of sick people, all human beings employ stereotypes and are prone to biased judgements. Also neglected was the social adjustment function of prejudice (Pettigrew, 1961). It reveals the social side of the phenomenon, and how deeply prejudice is embedded in the culture and structure of society.

3 Education by itself is a woefully insufficient remedy. Worse, the focus on speeches, dinners, and pamphlets steered the Human Relations Movement's efforts away from the real task – the systematic structural alterations necessary to eliminate intergroup separation and institutional discrimination. Altered institutions shape new inter-group behaviour which is the most effective means of changing intergroup attitudes. Just as the Movement's focus on sick bigots diverted attention from seeing the problem of prejudice in them-selves, its focus on educational remedies diverted attention from the difficult confrontation with the comfortable institutional arrange-ments that yield special privilege to the dominant group.

From its three key assumptions, the human relations movement constructed a sanguine theory of intergroup contact. Since it viewed individual prejudice as largely the result of ignorance, it believed that contact between groups could only be advantageous. Once together, all but the most extreme fringe would surely see the common humanity shared by the groups and prejudice would necessarily dissipate. Such a rosy and simple view of intergroup dynamics had surfaced on earlier occasions in Western thought, but it remained for the American human relations movement of the 1940s to elevate it to a cultural truism and a plan for action. Intergroup summer camps were begun, interracial dinners held and many other contact opportunities provided between the nation's various racial, religious and ethnic groups. Trew's pointed description (see chapter 5) of current efforts in Northern Ireland to arrange holidays with both Roman Catholic and Protestant children, while stoutly maintaining separate religious school systems, is reminis-cent of these earlier, American efforts.

This was the societal setting that inspired the original round of intensive research on intergroup contact in social science. Fresh from service in the Second World War, many young American social psychologists were concerned about intergroup relations. The discipline was entering a period of significant expansion; private resources were available for work in this area (in particular from American-Jewish organizations concerned with combating anti-Semitism); and social psychologists overwhelmingly shared the liberal political leanings of those active in the human relations movement. Besides, the movement was virtually 'the only game in town' concerned with intergroup relations. Thus, not surprisingly, the human relations movement's assumptions and hopes, in particular its remedial aspirations for intergroup contact, soon became a focus for research. Sympathetic as they were to the aims of the movement however, these early workers on the subject assumed a sceptical stance. This fact has often been obscured in later writing as new researchers entered the area; the contact hypothesis itself has sometimes been twisted beyond recognition to fit political aims. But a rereading of the best of this early work reveals that it anticipated most of the criticisms and qualifications raised once again in this book.

Much of this work in American social psychology was centred in New York City and originally published in the *Journal of Social Issues*, the publication of the activist Society for the Psychological Study of Social Issues (SPSSI). Two research organizations were especially active: the Research Center for Human Relations of New York University and the Commission on Community Interrelations of the American Jewish Congress. For several years, these two centres concentrated their efforts on a series of highly innovative intergroup contact studies conducted in the field. The young investigators involved soon became well-known, respected members of the discipline on both sides of the Atlantic – Morton Deutsch (later of Teachers College, Columbia University), Stuart Cook (later of the University of Colorado), John Harding (later of Cornell University), Maria Jahoda (later of the University of Sussex) and many others.

Long before quasi-experimentation in field settings came into vogue, these initial social-psychological tests of the contact hypothesis employed ingenious research designs to exploit the first instances of official governmental attempts to overcome racial segregation. Early efforts of New York State to combat racial discrimination centred on making available to black citizens opportunities previously closed to them in employment and public housing. By adroitly seizing the opportunity to study these new interracial job (e.g. Harding and Hogrefe, 1952; Saenger and Gilbert, 1950) and housing situations (e.g. Deutsch and Collins, 1951; Jahoda and West, 1951; Wilner, Walkley and Cook, 1955), these investigations provided the first systematic findings on the complexity of the phenomenon. The close agreement of these findings with those from the field experiments on racial desegregation in *The American Soldier*

(Stouffer et al., 1949b) and from less formal, non-experimental studies (e.g. Biesanz and Smith, 1951; Brophy, 1946; Lee and Humphrey, 1943; MacKenzie, 1948; Minard, 1952) gave social psychologists of the period confidence that they were beginning to grasp how interracial contact affected attitudes. Indeed, as seldom occurs in social psychology, there was a true triangulation of research results from quasi-experiments in the field, opinion surveys and observational studies. In broad outline, the consensus that emerged from this work in the early 1950s remains the core of intergroup contact theory under cross-cultural scrutiny in this book.

Values and hopes for future change were as explicit in this early work as they are in the chapters of this book. Thus, Deutsch and Collins (1951), in *Interracial Housing*, wasted no words:

frequently theory can be advanced equally well by any one of a number of alternative settings for research and, of course, when the research is intended to be immediately relevant to practical problems, the basic value premise has immediate implications for the formulation of the research problem. In such cases we believe *the research should be formulated so that it is strategically useful in facilitating democratic social change.* (Deutsch and Collins, 1951, p. xii; italics in original)

These sentiments led to the use of this early contact research in the efforts for racial change in the United States that culminated in the nation's civil rights movement in the 1960s. In fact, the Deutsch and Collins contact research, according to Jahoda and West (1951, pp. 138–9), soon contributed to 'the decision of the Newark Housing Authority to change from an area-segregated occupancy pattern to integrated occupancy'. Later, it was drawn on heavily in the social science statement that accompanied the brief to the Supreme Court against the racial segregation of public schools in 1954 (Clark, 1953; see also Cook, 1979 for a retrospective view of this effort). It also formed the research base upon which Allport (1954) formulated the modern form of the contact hypothesis under discussion throughout this book. Hence, we are not discussing here an abstract theory divorced from immediate application. The contact hypothesis has been, from its inception, value-laden and perceived as relevant for social policy.

Later work in the United States has refined and generalized the hypothesis without substantially altering it. Thus, it has been success-fully tested for blacks and their attitudes towards whites (Works, 1961) and for such other groups and situations as handicapped children in regular class-rooms. Nevertheless, does the contact hypothesis hold up as well under cultural and intergroup situations vastly different from those found in North America? Is there not a more generic theoretical framework in which to place the hypothesis? This book represents a concerted effort to address these questions from a variety of cultural and intergroup perspectives.

THE MACRO-CONTEXTS OF INTERGROUP CONTACT

The black American situation is unique in the world (Pettigrew, 1985). Black Americans are not immigrants, aliens, a colonized people or a group sharply distinguished by its religion and culture. They represent a long-standing, highly acculturated minority perceived by all as truly 'belonging' in American society (Landes, 1955), yet they have endured intense discrimination through a confluence of race, slavery and segregation. Black Americans are characterized even today by sharp group boundaries, as revealed by extremely low rates of residential contact and intermarriage with other Americans. This uniqueness argues for extreme caution in applying findings and principles based on racial contact in the United States to other minorities and national contexts.

The point is illustrated in these pages. Schofield in chapter 4 is concerned largely with 'second generation problems' – intergroup difficulties that arise only after such major structural changes as interracial education are formally achieved. More thoroughly than any other social science investigator in the United States, she has studied in patient detail the actual patterns of interracial interaction, in a so-called 'model' school in Pittsburgh, Pennsylvania. The practical problems Schofield raises contrast with those raised in settings where actual power shifts between groups are at stake: Israel, Northern Ireland, Quebec and South Africa.

To be sure, similarities do emerge. Strict group segregation of schools in Bavaria, Northern Ireland and South Africa rings familiar. So too does the operation of differences in power between the dominant and subordinate groups; language seems to be used as a separating device in German schools much in the same way as Schofield shows test scores are used in American schools. Some remedies also replicate. Wagner and Machleit report in chapter 3, a study where Aronson's jigsaw technique for co-operative learning proved effective in Germany. Even practices and assumptions of the old human relations movement re-emerge in chapters 2 and 5.

Differences with the American situation are however especially intriguing. Foster and Finchilescu provide an interesting discussion, in chapter 7, of how a thoroughly racist society poisons even intergroup contact with otherwise optimal conditions. Russell's (1961) study of an interracial neighbourhood in Durban is particularly relevant. Contact was associated with greater friendliness among the white, Indian and Coloured neighbours, but the larger context poisoned this predicted effect in two ways. First, the positive effects among Russell's white respondents appeared to generalize neither to other non-whites nor other situations – a replication of the findings of early contact studies (e.g. Deutsch and Collins, 1951; Harding and Hogrefe, 1952; Stouffer et al., 1949b). Second, Russell uncovered asymmetrical racial patterns of visiting and borrowing as whites subtly exploited their societal dominance. Soon after the study however the South African Government, with its Group Areas Act, eradicated this interracial neighbourhood. Apartheid as a system sets out to violate systematically each of Allport's key conditions for favourable intergroup contact. In a rough sense, the smouldering, ever-increasing intergroup conflict in South Africa since the Nationalists came to power in 1948 provides a case demonstration of the intergroup contact hypothesis in reverse.

Likewise, chapters 6 (on Quebec) and 5 (on Northern Ireland) reverse the traditional assumptions of intergroup research. The original contact studies assumed black-white interracial conflict as normative and aimed to develop intergroup harmony. However, these chapters set out to explain how widespread interpersonal harmony appears to continue in the midst of intense group conflict where power and sovereignty are at stake. This switch in orientation is refreshing. Social psychology, like social science in general, tends to over-explain conflict. By making harmony the problematic focus of enquiry, these writers expand our theoretical horizons and supply an overdue correction.

Taylor and his colleagues specify, in chapter 6, three interrelated hypotheses. First, they conjecture that much of this apparently frequent and friendly intergroup contact is subtly biased so that it 'is more illusory than real'. Second, when such contact does occur, it is qualitatively different from contact with ingroup members. Third, when the intergroup contact is occasionally frequent and intimate, 'individuals psychologically define themselves, the other person and the context in other than intergroup terms.' In short, as in Russell's South African study, the larger intergroup climate once again limits face-to-face interaction. It is often illusory and biased; when it is genuine, the contact can only occur if the larger conflictual context is essentially denied by both parties. The authors marshal considerable evidence from Quebec to support their contentions.

Two additional points concerning the Quebec phenomenon need to be considered. Like South Africa and Northern Ireland, intergroup tension in Quebec has a centuries-long history. Consequently, the cultural defences and skilled denial techniques delineated by Taylor, Dubé and Bellerose have had years to evolve and be perfected. Such apparent harmony at the interpersonal level might not be as possible in a situation of recent and acute intergroup tension, one in which these interpersonal skills of cross-group interaction had not had the opportunity to develop, Moreover, Quebec presents a situation where recent *selective* outmigration may well play a major role.[6] The substantial migration of anglophones out of Montreal since the Parti Québécois came to power in 1976 raises the distinct possibility that those who left for dominant English-speaking provinces tended to harbour the deepest fears and distrust of francophones and, perhaps, the most prejudice against and rejection of their French-speaking fellow Canadians. If this were true, it would supply a demographic explanation for Quebec's present inter-group situation: namely, that those anglophones who have remained in the Province are disproportionately more open to contact with franco-phones, have better French language and cultural skills and are therefore better equipped to engage in harmonious intergroup interaction than the typical member of the anglophonic community prior to 1976. This selective-migration explanation does not limit the arguments put forth by Taylor, Dubé and Bellerose. On the contrary, if this demographic phenomenon were true, it would only serve to heighten the significance of their argument and findings – for even a selectively open anglophonic population is apparently not able to overcome the legacy of centuries of intergroup separation and conflict.

The Quebec analysis assumes greater significance when Trew indicates that much the same phenomena operate between Roman Catholics and Protestants in Northern Ireland. She reports that divisive issues between the groups are rarely mentioned in intergroup interaction. Thus, similar to the arguments of Taylor and colleagues, Trew's suggestion is 'that short periods of contact between Catholics and Protestants . . . will allow individuals to discover their similarities but not delve into differences.' Consequently, interpersonal attraction principles, as focused on in traditional contact theory, operate but do not generalize to the intergroup level where 'the divisive issues . . . are not illusory.' The comparability of the Canadian and Irish results is made more remarkable by the differences that distinguish the two situations: the greater cultural division in Quebec and the longer and more intense pattern of sectarian violence in Northern Ireland.

Given these and other cross-cultural perspectives introduced in this book, what can now be said about the intergroup contact hypothesis itself? Are there indicated directions in which the hypothesis could be developed in the future?

NOTES TOWARDS AN EXPANDED INTERGROUP CONTACT HYPOTHESIS

This chapter's introduction cited six interrelated weaknesses of current social-psychological theories:

1 they are more often loose frameworks than testable theories;
2 they have centred on cold cognition to the relative exclusion of affective considerations;
3 they stress similarities (mechanical solidarity) to the virtual exclusion of differences (organic solidarity) as social bonds;
4 they focus largely on isolated, non-cumulative effects;
5 they too glibly assume universality across time, situations and cultures;
6 they are narrow- to middle-range in scope with bold generic theory that links various levels of analysis conspicuous by its absence.

The traditional contact hypothesis is no exception to most of these limitations – least of all the writer's version (Pettigrew, 1971). Thus, on the basis of the preceding chapters, the intergroup contact hypothesis on each of these features should be evaluated.

Loose frameworks rather than testable theory

This general criticism fits the traditional contact hypothesis like a glove. In a deep sense, it is not a testable hypothesis at all. Rather, as a laundry list of conditions, it has proved expandable and imprecise. No systematic arguments accounting for how these various conditions interact with each other have been advanced; and even the conditions themselves are often not well specified. For instance as Foster and Finchilescu point out, Allport had meant 'equal status' to refer only to equality of status *within* the situation itself, but it has sometimes been interpreted as meaning equality of status *outside* the situation.[7] Such a slippery hypothesis is extremely difficult to falsify definitively, for the addition of another condition or a re-specification of a condition seems all too easily possible.

This theoretical looseness reveals itself in two ways in the research literature and throughout this book. First, examples of intergroup contact are often claimed to be confirmations or disconfirmations of the hypothesis, even though the relevant conditions are either measured only in part or ignored altogether. Obviously, such unspecified cases are irrelevant to the hypothesis. Second, the openness of the theory tempts investigators to add further conditions to fit the special milieu under test.

Consider the many conditions suggested in this book as candidates to join Allport's basic four. Thus, from Germany, it is suggested that a common language, 'home turf', voluntary contact and prosperous economic times are important predictors of positive outcomes. From Israel, it is suggested that the contact should be intimate rather than casual, and should involve groups whose initial attitudes towards each other are not extremely negative. Other examples abound in the other chapters.

Naturally, this proliferation of specifying conditions weakens the original contact hypothesis; indeed, it cries out for a broader, more generic theory on several grounds. Many of these suggested conditions make sense in the specific context under discussion, but do not necessarily generalize to other cultures. Hence, Wagner and Machleit's emphasis on voluntary contact does not appear to apply to school contact between black and white children in the United States (Crain and Mahard, 1978). More importantly, this growing string of limiting conditions threatens to remove all practical interest from the hypothesis. Contact theory would in time fall of its own weight. An ever-increasing list of conditions rapidly excludes the vast majority of intergroup situations in the world and renders the hypothesis trivial.

Put differently, contact theory and research have concentrated on avoiding Type I errors – false positives. Its numerous conditions remove from contention all too many situations where positive changes are not predicted. Far less attention has been granted Type II errors – false negatives. Groups interact in harmony throughout the world in situations that typically do not meet these stringent conditions. Yet beneficial effects – often modest, to be sure – seem generally to result. Social psychology has once again overexplained conflict, and, as we have seen in the Quebec, South African and Northern Ireland chapters, some positive contact can occur even under the restrictive circumstances imposed by major political conflict. The broader theory of intergroup contact, which is needed, must therefore be more than a listing of conditions and must account for the widespread degree of harmony as well as conflict between groups around the globe.

Cold cognition stressed to the near exclusion of affective factors

As a discipline that attempts to specify the processes that link the individual and structural levels of social analysis, social psychology must necessarily pay primary attention to cognitive phenomena. The dictum of W. I. Thomas (Thomas and Thomas, 1928) – 'If men define situations as real they are real in their consequences' – remains a corner-stone of social-psychological thinking. As such, social cognition, the study of how human beings 'define' their social world, understandably plays a central role in most of the discipline's theories. The exciting rise of cognitive theory and research in general psychology in recent decades enhanced socio-psychological work in this area. Social cognition has become a major sub-field in the discipline, one that both 'socializes' cognitive theory while it provides a fundamental basis for social-psychological theory generally. A problem arises however when these significant advances in both cognition and social cognition so overwhelm the field that affective considerations are virtually ignored.

The contact hypothesis is no exception. While emotional factors were included in Allport's (1954) early discussion, treatment of the hypothesis has lavished almost exclusive attention on the cognitive processes involved in contact. This neglect of affect may be more serious for contact theory than for other theoretical domains. After all, affect is a central component of the phenomenon and definition of intergroup prejudice: an *antipathy against* groups acompanied by faulty generalizations (Pettigrew, 1982, p. 3). To treat intergroup contact as if it were dealing simply with cold cognition is to slight what makes the entire area of intergroup conflict problematic – its *heat*.

This systematic bias is not directly addressed in this book: in fact, the bias is demonstrated throughout. Reicher's interesting analysis in chapter 9, for example employs cognitive concepts exclusively – 'categorization', 'meaningfulness of experience', etc. Consider too the important findings of the Allen and Stephenson (1985) study of industrial organizations. It assessed the social-psychological processes that help to explain 'the size effect' – the strong positive relationship between size of firm and labour-management 'friction'. As Allen describes, in chapter 8 of this book, these processes involve systematic misperceptions by both workers and managers whereby in smaller firms each group incorrectly sees the other as less extreme than the accepted general stereotypes. However, Allen notes, since these are in fact misperceptions and the general stereotypes are just as prevalent in the smaller firms, these typically 'quieter' situations are 'potentially unstable'. Indeed, when the small firms' labour–management relations do become strained, they often explode.

The point at issue is that Allen provides a singularly cognitive account of this phenomenon. Though it employs such affect-laden terms as 'expressive rewards', 'neighbourliness', 'friendly', and 'trust', his basic explanation is almost totally cognitive: attributed intergroup attitudes set the industrial scene for labour–management strife. I find this argument persuasive, but incomplete in its neglect of affect.[8] A more balanced affective–cognitive argument can also be advanced. Face-to-face contact between workers and managers in small firms tends to engender trust and some degree of mutual acceptance – even though by definition this interaction violates the status-equality requirement of contact theory. Social-psychological theory would anticipate this result for at least three reasons: the requirements of smooth and repeated interaction, the probable disconfirmation of the most harsh aspects of the negative outgroup stereotype and the public commitment created by the interaction with 'the enemy'. Using the critical Brown and Turner (1981) distinction, this trust and acceptance may well be justified on the basis of the *interpersonal* behaviour of individual actors. It proves wrong in *intergroup* issues, when the two sides act collectively and thus more ideologically. Tension in the firm should also enhance fraternal over egoist concerns (Walker and Pettigrew, 1984) and shift the relevant reference from the firm to the group. This is not a substitute for Allen's argument. Rather it is simply supplying a more balanced affective-cognitive account in addition to the exclusively cognitive one he describes. Not incidentally, this extension helps to account for the fact that when small firms do finally experience industrial strains they often erupt with greater heat than large firms: perceived betrayal is a strong emotion.

Future accounts of intergroup contact need to balance affective with cognitive considerations. A promising start in this direction is provided by Tajfel's (1982a) emphasis on social identity, since threats to identity have powerful emotional consequences. Hewstone and Brown pick up on this point in their chapter with their claim 'that motivational as well as cognitive factors underlie intergroup differentiation.' Yet even their extended model allows for varying 'cognitive processes at work in contact' (Stage V of their Model of intergroup contact), but no equivalent differentiation for levels of affective arousal.

Similarities stressed as social bonds to the near exclusion of differences

The sociological branches of social psychology note the operation of differences in social bonds with such concepts as role reciprocity. But the psychological branches have tended to focus on similarity as the key to social attraction. This one-sided emphasis is apparent throughout the intergroup contact literature. Following this tradition, Brewer and Miller (1984) attend excusively to mechanical solidarity – similarity at the interpersonal level – in their recent model of intergroup contact.

In their 'conceptual framework', Brewer and Miller elaborate Tajfel's use of both social categorization and social comparison ideas. Their chief thrust is to reinterpret contact theory in terms of the salience of social categories. In their examination of the conditions related to group salience, these authors maintain that *differentiation* and *personalization* are the principal features of decategorization. An interesting aspect of their argument is their insistence that these features should be sharply distinguished, that 'differentiation [is] a necessary but not sufficient condition for personalization' (Brewer and Miller, 1984, p. 288). They then apply their framework to explain in salience terms the various conditions under which intergroup contact leads to reduced prejudice and discrimination. In particular, they join the numerous theorists who emphasize the significance of cross-cutting social bonds. Such bonds blur group boundaries and thereby render group categories less salient. Note that the two fundamental concepts of their analysis, differentiation and personalization, apply only to cognitive states at the interpersonal level. The decategorization of groups is the desired result from which reduced intergroup prejudice and discrimination can be anticipated.

The virtue of this formulation, one often missing in social-psychological theory, is that it leads to several clear and falsifiable predictions. One such derivable prediction of special interest to this discussion is: *any aspects internal or external to the contact situation that act to heighten group categorization will result in negative intergroup effects.* Brewer and Miller (1984) cite supporting evidence from a variety of experimental investigations at the interpersonal level. However, they do not explore the many apparent exceptions to their cognitive predictions.[9] Consider first the Crain and Mahard (1982) survey of students and teachers in 1975 bi-racial high schools in American southern states. They found that community conflict early in the desegregation process is associated with *less* racial tension and black student alienation a few years later.

Why? Since Brewer and Miller (1984) assume that conflict increases the salience of race, greater tension and alienation should have resulted. A parsimonious explanation is ruled out by the fact that early conflict is not related to improved school practices. Crain and Mahard (1982, p. 697) conclude that 'conflict had led to stronger cohesion within the black community and greater support for school desegregation among blacks, which in turn led to less tension in the schools.' In other words, these investigators see the enhancement of *group* cohesion as a positive force in this type of highly charged situation. Presumably, early conflict *did* create heightened salience, but this led to positive rather than negative outcomes for the intergroup contact.

The voluntary nature of intergroup contact provides another illustration. Wagner and Machleit report that only voluntary contact between

Germans and foreigners seems to be associated with lessened prejudice. This finding is consistent with the Brewer and Miller (1984, p. 295) analysis, for they endorse the importance of voluntary contact as one means of reducing group category salience. However, once again Crain and Mahard (1978), in their meta-analysis of school desegregation effects, cast doubt on the universality of this finding.[10] Black achievement gains from school desegregation appear to be as high or higher on average in *non-voluntary* desegregation programmes as in voluntary programmes.

In her chapter on racial contact in American schools, Schofield outlines the practical problems of the colour-blind perspective – which, as Hewstone and Brown point out, is essentially what Brewer and Miller advocate for intergroup contact generally. Schofield notes how the perspective, when carried to the point of a normative taboo against any reference to race, can inhibit 'constructive problem solving'. Further, she argues, the colour-blind approach is 'at odds with reality'. In a society where race and skin colour are salient perceptual features, such insistence on racial denial endangers the learning of the critical lesson that race is basically an irrelevant social category.

Nor are these reversals to Brewer–Miller predictions limited to field research on the racial desegregation of schools in the United States. Hewstone and Brown cite two relevant experimental studies. Group categorization should be *more* likely when the outgroup member with whom one is interacting is thought to be 'typical' of the outgroup. Yet, counter to the Brewer–Miller model, Wilder (1984) found that a significant improvement in the evaluation of an outgroup occurred only after a pleasant encounter with a 'typical' outgrouper. Likewise, Weber and Crocker (1983) demontrated that their subject's stereotypes of 'corporate lawyers' were altered more by disconfirming instances who were representative of the group. Since a group's distribution of traits is largely unknown, outgroup typicality must necessarily involve stereotypic traits that generally distinguish the outgroup from the ingroup. Here we see a genuine conflict between the interpersonal and intergroup levels. Considerable evidence supports the Brewer–Miller contentions of the importance of group categorization at the interpersonal level: in general, liking and acceptance at the personal level is enhanced by similarities and lowered salience of group membership.[11] Yet the opposite is often the case at the intergroup level. That is atypical outgroupers may be more readily accepted at the interpersonal level, but their very atypicality limits the generalization of this change at the intergroup level. Similarities and differences are therefore both important, and we need a broader theory of intergroup contact that addresses the complex trade-offs between them.

This is the significance of the formulation advanced in these pages by Hewstone and Brown. Building on Tajfel's (1982a) social identity theory (as did Brewer and Miller) as well as the firm distinction of Brown and Turner (1981) between the interpersonal and intergroup levels of analysis, they offer the broadest model yet proposed for intergroup contact. It addresses several weaknesses of the current contact hypothesis. However, its special contributions lie in its emphasis on differences as well as similarities and in its ability to account at the intergroup level for findings that are anomalous at the interpersonal level.

The Hewstone–Brown model is as yet untested. It seems premature, as Ben-Ari and Amir do in chapter 2, to compare it with the Brewer–Miller model. Indeed, as the present formulation largely subsumes the earlier effort, they are not directly competing theories. It accepts the accumulated evidence in support of group decategorization at the interpersonal level, but it holds the cognitive emphasis on interpersonal similarity to be only part of the story. The ultimately more critical intergroup level, Hewstone and Brown contend, has been either ignored or confused with interpersonal dynamics – not just by Brewer and Miller, but by virtually all contact theorists from the 1950s onwards.

The critical test comes with the group generalization of the interpersonal effects of contact. The difficulty of obtaining group generalization was recognized by Allport (1954) and most of the writers on contact who have followed him. None the less, the Hewstone–Brown formulation allows specific predictions of when group generalization can be expected to follow from interpersonal effects: only when group categorization *is* invoked – as when the individual is seen as representative of the outgroup. Following along the lines established by Wilder's (1984) investigation, future research must focus on this clarifying conjecture. In doing so, two modifying points may prove important: the first, specifying the links between the interpersonal and intergroup levels, and the second, the time sequence of intergroup contact.

1 To make their critical distinction clear, Brown and Turner (1981) and now Hewstone and Brown draw a rather firm boundary between the two levels of analysis. I suspect their demarcation is too firmly drawn, and that this could cause future workers to overlook the many important connections between the interpersonal and intergroup realms. Indeed, the specification of these connections should be a prime focus of attention by contact investigators.

Cook (1984, p. 183) provides an illustration of such a link. In an extended series of skilful experiments, he confirms earlier research: 'task interdependence induces cooperative, friendly behavior and develops liking and respect for one's [multi-ethnic] groupmates.' However, Cook goes further. His studies introduce explicit procedures for ensuring that participants understand how the adoption of equalitarian social policies make it less likely that their new friends from the outgroup will encounter discrimination and prejudice. He shows that this individuation procedure promotes 'the generalization of positive affect felt for other-ethnic friends to race-relations policies that would benefit them.' In other words, using the vivid case of the well-liked outgrouper as 'the foot in¯ the door', Cook achieves generalization to the outgroup itself by deliberately making group categorization salient in order to personalize prejudice and discrimination. Widespread anecdotal evidence suggests that this laboratory procedure is not an uncommon occurrence in modern society, and the method reveals how closely entwined the interpersonal and intergroup levels are in practice.

2   The time-sequence of intergroup contact: the Cook technique for enhancing generalization from outgrouper to outgroup suggests that we consider the Hewstone–Brown model in a sequential perspective. In 'the bottom-up', micro-to-macro model of change, the initial emphasis is placed on interpersonal attraction. Here the traditional analyses of contact conditions as well as the Brewer–Miller focus on group decategorization retain their force. However, as Hewstone and Brown insist, for the success of this initial contact to have intergroup consequences, the later phases must make group membership salient. In 'the top-down', macro-to-micro model of change, this sequence is reversed. The surprising benefits of interracial tension prior to contact in desegregated schools, previously noted, afford an example (Crain and Mahard, 1982). Future work in this area should therefore adopt a longer, sequential perspective than most earlier efforts did. It is not so much a test between the more traditional Brewer–Miller model and the newer Hewstone–Brown model as it is a test of *when* in the contact each is optimally effective.

An emphasis on isolated, rather than cumulative, effects

Following from the sequential point, contact theory and research resemble much of social-psychological work in their focus on relatively isolated effects. To be sure, contact studies have investigated both changed attitudes and behaviour, but typically they have done so by looking at intergroup contact in a fixed, non-cumulative manner. Allen's approach to labour–management situations seems appropriate for contact situations generally:

behaviour in the firm is the result of interaction between the sides over time and . . . the situation is not only perceived by both sides in ways reflecting their positions but . . . mutual perceptions of one another contribute to a tradition of interpretation in the firm that helps pre-define situations and determine outcomes. (p. 147)

Contact situations do not occur *de nova*. They have a history, 'a tradition of interpretation' that 'pre-defines' and shapes the intergroup interaction. Obvious as this point may appear, most contact studies have ignored it. Its recognition however raises the distinct possibility that the measurement of isolated consequences of a single contact episode will fail to detect more subtle, latent effects that become manifest only after repeated contact situations. This possibility is relevant to the central issue of generalization highlighted by Hewstone and Brown. There may well be *cumulative* effects across repeated contact situations involving varying people and social contexts. Learning theory predicts such an accumulation, and Sherif's (1966a) famous 'Robbers Cave' study provides evidence for precisely such a phenomenon.

After developing intense conflict between two groups of young boys, Sherif and his associates set out to reduce the social distance, hostile attitudes and negative stereotypes that had arisen between them. The central focus of the investigation was to demonstrate the efficacy of co-operative contact in the pursuit of *superordinate* goals – goals unattainable by one group alone. With such joint experiences as fixing the broken water-supply system, working together to afford attendance at a jointly chosen motion picture and pulling a rope together to start up a truck for a picnic, intergroup conflict between the 'Eagles' and the 'Rattlers' was sharply reduced. However, what is often overlooked about this famous finding is that these co-operative efforts considered singly did not achieve the dramatic change. It was a gradual, *cumulative* effect. The attainment of the first superordinate goal, the plumbing repairs, aroused 'good spirits' at the time, but 'the groups fell back on their old recriminations once the immediate crisis was over' (Sherif, 1966, p. 89). Sherif writes:

Joint efforts in situations such as these did not *immediately* dispel hostility. But gradually, the series of activities requiring interdependent action reduced conflict and hostility between the groups. . . . A series of cooperative activities towards superordinate goals has a cumulative effect on reducing intergroup hostility. This cumulative effect involves the successful development of procedures for cooperating in specific activities and their transfer to new situations, so the established modes of intergroup cooperation are recognized. (Sherif, 1966, pp. 89, 93)

Compare Sherif's cumulative effect finding with the many contact examples described in this book. The vast majority of the contact situations that did not have positive consequences possess several characteristics in common:

1   They violated one or more of Allport's (1954) critical four conditions (especially the requirement for authority sanction).
2   If they did achieve positive interpersonal bonds, these changes failed to generalize to the intergroup level because of the systematic denial of group salience (the Hewstone and Brown emphasis).
3   They consisted largely of brief, often one-off contact situations that did not permit *cumulative* effects to develop

It is this third factor that has not been emphasized enough. It helps to account for the numerous striking exceptions that are reported in these pages. Recall the surprisingly positive interpersonal results from Russell's (1961) intergroup neighbourhood in Durban, South Africa and Lockhart and Elliott's (1980) five-week-long residential assessment centre for young offenders in Northern Ireland. Prolonged contact in neighbourhoods and 'total institutions' are ideal settings for cumulative effects to occur.

Untested assumptions of universality across time, situations and cultures

The contact hypothesis is as easily challenged on this count as most social-psychological theories. We noted, when tracing the history of the hypothesis, that contact theory was originally set in the special, post-World War II context of slowly improving American race relations. Early papers were blunt in their value concerns and direct in their application toward the eradication of racial segregation policies. Necessarily, these initial statements of the contact hypothesis assumed the conditions of US black–white relations of their time. They expressed an optimism borne of structural reform and fitted to a unique minority that sought only equal treatment rather than fundamental power alterations. Such optimism and restricted reform do not generally characterize intergroup relations in the world today – as indicated by the pessimistic tone of this book.

The chapters on Israel, Northern Ireland and South Africa make clear the many differences from the American scene that colour intergroup interaction in these embattled countries; and Reicher provides a detailed account of the special characteristics of race relations in the United Kingdom. His analysis highlights the many contrasts between the racial patterns of the UK and the US. In particular, racial minorities in Britain have far higher rates of intermarriage with Caucasians, while at the same time they are not seen as truly 'belonging' to the country as are black Americans (Landes, 1955). Reicher also stresses the cultural distinctiveness of the Asian minorities in Britain. Using an argument that resembles ethnomethodological analysis (Garfinkel, 1967; Handel, 1982), he concludes that the typical conditions for intergroup contact in the United Kingdom make it 'most unlikely to have favourable consequences'. He believes the American-cast hypothesis does not allow direct extrapolation to such a different situation. The simple effects of the 'multiplicity of variables . . . were not fully understood, their interactions even less so.'

Reicher's conclusion is repeated in varying degrees in most of the previous chapters and requires discussion. However, first a small caveat is in order. Some examples cited against the original statements of contact theory are irrelevant. Cases of intergroup contact that failed to lead to positive effects are cited without their conditions being specified. Such cases of course are irrelevant since they could potentially confirm Allport's (1954) contentions if any of his four conditions were violated. The use of such examples slips back to the erroneous notion that the contact hypothesis generally predicted positive effects. As noted above, the problem with the theory is quite the reverse: the hypothesis, as originally stated, is too restrictive and unconcerned with type II errors. Moreover, 'racial compositions' and group percentages in an area or an institution cannot be used as surrogate measures for actual intergroup contact and interaction.

This caveat aside, significant challenges to the original statements of contact theory are effectively made throughout this book. One way to view these challenges is to see them as illustrations of the importance of the broader social context of the intergroup contact.[12] The limited laundry list of conditions that constituted the first statements of contact theory fitted the applied needs of the American scene in a time of progressive change. They helped to clarify for instance the difference between a merely racially 'desegregated' school and a truly 'integrated' school (Pettigrew, 1971). However, this listing did not meet the needs of a broader, generic theory that was equally applicable to other societies and times. It was however an important first step – one that both the Brewer–Miller and Hewstone–Brown models have built upon.

There are two additional implications for intergroup attitudes and behaviour. *Contact is not the only – in fact, it is probably not even the principal – mechanism of social influence across social groups.* The social-psychological literature on social influence is rich in possibilities, and intergroup relations studies provide numerous examples of their operation. Hewstone and Brown mention several such mechanisms that in practice often boost the effects of contact – 'the achievement of superordinate goals, co-operation, cross-cutting categories or the manipulation of expectation states'. These and other influence processes also often operate without any face-to-face contact whatsoever.

Consider how intergroup contact is not the prime variable for attitude change in research on the residential desegregation of blacks and whites in the United States. Using longitudinal data from suburban neighbourhoods, Hamilton, Carpenter and Bishop (1984, p. 116) found after one year that 'the experience of having black neighbors had a positive effect on the white residents' racial attitudes . . . .' Nevertheless, intergroup contact during this period was minimal. Reminiscent of Thibaut and Kelley's (1959) concept of 'comparison of alternatives', Hamilton and his colleagues believe the effect was generated by a disconfirmation of highly negative expectancies – a process that helps to explain many similar findings in American race relations research. Racial segregation has generated such deep fears in America that even less than ideal desegregation can dispel them without significant contact. However, once again the social context is critical. The Hamilton study took place at a time of positive national change and with middle-class blacks who did indeed alleviate the fears of the middle-class whites. Foster and Finchilescu remind us that in South Africa the social context makes it likely that racial fears will be confirmed rather than disconfirmed in comparable situations.

Public commitment to another primary mechanism of social influence that requires no direct contact. Major shifts in white support of racially desegregated schools occurred in the United States after, and not before, the schools in an area were desegregated (e.g. Jacobson, 1978). These changes were especially notable among white parents of the schoolchildren involved, although they were obviously not directly involved in the intergroup contact. However, their act, in daily public view, of sending their children to the interracial school was deeply committing in the midst of controversy and opposition to the change in the white community. The same influence principles help to explain the fact that white parents who sent their children to other schools often became more resistant to racial change (Jacobson, 1978).

Mass-media communication also gets involved. Much is made of the ways the media contribute to group stereotypes, most of which are formed without contact with the stereotyped outgroup. Yet they can also play a role in improving intergroup images when they communicate information that indicates common humanity across group lines. Dramatic events are especially salient. One quasi-experiment studied the effects of the murder of Dr Martin Luther King, Jr on the attitudes of white Texans towards racial change. This tragic and much-publicized event in 1968 caused significant shifts towards a greater acceptance of change, but the general trend masked several phenomena. Just as social judgement theory would predict (Sherif and Hovland, 1961), counter-ceiling effects emerged for both respondents and types of attitudes. Those types of white Texans who were already among the most accepting of racial change prior to King's murder showed the most positive shifts; those types of racial change that were the most favoured prior to the murder were those that gained even more acceptance after the murder (Riley and Pettigrew, 1976).

The operation of social influence sources that do not require contact is therefore one response to the pessimism of this book. To be sure, many of these other sources are no more likely than contact to be powerful mechanisms for intergroup change in such strife-torn societies as Israel, Northern Ireland and South Africa. That obvious fact raises the second and more generic response to this book's tone – a response that is indeed documented throughout it. *The use of intergroup contact as a means of alleviating conflict is largely dependent on the societal structure that patterns relations between the groups.*

If the optimal situational conditions of contact theory can be met, it usually signifies that the important structural issues, from power to resource allocations, have already been equitably worked out. Put differently, contact theory – like most social-psychological processes – does not typically have causal primacy. In broad strokes, the top-down theory of social change generally applies. For a variety of reasons, the structure of intergroup relations typically initiates change and triggers micro-processes that lead to the accommodation of individuals to the changes and in turn to a favourable climate for further structural changes (the bottom-up side of the cycle). Within this context, social psychology makes its essential contribution to social change theory by specifying those micro-processes that translate institutional alterations into individual change and back again. For intergroup relations, face-to-face contact is one, but just one among many, of those micro-processes.

From this perspective, the role of social-psychological theory is more modest than some would have it. Like other social-scientific disciplines, social psychology carves out only a slice of the pie and can contribute only part of the answer to the riddle of social life. This view agrees with the many authors of this book, particularly Reicher, who stress the importance of structure and the larger social context. It differs from several of them however in expecting less from social-psychological theories; it therefore leads to less despair over the failure of contact and similar micro-theories to account for the wide range of intergroup relations found throughout the globe.

The absence of bold generic theory that links various levels of analysis

Contact theory has been a typical middle-range theory. It is hoped that this book will serve to stimulate its development into a bolder, broader statement that more closely resembles what Popper suggests is the hallmark of more testable theories in science. Hewstone and Brown's enlargement of it widens its scope considerably. Allen extends it to labour-management interaction. Taylor and his colleagues as well as Trew extend it further to cover the apparently harmonious intergroup interactions that take place in the midst of considerable tension. Other chapters broaden its cross-cultural base by following through its operation from West Germany and Israel to South Africa.

Responding to these interesting arguments, this chapter's discussion leads to eight suggested directions that this bolder contact theory of the future might profitably pursue.

1   Rather than consisting of simply a loose listing of highly limited conditions, new theoretical treatments of intergroup contact must account for the widespread degree of harmony as well as conflict between groups. Type II errors must therefore be considered in addition to Type I errors.
2   Future contact theorizing must balance affective and motivational concerns with cognitive factors.
3   Perceived group differences in addition to similarities should be accounted for in models. This direction is intimately related to the problem of generalization across both situations and people. Building on previous interpersonal theories of contact, Hewstone and Brown offer a promising and testable model that directly confronts these issues.
4   The next task is a careful specification of the links between the interpersonal and intergroup levels.
5   A sequential perspective may help to address the trade-off between similarities and differences at the interpersonal and intergroup levels of analysis.
6   Intergroup contact theory and research of the future should assess cumulative effects over repeated contact, rather than simply looking for isolated effects from one-off contact situations.
7   Another promising direction would involve work that systematically compares the intergroup changes that result from direct contact with

changes that result from other processes of social influence that do not require face-to-face interaction.

8   To overcome its special vulnerability to differences across time, cultures and societies, future approaches to intergroup contact need to include explicit structural considerations. This requirement could be modestly met by placing the theory within a particular structural context. However, to secure greater scope, contact theory needs to include varying structural specifications as integral parts of the theory itself.

NOTES

1   I omit Gergen's (1973) historical criticism of social-psychological theory: 'theories of social behavior are primarily reflections of contemporary history' and therefore their 'premises are often invalidated' over time. At a broad level, this argument can be viewed as a special case of what Karl Popper (1957) terms 'historicism'; And I agree with both Popper's (1957) and Urbach's (1985) rejections of this perspective. At a narrower level, Gergen's argument is a special-case call for social-psychological theory and research to be nested systematically in their macro-social contexts. In this second interpretation, I regard Gergen's criticism to be correct, but it is more precisely stated generically, for the needed social contexts vary not only across time but across cultures and situations in the same time.

2   Bales (1970) offers a rare and explicit attempt to include both approaches. While his is fundamentally a bottom-up theory, he ingeniously employs a three-dimensional-space analysis that focuses specifically on self-analytic groups. Within this situational context, Bales carefully developed, over decades of theory-directed investigation, a system that simultaneously looks at personality (as 27 interacting types), role structure (as with his famous distinction between task-oriented and socio-emotional roles) and group structure (with a direct analysis of group interaction). Significantly, Bales (1940) began his career by writing a Masters thesis on 'The Concept "Situation" as a Methodological Tool'. The richness and rarity of Bales's important contribution supports the argument proposed in this chapter; indeed, this work helped to shape these views.

3   In an interesting paper directed to the problem of establishing links betwen the micro- and macro-levels of analysis, Coleman (1983) emphasizes the critical difference in these two types of social factors. He demonstrates how the 'pseudo-macro' aggregations of individual data create special problems for both method and theory. He also decries the widespread use in sociology of such variables. However, in social psychology the use of such variables as indicators of situational structure is even more prevalent and their limitations less appreciated.

4   Though it was largely developed after the initial statements of the contact

hypothesis by Williams (1947) and Allport (1954), balance theory offers a generic approach to the problem at the micro-level of individual dynamics. Each of the prejudice-reducing situational conditions listed by various writers on intergroup contact can be viewed as a structural inducement for initiating the development and perception of similarities across groups. Consequently, the operation of these structural arrangements is intended to produce positive 'balance' in the sense of such theorists as Heider (1958). This relationship reveals clearly how the contact hypothesis is yet another social-psychological theory that depends almost exclusively on mechanical solidarity (Davis, 1963).

5   A representative statement of this movement can be found in Kilpatrick and Van Til's (1947) edited book, *Intercultural Attitudes in the Making*. It addresses 'parents, youth leaders, and teachers,' provides educational means of combating prejudice, omits mention of structural changes in society and yet aims 'to build sound democratic relations for the future'.

6   There may also be a counter-selective migration phenomenon operating in Quebec among francophones. Although the proportion of the group affected must necessarily be smaller, it is reasonable to conjecture that those francophones most at ease in the English-speaking world are more likely to migrate out of the Province to other parts of Canada and to the United States in search of wider economic opportunities. If true, this selectivity would leave behind in Quebec those francophones least comfortable in intergroup interaction.

7   Some of the mistranslation of Allport has political motivations. A few American social scientists, paid by school systems to defend racially segregated schools, prefer to stress status equality in the larger society as a necessary condition for effective interracial contact as a reason for limiting desegregation plans to the minority of black children who come from middle-class homes (Pettigrew et al., 1973).

8   Parts of Allen's analysis, especially those that assume that widespread industrial conflict is a natural state of affairs, reflect the intense labour-management tensions in Great Britain. Some Western nations, lacking the sharp class conflict that underlies British industrial relations, have remarkably little strife. The Netherlands for example has a strike record that is a fraction of that of the UK, partly as a result of a cultural tradition of protracted negotiation between labour and management.

9   Though they cite them once in another context, Brewer and Miller (1984, p. 282) make no use whatsoever of the interpersonal–intergroup distinction of Brown and Turner (1981).

10   Interestingly, Brewer and Miller (1984, p. 286) regard the racial desegregation of American schools as a prime example of institutional change that leads to situations that accentuate group categorization. This belief may explain Miller's role in several school desegregation court suits as an expert witness representing urban school systems defending their racially segregated schools. At any rate, they overlook the many research reports on this much-studied phenomenon, such as the Crain and Mahard (1978; 1982)

studies, that appear to falsify – or at least modify – their basic categorization salience predictions.

11 Even at the interpersonal level however differences can be important too. Recall the many examples from the interpersonal attraction and social influence research literatures where differences are valued over similarities. For example under conditions when the 'implications for self-esteem are heightened, it is easier to like the dissimilr person who dislikes us than the similar person' (Jones, Bell and Aronson, 1972, p. 176).

12 Hewstone and Brown regard it as a mere 'truism that any social behaviour must be located in a social context.' At the level of lip-service within social psychology, they are certainly correct, but in actual practice, it is a 'truism' that is generally ignored.

References

Adam, H. (1971) *Modernizing Racial Domination*. Berkeley: University of California Press.

Adar, L., and Adler, H. (1965) *Education for Values in Schools for Immigrant Children*. Jerusalem: The Hebrew University, School of Education.

Adorno, T. W., Frenkel-Brunswik, E., Levinson, D. J. and Sanford, R. N. (1950) *The Authoritarian Personality*. New York: Harper and Row.

Alevy, D. L., Bunker, B. B., Doob, L. W., Foltz, W. J., French, W., Klein, E. B. and Miller, J. C. (1974) Rationale research and role relations in the Stirling Workshop. *Journal of Conflict Resolution*, *18*(2), 276–84.

Allen, P. T. (1981) Behaviour and Imagery of a 'traditional' Workforce. PhD Thesis, University of Southampton.

Allen, P. T. (1982) Size of Workforce, Morale and Absenteeism. *British Journal of Industrial Relations*, *20*(1), 83–100.

Allen, P. T. (1983) Understanding in Industry: Who gets it right? *Employee Relations*, *5*(3), 13–16.

Allen, P. T. (1984) The class imagery of 'traditional proletarians'. *British Journal of Sociology*, *35*(1), 93–111.

Allen, P. T. and Stephenson, G. M. (1983) Inter-group understanding and size of organisations. *British Journal of Industrial Relations*, *21*(3), 312–29.

Allen, P. T. and Stephenson, G. M. (1985) The relationship of inter-group understanding and inter-party friction in industry. *British Journal of Industrial Relations*, *23*(2), 203–13.

Allen, V. L. and Wilder, D. A. (1975) Categorisation, belief similarity, and intergroup discrimination. *Journal of Personality and Social Psychology*, *32*(6), 971–7.

Allport, G. W. (1954/1979 ed.) *The Nature of Prejudice*. Cambridge/Reading, MA: Addison-Wesley.

Alverson, H. (1970) Labour migrants in South African industry. In R. F. Spencer (ed.), *Migration and Anthropology*. Seattle: University of Washington Press.

Amir, Y. (1969) Contact hypothesis in ethnic relations. *Psychological Bulletin*, *71*, 319–42.

Amir, Y. (1976) The role of intergroup contact in change of prejudice and ethnic relations. In P. A. Katz (ed.), *Towards the Elimination of Racism*. Elmsford, N.Y.: Pergamon Press.

Amir, Y. (1979) Interpersonal contact between Arabs and Israelis. *The Jerusalem Quarterly*, *13*, 3–17.

Amir, Y. and Ben-Ari, R. (1985) International tourism, ethnic contact and attitude change. *Journal of Social Issues*, *41*(3), 105–15.

Amir, Y., Ben-Ari, R., Bizman, A. and Rivner, M. (1982) Objective versus subjective aspects of interpersonal relations between Jews and Arabs. *Journal of Conflict Resolution*, *26*, 485–506.

Amir, Y., Bizman, A., Ben-Ari, R. and Rivner, M. (1980) Contact between Israelis and Arabs: a theoretical evaluation of effects. *Journal of Cross-Cultural Psychology*, *11*, 426–43.

Archer, R. and Bouillon, A. (1982) *The South African Game: Sport and Racism*. London: Zed Press.

Aronson, E., Blaney, N., Stephan, C., Sikes, J. and Snapp, M. (1978) *The Jigsaw Classroom*. Beverly Hills: Sage.

Arrington, K. M. (1981) *With All Deliberate Speed: 1954–19??*. Washington, DC: United States Commission on Civil Rights Clearinghouse (Publication 69).

Asch, S. (1951) Effects of group pressure on the modification and distortion of judgments. In H. Guetzkow (ed.), *Groups, Leadership and Men*. Pittsburgh: Carnegie Press.

Ashmore, R. D. (1970) Solving the problem of prejudice. In B. E. Collins (ed.), *Social Psychology*. Reading, MA: Addison-Wesley.

Bagley, C. (1972) Patterns of inter-ethnic marriage in Britain. *Phylon*, *4*, 373–9.

Bagley, C. and Verma, G. (1978) Development, norms and factorial validity of scales for measuring racial attitudes in adolescents in multi-ethnic settings. *Educational Studies*, *4*, 189–200.

Bagley, C. and Verma, G. (1979) *Racial Prejudice, the Individual and Society*. Farnborough: Saxon House.

Bain, G. S. and Clegg, H. (1974) A strategy for industrial relations research in Great Britain. *British Journal of Industrial Relations*, *12*, 91–114.

Bales, R. F. (1940) The concept 'situation' as a methodological tool. Unpublished Masters thesis, University of Oregon, Eugene, OR.

Bales, R. F. (1970) *Personality and Interpersonal Behavior*. New York: Holt, Rinehart and Winston.

Banton, M. (1983) The influence of colonial status upon Black-White relations in England, 1948–1958. *Sociology*, *17*, 546–59.

Barker, M. (1981) *The New Racism*. Frederick, MD: University Publications of America.

Batstone, E., Boraston, I. and Frenkel, S. (1978) *The Social Organisation of Strikes*. Oxford: Basil Blackwell.

Beattie, G. W. (1979) The 'troubles' in Northern Ireland. *Bulletin of the British Psychological Society*, *32*, 249–52.

Bellerose, J., Hafer, C. and Taylor, D. M. (1984) The nature of contact between anglophones and francophones in Quebec. Unpublished manuscript, McGill University.

Bellerose, J. and Taylor, D. M. (1984) Interpersonal harmony in the context of intergroup conflict. Paper presented at the Canadian Psychological Association meeting, Ottawa.

Benjamin, A. (1970) *A Report on a Sensitivity Training Workshop for Arabs and Jewish Students*. Haifa: The American Jewish Committee and B'nai B'rith Hillel Foundation.

Benyamini, K. (1980) The image of the Arab in the eyes of Israeli youth: changes over the past 15 years. *Studies in Education*, 27, 65–74.

Berger, C. R. and Calabrese, R. J. (1975) Some explorations in initial interaction and beyond: toward a developmental theory of interpersonal communication. *Human Communication Research*, 1, 99–112.

Berger, J., Cohen, S. P. and Zelditch, M. (1972) Status characteristics and social interaction. *American Sociological Review*, 37, 241–55.

Bergius, R., Werbik, H., Winter, G. and Schubring, G. (1970) Urteile deutscher Arbeitnehmer über Völker in Relation zur Zahl ihrer ausländischen Bekannten. *Psychologische Beiträge*, 12, 485–532.

Berry, J. W. (1984) Cultural relations in plural societies: alternatives to segregation and their sociopsychological implications. In N. Miller and M. B. Brewer (eds), *Groups in Contact: The Psychology of Desegregation*. New York: Academic Press.

Biko, S. (1978) *I Write What I Like*. London: Heinemann.

Biesanz, J. and Smith, L. M. (1951) Race relations of Panama and the Canal Zone. *American Journal of Sociology*, 57, 7–14.

Billig, M. (1976) *Social Psychology and Intergroup Relations*. London: Academic Press.

Billig, M. (1978) *Fascists: A Social Psychological View of the National Front*. London: Academic Press.

Bizman, A. (1978) Status similarity, status level and the reduction of prejudice following contact between national groups. Unpublished doctoral dissertation, Bar-Ilan University, Ramat-Gan, Israel.

Blalock, H. M. (1967) *Toward a Theory of Minority Group Relations*. New York: Wiley.

Blalock, H. M. (1982) *Race and Ethnic Relations*. Englewood Cliffs, NJ: Prentice-Hall.

Blanchard, F. A., Adelman, L. and Cook, S. W. (1975) The effect of group success and failure upon interpersonal attraction in co-operating interracial groups. *Journal of Personality and Social Psychology*, 31, 1020–30.

Boal, F. W. (1982) Segregating and Mixing: space and residence in Belfast. In F. W. Boal and J. N. M. Douglas (eds), *Integration and Division: Geographic Aspects of the Northern Ireland Problem*. Middlesex: Head Press.

Boehringer, E. H., Bayley, J., Zeruolis, V. and Boehringer, K. (1974) Stirling: The destructive application of group techniques to a conflict. *Journal of Conflict Resolution*, 18(2), 257–75.

Bogardus, E. S. (1925) Measuring social distance. *Journal of Applied Sociology*, 9, 299–308.

Boos-Nünning, U. (1981) Muttersprachliche Klassen für ausländische Kinder:

Eine kritische Diskussion des bayerischen 'Offenen Modells'. *Deutsch lernen*, 2, 40–70.

Bourhis, R. Y. (1984) *Conflict and Language Planning in Quebec*. Clevedon, England: Multilingual Matters.

Bradburn, N. M., Sudman, S. and Gockel, G. L. (1971) *Side by Side: Integrated Neighborhoods in America*. Chicago: Quadrangle Books.

Brehm, J. W. and Cohen, A. R. (1962) *Explorations in Cognitive Dissonance*. New York: Wiley.

Brewer, M. B. (1979) In-group bias in the minimal intergroup situation: a cognitive-motivational analysis. *Psychological Bulletin*, 86, 307–34.

Brewer, M. B. and Campbell, D. T. (1976) *Ethnocentrism and Intergroup Attitudes: East African Evidence*. New York: Halstead Press.

Brewer, M. B. and Miller, N. (1984) Beyond the contact hypothesis: theoretical perspectives on desegregation. In N. Miller and M. B. Brewer (eds), *Groups in Contact: The Psychology of Desegregation*. New York: Academic Press.

Brigham, J. C. (1971) Ethnic stereotypes. *Psychological Bulletin*, 76, 15–38.

Brislin, R. and Pedersen, P. (1976) *Cross-Cultural Orientation Programs*. New York: Wiley/Halsted.

Brophy, I. N. (1946) The luxury of anti-Negro prejudice. *Public Opinion Quarterly*, 9, 456–66.

Brown, R. (1978) Divided we fall: an analysis of relations between sections of a factory workforce. In H. Tajfel (ed.), *Differentiation Between Social Groups*. London: Academic Press.

Brown, R. J. (1984) The effects of intergroup similarity and co-operative vs. competitive orientation on intergroup discrimination. *British Journal of Social Psychology*, 23, 21–33.

Brown, R. and Abrams, D. (1986) The effects of intergroup similarity and goal interdependence on intergroup attitudes and task performance. *Journal of Experimental Social Psychology*, 22, 78–92.

Brown, R. J. and Turner, J. C. (1979) The criss-cross categorisation effect in intergroup discrimination. *British Journal of Social and Clinical Psychology*, 18, 371–83.

Brown, R. and Turner, J. C. (1981) Interpersonal and intergroup behaviour. In J. Turner and H. Giles (eds), *Intergroup Behaviour*. Oxford: Basil Blackwell.

Brown, R. and Wade, G. (1986) Superordinate goals and intergroup behaviour: the effects of role ambiguity and status on intergroup attitudes and task performance. *European Journal of Social Psychology*, in press.

Brown, W. (ed.) (1981) *The Changing Contours of British Industrial Relations*. Oxford: Basil Blackwell.

Brown, W. G. (1934) Culture contact and race conflict. In E. B. Reuter (ed.), *Race and Culture Contacts*. New York: McGraw-Hill.

Bruner, J. S. (1957) On perceptual readiness. *Psychological Review*, 64, 123–51.

Buchanan, R. H. (1982) The planter and the Gael: cultural dimensions of the Northern Ireland Problem. In F. W. Boal and J. N. H. Douglas (eds), *Integration and Division: Geographical Aspects of the Northern Ireland Problem*. Middlesex: Head Press.

Bulmer, M. (ed.) (1975) *Working-Class Images of Society*. London: Routledge & Kegan Paul.

Bundesminister für Arbeit und Sozialordnung (1980) *Untersuchung von Möglichkeiten der außerschulischen Integration ausländischer Kinder und Jugendlicher vor dem Hintergrund spezifischer Sozialisationsbedingungen*. Bonn: Bundesminister für Arbeit und Sozialordnung.

Bundesminister des Innern (1983) *Aufzeichnung zur Ausländerpolitik und zum Ausländerrecht in der Bundesrepublik Deutschland*. Aktenzeichen V II – 937 020/19.

Burton, F. (1978) *The Politics of Legitimacy: Struggles in a Belfast Community*. London: Routledge & Kegan Paul.

Byrne, D. (1969) Attitudes and attraction. In L. Berkowitz (ed.) *Advances in Experimental Social Psychology*. New York: Academic Press, vol. 4.

Byrne, D. (1971) *The Attraction Paradigm*. New York: Academic Press.

Cagle, L. T. (1973) Interracial housing: a reassessment of the equal-status contact hypothesis. *Sociology and Social Research*, 57, 342–55.

Cairns, E. (1980) The development of ethnic discrimination in children in Northern Ireland. In J. Harbison and J. Harbison (eds) *A Society under Stress*. Somerset: Open Books.

Campbell, A. (1971) *White Attitudes Toward Black People*. Ann Arbor: Institute for Social Research.

Castles, S., Booth, H. and Wallace, T. (1984) *Here for Good: Western Europe's New Ethnic Minorities*. London: Pluto Press.

Clark, K. B. (1953) Desegregation: An appraisal of the evidence. *Journal of Social Issues*, 9(4), 2–76.

Cock, J. (1980) *Maids and Madams: A study in the politics of exploitation*. Johannesburg: Ravan.

Cohen, E. (1972) Interracial interaction disability. *Human Relations*, 25(1).

Cohen, E. G. (1980) Design and redesign of the desegregated school: problem of the status, power, and conflict. In W. G. Stephan and J. R. Feagin (eds), *School Desegregation: Past, Present, and Future*. New York: Plenum.

Cohen, E. G. (1982) Expectation states and interracial interaction in school settings. *Annual Review of Sociology*, 8, 209–35.

Cohen, E. G. (1984) The desegregated school: problems in status power and interethnic climate. In N. Miller and M. B. Brewer (eds), *Groups in Contact: The Psychology of Desegregation*. New York: Academic Press.

Cohen, E. and Roper, S. (1972) Modification of interracial interaction disability: an application of status characteristics theory. *American Sociological Review*, 36, 643–57.

Coleman, J. S. (1983) Micro foundations and macrosocial theory. Unpublished paper, Department of Sociology, University of Chicago, Chicago, IL.

Coleman, J. S., Campbell, E. O., Hobson, C. J., McPartland, J., Mood, A. M., Weinfeld, F. D. and York, R. L. (1966) *Equality of educational opportunity*. Washington, DC: U.S. Government Printing Office.

Collins, T. (1979) From courtrooms to classrooms: managing school desegregation in a deep south high school. In R. Rist (ed.), *Desegregated Schools:*

Appraisals of an American Experiment. New York: Academic Press, pp. 89–114.

Collins, T. W. and Noblit, G. W. (1977) Crossover High. Unpublished manuscript, Department of Anthropology, Memphis State University.

Commins, B. and Lockwood, J. (1978) The effects on intergroup relations of mixing Roman Catholics and Protestants: an experimental investigation. *European Journal of Social Psychology, 8,* 383–6.

Cook, S. W. (1962) The systematic analysis of socially significant events: a strategy for social research. *Journal of Social Issues, 18,* 66–84.

Cook, S. W. (1969) Motives in a conceptual analysis of attitude-related behavior. In W. J. Arnold and D. Levine (eds), *Nebraska Symposium on Motivation.* Lincoln: University of Nebraska Press, vol. 17, pp. 179–235.

Cook, S. W. (1970) Motives in a conceptual analysis of attitude-related behavior. In W. J. Arnold and D. Levine (eds), *Nebraska Symposium on Motivation, 1969.* Lincoln: University of Nebraska Press.

Cook, S. W. (1971) The effect of unintended interracial contact upon racial interaction and attitude change. Final report, U.S. Department of Health, Education and Welfare, Office of Education, Project no. 5–1320, Mimeo.

Cook, S. W. (1978) Interpersonal and attitudinal outcomes in cooperating interracial groups. *Journal of Research and Development in Education, 12,* 97–113.

Cook, S. W. (1979) Social science and school desegregation: 'Did we mislead the Supreme Court?' *Personality and Social Psychology Bulletin, 5,* 420–37.

Cook, S. W. (1984) Cooperative interaction in multiethnic contexts. In N. Miller and M. B. Brewer (eds), *Groups in Contact.* New York: Academic Press.

Cook, S. W. and Selltiz, C. (1955) Some factors which influence the attitudinal outcomes of personal contacts. *International Sociological Bulletin, 7,* 51–8.

Cooper, J. and Fazio, R. H. (1979) The formation and persistence of attitudes that support intergroup conflict. In W. G. Austin and S. Worchel (eds), *The Social Psychology of Intergroup Relations.* Monterey, Ca.: Brooks/Cole.

Crain, R. L. and Mahard, R. E. (1978) Desegregation and black achievement: a review of the research. *Law and Contemporary Problems, 43*(3), 17–56.

Crain, R. L. and Mahard, R. E. (1982) The consequences of controversy accompanying institutional change: the case of school desegregation. *American Sociological Review, 47,* 697–708.

Curran, J. and Stanworth, J. (1979) Worker involvement and social relations in the small firm. *The Sociological Review, 27*(2), 312–42.

Cusick, P. and Ayling, R. (1973) Racial interaction in an urban secondary school. Paper presented at the annual meeting of the American Educational Research Association, New Orleans, LA.

Darby, J. (1976) *Conflict in Northern Ireland: the Development of a Polarised Community.* Dublin: Gill and Macmillan.

Davey (1983) *Learning to be Prejudiced.* London: Edward Arnold.

Davis, J. A. (1963) Structural balance, mechanical solidarity, and interpersonal relations. *American Journal of Sociology, 68,* 444–62.

Delgado, M. J. (1972) *Die 'Gastarbeiter' in der Presse.* Opladen: Leske.

Der Spiegel, 1982, vol. 82.

Deschamps, J. C. and Brown, R. (1983) Superordinate goals and intergroup conflict. *British Journal of Social Psychology*, 22, 189–95.

Deschamps, J. C. and Doise, W. (1978) Crossed category memberships in intergroup relations. In H. Tajfel (ed.), *Differentiation between Social Groups*. London: Academic Press, pp. 141–58.

Deutsch, M. and Collins, M. (1951) *Interracial Housing: A Psychological Evaluation of a Social Experiment*. Minneapolis: University of Minnesota Press.

DeVries, D. L., Edwards, K. J. and Slavin, R. E. (1978) Biracial learning teams and race relations in the classroom: four field experiments using Teams-Games-Tournament. *Journal of Educational Psychology*, 70, 356–62.

Diab, L. N. (1970) A study of intragroup and intergroup relations among experimentally produced small groups. *Genetic Psychology Monographs*, 82, 49–82.

Dickopp, K. H. (1982) *Erziehung ausländischer Kinder als pädagogische Herausforderung – Das Krefelder Modell*. Düsseldorf: Schwann.

Doise, W. (1978) *Groups and Individuals: Explanations in Social Psychology*. Cambridge: Cambridge University Press.

Donnan, H. and McFarlane, G. (1983) Informal social organization. In J. Darby (ed.), *Northern Ireland: the Background to the Conflict*. Belfast: Appletree Press.

Doob, L. W. and Foltz, W. J. (1973) The Belfast workshop. An application of group technique to destructive conflicts. *Journal of Conflict Resolution*, 17(3), 489–512.

Doob, L. W. and Foltz, W. J. (1974) The impact of a workshop upon grass-roots leaders in Belfast. *Journal of Conflict Resolution*, 18(2), 237–56.

Douglas, S. E. (1983) Differences in group identity and intergroup attitudes in children attending integrated or segregated schools in Northern Ireland. Unpublished BSSc thesis, Queen's University of Belfast.

Drucker, P. (1955) *The Practice of Management*. London: Heinemann.

Duncan, B. L. (1976) Differential racial perception and attribution of intergroup violence. *Journal of Personality and Social Psychology*, 34, 590–8.

Durkheim, E. (1960) *The Division of Labor in Society*. Glencoe, Ill.: Free Press. English translation of *De la Division du Travail Social* (1893).

Edwards, P. K. (1977) A critique of the Kerr-Siegel hypothesis of strikes and the isolated mass. *The Sociological Review*, 25(3), 551–74.

Elkin, S. and Panning, W. (1975) Structural effects and individual attitudes: racial prejudice in English cities. *Public Opinion Quarterly*, 39, 159–77.

Ellison, R. (1952/1965 2nd ed.) *Invisible Man*. Harmondsworth: Penguin Books.

EMNID (1982) *Ausländer – Rausländer*. Emnid-Informationen, Nr. 1/2.

Esser, H. (1980) *Aspekte der Wanderungssoziologie*. Darmstadt: Luchterhand.

Evans-Pritchard, E. E. (1940) *The Nuer*. London: Oxford University Press.

Feshbach, S. and Singer, R. (1957) The effects of personality and shared threats upon social prejudice. *Journal of Abnormal and Social Psychology*, 54, 411–16.

Fishbein, M. and Ajzen, I. (1975) *Belief, Attitude, Intention and Behavior: An Introduction to Theory and Research*. Reading, MA.: Addison-Wesley.

Forehand, G. A. and Ragosta, M. (1976) *A Handbook for Integrated Schooling.* Princeton, NJ: Educational Testing Service.

Forschungsverbund (1979) *Probleme der Ausländerbeschäftigung – Integrierter Endbericht.* Bochum/Mannheim/München: Selbstverlag.

Fraser, M. (1979) *Children in Conflict.* London: Penguin.

Frazier, E. F. (1957) *Race and Culture Contacts in the Modern World.* New York: Knopf.

Gaertner, S. and Dovidio, J. (1977) The subtlety of white racism, arousal and helping behavior. *Journal of Personality and Social Psychology, 35,* 691–707.

Gaertner, S. and Dovidio, J. (1986). In S. Gaertner and J. Dovidio (eds), *Prejudice and Racism.* New York: Academic Press.

Garcia, L. T., Erskine, N., Hawn, K. and Casmay, S. R. (1981) The effect of affirmative action on attributions about minority group members. *Journal of Personality, 49,* 427–37.

Garfinkel, H. (1967) *Studies in Ethnomethodology.* Englewood Cliffs, NJ: Prentice-Hall.

Gerard, H. and Miller, N. (1975) Introduction. In H. Gerard and N. Miller (eds), *School Desegregation.* New York: Plenum.

Gerard, H., Jackson, T. and Connolley, E. (1975) Social contact in the desegregated classroom. In H. Gerard and N. Miller (eds), *School Desegregation.* New York: Plenum.

Gergen, K. J. (1973) Social psychology as history. *Journal of Personality and Social Psychology, 26,* 309–20.

Ghosh, E. S. K. and Huq, M. M. (1985) A study of social identity in two ethnic groups in India and Bangladesh. *Journal of Multilingual and Multicultural Development, 6,* 239–51.

Giles, H. and Johnson, P. (1981) The role of language in ethnic group relations. In J. C. Turner and H. Giles (eds), *Intergroup Behaviour.* Oxford: Basil Blackwell.

Giles, H. and Wiemann, J. (in preparation) Verbal and non-verbal communication. To appear in M. Hewstone, W. Stroebe, G. Stephenson and J.-P. Codol (eds), *Introduction to Social Psychology.* Oxford: Basil Blackwell.

Glaser, N. (1954) Ethnic groups in America: from national culture to ideology. In M. Berger, T. Abel and C. Poze (eds), *Freedom and Control in Modern Society.* New York: Van Nostrand.

Glaser, N. and Moynihan, P. (1970) *Beyond the Melting Pot* (2nd ed.). Cambridge, MA: MIT Press.

Gordon, H. (1980) Buberian learning groups: a response to the challenge of education for peace in the Middle East. *Teacher College Record, 82,* 291–310.

Gordon, R. J. (1977) *Mines, Masters and Migrants.* Johannesburg: Ravan.

Gouldner, A. W. (1955) *Wildcat Strike.* London: Routledge & Kegan Paul.

Greeley, A. M. and Sheatsley, P. B. (1971) Attitudes toward racial integration. *Scientific American, 222,* 13–19.

Greenbaum, C. and Abdul Razak, A. (1972) An Arab-Jewish student workshop. Unpublished manuscript, The Hebrew University, Jerusalem, Israel.

Groenewald, D. C. and de Kock, C. (1979) Enkele aspekte van 'n groep

Kleurlingmans in Wes-Kaapland se verhouding met Blanke, Indiërs en Swartes. In J. M. Lötter (ed.), *Social Problems in the Republic of South Africa*. Pretoria: Human Sciences Research Council, pp. 571–7.

Grundy, K. W. (1983) *Soldiers Without Politics*. Berkeley: University of California Press.

Gudykunst, W. B., Hammer, M. R. and Wiseman, R. L. (1977) An analysis of an integrated approach to cross-cultural training. *International Journal of Intercultural Relations*, *1*, 99–110.

Gurwitz, S. B. and Dodge, K. A. (1977) Effects of confirmations and disconfirmations on stereotype-based attributions. *Journal of Personality and Social Psychology*, *35*, 495–500.

Hahlo, K. (1969) A European-African worker relationship in South Africa. *Race*, *11*, 13–34.

Hamill, R., Wilson, T. D. and Nisbett, R. E. (1980) Insensitivity to sample bias: generalising from atypical cases. *Journal of Personality and Social Psychology*, *39*, 578–89.

Hamilton, D. L. (1979) A cognitive-attributional analysis of stereotyping. In L. Berkowitz (ed.), *Advances in Experimental Social Psychology*. New York: Academic Press, vol. 12.

Hamilton, D. L. (ed.) (1981) *Cognitive Processes in Stereotyping and Intergroup Behavior*. Hillsdale, NJ: Erlbaum.

Hamilton, D. L. and Bishop, G. D. (1976) Attitudinal and behavioural effects of initial integration of white suburban neighbourhoods. *Journal of Social Issues*, *32*, 47–67.

Hamilton, D. L., Carpenter, S. and Bishop, G. D. (1984) Desegregation of suburban neighborhoods. In N. Miller and M. B. Brewer (eds), *Groups in Contact: The Psychology of Desegregation*. New York: Academic Press.

Hamilton, D. L. and Trolier, T. K. (in press) Stereotypes and stereotyping: an overview of the cognitive approach. In J. Dovidio and S. L. Gaertner (eds), *Prejudice, Discrimination and Racism: Theory and Research*. New York: Academic Press.

Handel, W. (1982) *Ethnomethodology: How People Make Sense*. Englewood Cliffs, NJ: Prentice-Hall.

Hanf, T., Weiland, H. and Vierdag, G. (1981) *South Africa: The Prospects of Peaceful Change*. London: Rex Collings.

Harding, J. and Hogrefe, R. (1952) Attitudes of white department store employees towards negro co-workers. *Journal of Social Issues*, *8*, 18–28.

Harding, J., Proshansky, H., Kutner, B. and Chein, I. (1969) Prejudice and ethnic relations. In G. Lindzey and E. Aronson (eds), *The Handbook of Social Psychology*, vol. 5. Reading, MA: Addison-Wesley.

Harris, R. (1972) *Prejudice and Tolerance in Ulster: A Study of Neighbours and 'Strangers' in a Border Community*. Manchester: Manchester University Press.

Harris, R. (in press) Myth and reality in Northern Ireland: an anthropological study. In L. McWhirter and K. Trew (eds), *The Northern Ireland Conflict: Myth and Reality*. Ormskirk: Hesketh.

Hartmann, P. and Husband, C. (1970) The mass media and racial conflict. *Race*, *12*, 267–82.

Hartmann, P. and Husband, C. (1974) *Racism and the Mass Media*. London: Davis-Poynter.

Hawley, W., Smylie, M. D., Crain, R. L., Rossell, C. H., Fernandez, R. R., Schofield, J. W. and Trent, W. P. (1983) *Strategies for Effective Desegregation: Lessons from Research*. Lexington, MA: Lexington Books, D. C. Heath.

Heath, S. B. (1982) Questioning at home and at school: a comparative study. In G. Spindler (ed.), *Doing the Ethnography of Schooling: Educational Anthropology in Action*. New York: Holt, Rinehart and Winston.

Heaven, P. C. L. (1983) Ethnic polarization in South Africa: myth or reality. *Ethnic and Racial Studies*, *6*, 356–62.

Heider, F. (1944) Social perception and phenomenal causality. *Psychological Review*, *51*, 358–74.

Heider, F.. (1958) *The Psychology of Interpersonal Relations*. New York: Wiley.

Herzberg, G. (1966) *Work and the Nature of Man*. New York: World Publishing Company.

Heskin, K. (1980) *Northern Ireland: A Psychological Analysis*. Dublin: Gill and Macmillan.

Hewstone, M. (ed.) (1985) Social psychology and intergroup relations: cross-cultural perspectives. Special issue of the *Journal of Multicultural and Multilingual Development*, 6.

Hewstone, M. and Giles, H. (1984) Intergroup conflict. In A. Gale and A. J. Chapman (eds), *Psychology and Social Problems*. Chichester: J. Wiley.

Hewstone, M. and Giles, H. (1986) Social groups and social stereotypes in intergroup communication. In W. B. Gudykunst (ed.), *Intergroup Communication*. London: Edward Arnold.

Hewstone, M. and Jaspars, J. (1982) Intergroup relations and attribution processes. In H. Tajfel (ed.), *Social Identity and Intergroup Relations*. Cambridge/Paris: Cambridge University Press/Maison des Sciences de l'Homme.

Hewstone, M. and Jaspars, J. (1984) Social dimensions of attribution. In H. Tajfel (ed.), *The Social Dimension: European Developments in Social Psychology*. Cambridge/Paris: Cambridge University Press/Maison des Sciences de l'Homme.

Hofman, J. E. (1972) Readiness for social relations between Arabs and Jews in Israel. *Journal of Conflict Resolution*, *16*, 241–51.

Hofman, J. E. (1976) *Identity and Intergroup Perception in Israel: Jews and Arabs*. Occasional papers in the Middle East, no. 7. Haifa: Haifa University, Institute of Middle-Eastern Studies.

Hofman, J. E. (1985) A social psychological perspective on relations between Jews and Arabs. Unpublished manuscript, University of Haifa, Israel.

Hoffman, L. W. (1984) Foreword. In N. Miller and M. B. Brewer (eds), *Groups in Contact: The Psychology of Desegregation*. New York: Academic Press.

Hoffmann, L. and Even, H. (1983) 'Die Belastungsgrenze ist überschritten' –

Entwurf einer Theorie des Ausländerfeindlichkeit. Bielefeld, *Materialien des Zentrums für Wissenschaft und berufliche Praxis, Heft 15.*

Holfort, F. (1982) *Benachteiligung ohne Ende? Zur sozialen Integration ausländischer Kinder.* Düsseldorf: Schwann.

Hopf, D. (1981) Schulprobleme der Ausländerkinder. *Zeitschrift für Pädagogik,* 27, 839–61.

Horowitz, E. L. (1936) The development of attitudes toward the Negro. *Archives of Psychology, 194.*

Horowitz, E. and Horowitz, R. (1937) Development of social attitudes in children. *Sociometry, 1,* 301–20.

Horrell, M. (1978) *Laws Affecting Race Relations in South Africa 1948–1976.* Johannesburg: South African Institute of Race Relations.

Hunter, J. (1982) An analysis of the conflict in Northern Ireland. In D. Rae (ed.), *Political Co-operation in Divided Societies.* Dublin: Gill and Macmillan.

Husbands, C. T. (1979) The threat hypothesis and racist voting in England and in United States. In R. Miles and A. Phizacklea, *Racism and Political Action in Britain.* London: Routledge & Kegan Paul.

Indik, B. P. (1965) Organisation size and member participation. *Human Relations, 18,* 339–49.

INFAS (1982) *Meinungen und Einstellungen zu Ausländerproblemen.* Bonn: Selbstverlag.

Ingham, G. K. (1967) Organisation size, orientations to work and industrial behaviour. *Sociology, 1,* 239–58.

Jabes, J. (1978) *Individual Processes in Organisational Behaviour.* Illinois: AHM Publishing Corp.

Jacobson, C. K. (1977) Separatism, integrationism, and avoidance among Black, White, and Latin adolescents. *Social Forces, 55,* 1011–27.

Jacobson, C. K. (1978) Desegregation rulings and public attitude changes: white resistance or resignation? *American Journal of Sociology, 84,* 698–705.

Jahoda, M. and West, P. (1951) Race relations in public housing. *Journal of Social Issues, 7,* 132–9.

Jaspars, J. and Hewstone, M. (1982) Cross-cultural interaction, social attribution and intergroup relations. In S. Bochner (ed.), *Cultures in Contact: Studies in Cross-Cultural Interaction.* Oxford: Pergamon Press.

Jaspars, J. and Warnaen, S. (1982) Intergroup relations, ethnic identity and self-evaluation in Indonesia. In H. Tajfel (ed.), *Social Identity and Intergroup Relations.* Cambridge/Paris: Cambridge University Press/Maison des Sciences de l'Homme.

Johnson, D. W. and Johnson, R. T. (1982) The study of cooperative, competitive, and individualistic situations: state of the area and two recent contributions. *Contemporary Education: A Journal of Reviews, 1*(1), 7–13.

Johnson, D. W., Johnson, R. T. and Maruyama, G. (1984) Goal interdependence and interpersonal attraction in heterogeneous classrooms: a meta-analysis. In N. Miller and M. B. Brewer (eds), *Groups in Contact: The Psychology of Desegregation.* New York: Academic Press.

Johnston, N. (1983) The flag that closed a factory. *Belfast Telegraph*, 25 August, p. 7.

Jones, E. E., Bell, L. and Aronson, E. The reciprocation of attraction from similar and dissimilar others: a study in person perception and evaluation. In C. G. McClintock (ed.), *Experimental Social Psychology*. New York: Holt, Rinehart & Winston.

Joubert, D. (1974) Maar nie met iemand van 'n ander kleur nie – regverdigings vir wette teen intieme verhoudings oor die kleurgrens. *South African Journal of Sociology*, 9, 71–81.

Joy, R. J. (1972) *Languages in Conflict*. Toronto: McClelland & Stewart.

Joy, R. J. (1978) *Canada's Official Language Minorities*. Montreal: C. D. Howe.

Kagan, S. (1977) Social motives and behaviors of Mexican-American and Anglo-American children. In J. L. Martinez and R. H. Mendoza (eds), *Chicano Psychology*. New York: Academic Press.

Kagan, S. (1979) Cooperation-competition, culture and structural bias in classrooms. In S. Sharan, P. Hare, C. Webb and R. Hertz-Lazarocty (eds), *Cooperation in Education*. Provo, Utah: Brigham Young University Press.

Kane, J. (1983) Union bid to protect jobs in Union Jack dispute. *Belfast Telegraph*, 23 August, p. 2.

Katz, I. (1964) Review of evidence relating to the effects of desegregation on the intellectual performance of Negroes. *American Psychologist*, 19, 381–99.

Katz, I. (1970) Experimental studies of Negro-white relationships. In L. Berkowitz (ed.), *Advances in Experimental Social Psychology*. New York: Academic Press, vol. 5.

Katzen, M. F. (1969) White settlers and the origin of a new society. In M. Wilson and L. Thompson (eds), *The Oxford History of South Africa*. Oxford: Oxford University Press, vol. 1, pp. 187–232.

Kawwa, T. (1968) A survey of ethnic attitudes of some British secondary school pupils. *British Journal of Social and Clinical Psychology*, 7, 161–8.

Kelley, H. H. (1983) The situational origins of human tendencies: a further reason for the formal analysis of structures. *Personality and Social Psychology Bulletin*, 9, 8–30.

Kerr, C. (1964) *Labor and Management in Industrial Society*. New York: Doubleday.

Kerr, C. and Siegel, A. (1954) The inter-industry propensity to strike. In A. Kornhauser, R. Dubin and A. M. Ross (eds), *Industrial Conflict*. New York: McGraw-Hill.

Kidder, L. H. and Stewart, V. M. (1975) *The Psychology of Intergroup Relations*. New York: McGraw-Hill.

Kiesler, S. B. (1978) *Interpersonal Processes in Groups and Organisations*. Illinois: AHM Publishing Corp.

Kilpatrick, W. H. and Van Til, W. (eds) (1947) *Intercultural Attitudes in the Making: Parents, Youth Leaders, and Teachers at Work*. New York: Harper.

Kimble, G. A. (1961) *Hilgard and Marquis' Conditioning and Learning* (2nd ed.). New York: Appleton-Century-Crofts.

Klee, E. (ed.) (1972) *Gastarbeiter. Analysen und Berichte.* Frankfurt-am-Main. Suhrkamp Verlag.

Knight, G. P. and Kagan, S. (1977) Development of prosocial and competition behaviors in Anglo-American and Mexican-American children. *Child Development*, 48, 1385–94.

Knowles, K. G. J. C. (1952) *Strikes: A Study in Industrial Conflict.* Oxford: Basil Blackwell.

Kochman, T. (1981) *Black and White Styles of Conflict.* Chicago, IL: University of Chicago Press.

Kohler, D. (1973) Public opinion and the Ugandan Asians. *New Community*, 2, 194–7.

Kramer, B. (1950) *Residential Contact as a Determinant of Attitudes towards Negroes*, Unpublished PhD Dissertation, Harvard University.

Kühn, H. (1979) *Stand und Weiterentwicklung der Integration der ausländischen Arbeitnehmer und ihrer Familien in der Bundesrepublik Deutschland.* Bonn: Beauftragter der Bunolesregierung für die Integration ausländischer Arbeitnehmer und ihrer Familienangehörigen.

Kuper, L., Watts, H. and Davies, R. (1958) *Durban: A Study in Racial Ecology.* London: Jonathan Cape.

Lakin, H., Lomeranz, J. and Lieberman, M. (1969) *Arab and Jew in Israel: A Case Study in Human Relations Training Approach to Conflict.* New York: American Academic Association for Peace in the Middle East.

Lambert, W. E. and Klineberg, O. (1967) *Children's Views of Foreign Peoples: A cross-national study.* New York: Appleton-Century-Crofts.

Landes, R. (1955) Biracialism in American society: A comparative view. *American Anthropologist*, 57, 1253–63.

Landis, D., Hope, R. O. and Day, H. R. (1984) Training for desegregation in the military. In N. Miller and M. B. Brewer (eds), *Groups in Contact: The Psychology of Desegregation.* New York: Academic Press.

Lee, A. M. and Humphrey, N. D. (1943) *Race Riot.* New York: Dryden.

Legassick, M. (1975) South Africa, forced labour, industrialization and racial discrimination. In R. Harris (ed.), *The Political Economy of Africa.* Cambridge, MA: Schenkman, pp. 229–270.

Legassick, M. (1980) The frontier tradition in South African historiography. In S. Marks and A. Atmore (eds), *Economy and Society in Pre-Industrial South Africa.* London: Longmore, pp. 44–79.

Lemaine, G., Kasterszstein, J. and Personnaz, B. (1978) Social differentiation. In H. Tajfel (ed.), *Differentiation between Social Groups.* London: Academic Press.

Lever, H. (1971) Programme to reduce inter-group tensions. In P. Randall (ed.), *Towards Social Change.* Johannesburg: SPROCAS, pp. 136–55.

Lever, H. (1978) *South African Society.* Johannesburg: Jonathan Ball.

LeVine, R. A. and Campbell, D. T. (1972) *Ethnocentrism: Theories of Conflict, Ethnic Attitudes and Group Behavior.* New York: Wiley.

Levy, S. and Guttman, L. (1976) *Values and Attitudes of Israeli Youth.* Jerusalem: The Institute of Applied Social Research.

Leyton, E. (1974) Opposition and integration in Ulter. *Man*, *9*, 185–98.

Lieberson, S. (1961) A societal theory of race and ethnic relations. *American Sociological Review*, *26*, 902–10.

Lieberson, S. (1970) *Language and Ethnic Conflict in Canada*. New York: Wiley.

Linville, P. W. and Jones, E. E. (1980) Polarised appraisals of outgroup members. *Journal of Personality and Social Psychology*, *38*, 689–703.

Little, A., Ejionye, V., Nanton, P. and Gardiner, S. (1977) *Housing Choice and Ethnic Concentration*. London: London Commission for Racial Equality.

Lockhart, W. H. and Elliott, R. (1980) Changes in the attitudes of young offenders in an integrated assessment centre. In J. Harbison and J. Harbison (eds), *A Society Under Stress*. Somerset: Open Books.

Lockwood, D. (1966) Sources of variation in working-class images of society. *The Sociological Review*, *14*, 249–67.

Lockwood, J. (1982) Working for them versus working for us. A theoretical case-study in intergroup relations between science and society. In P. Stringer (ed.), *Confronting Social Issues. Applications of Social Psychology*. London: Academic Press, vol. 2.

Lodge, T. (1983) *Black Politics in South Africa Since 1945*. Johannesburg: Ravan.

Luiz, D. and Krige, P. (1981) The effect of social contact between South African white and coloured adolescents. *Journal of Social Psychology*, *113*, 153–8.

Lupton, T. (1983) *Management and the Social Sciences*. Harmondsworth: Penguin.

Lyon, M. (1970) The role of the settlement area in British race relations. *Journal of Biosocial Science, Supplement 1*, 163–70.

MacCrone, I. D. (1937) *Race Attitudes in South Africa*. London: Oxford University Press.

Machleit, U. and Wagner, U. (1983) *Der Abbau ethnischer Vorurteile*. Essen/Bochum: RAA-Selbtsverlag.

Mackenzie, B. (1948) The importance of contact in determining attitudes towards Negroes. *Journal of Abnormal and Social Psychology*, *43*, 417–41.

Malhotra, M. K. (1978) Das Bild vom Gastarbeiterkind bei deutschen Schulkindern. *Pädagogische Rundschau*, *32*, 207–32.

Mayer, P. (1975) Class, status and ethnicity as perceived by Johannesburg Africans. In L. Thompson and J. Butler (eds), *Change in Contemporary South Africa*. Berkeley: University of California Press, pp. 138–67.

McClendon, M. J. (1974) Interracial contact and the reduction of prejudice. *Sociological Focus*, *7*, 47–65.

McConahay, J. B. and Hough, J. C. (1976) Symbolic racism. *Journal of Social Issues*, *32*, 23–45.

McConahay, J. B., Hardee, B. B. and Batts, V. (1982) Has racism declined? It depends upon who's asking and what is asked. (Working paper) Institute of Policy Sciences and Public Affairs, Duke University.

McWhirter, L. (1983) Contact and conflict: the question of integrated education. *The Irish Journal of Psychology*, *6*, 13–27.

McWhirter, L. (1985) Evaluation of Protestant-Catholic Workshops. Paper presented at conference on Contact and the Reconciliation of Conflict,

Northern Ireland Regional Office of the British Psychological Society, Belfast.

Mehrländer, U., Hofmann, R., König, P. and Krause, H.-J. (1981) *Situation der ausländischen Arbeitnehmer und ihrer Familienangehörigen in der Bundesrepublik Deutschland*, Forschungsbericht im Auftrag des Bundesministers für Arbeit und Sozialordnung. Bonn: Bundesminister für Arbeit und Sozialordnung.

Meinhard, R. (1982) Wir spielen 'Keloglan'. Interkulturelles Lernen im Schultheaterspiel. *Ausländerkinder in Schule und Kindergarten*, 2, 6–9.

Miles, R. and Phizacklea, A. (1984) *White Mans Country*. London: Pluto Press.

Milgram, S. (1974) *Obedience to Authority*. New York: Harper & Row.

Miller, D. (ed.) (1985) *Popper Selections*. Princeton, NJ: Princeton University Press.

Miller, N. and Brewer, M. B. (eds) (1984) *Groups in Contact: The Psychology of Desegregation*. New York: Academic Press.

Milroy, J. (1981) *Regional Accents in English: Belfast*. Belfast: Blackstaff Press.

Minard, R. D. (1952) Race relationships in the Pocahontas coal fields. *Journal of Social Issues*, 25, 29–44.

Montagu, A. (ed.) (1964) *The Concept of Race*. New York: Free Press.

Montagu, A. (ed.) (1972) *Statement on Race* (3rd ed.). London: Oxford University Press.

Moorehead, A. (1969) *Darwin and the Beagle*. London: Hamish Hamilton, p. 93.

Morley, I. E. and Stephenson, G. M. (1977) *The Social Psychology of Bargaining*. London: Allen & Unwin.

Moxon-Browne, E. P. (1983) *Nation, Class and Creed in Northern Ireland*. Aldershot: Gower.

Mummendey, A. and Schreiber, H.-J. (1983) Better or just different? Positive social identity by discrimination against or by differentiation from outgroups. *European Journal of Social Psychology*, 13, 389–97.

Mummendey, A. and Schreiber, H.-J. (1984) 'Different' just means 'better': some obvious and some hidden pathways to ingroup favouritism. *British Journal of Social Psychology*, 23, 363–8.

Myers, D. (1983) *Social Psychology*. New York: McGraw-Hill.

Mynhart, J. C. (1982) Etniese houdings in 'n kontaksituasie. Unpublished doctoral dissertation. University of South Africa.

Myrdal, G. (1944) *An American Dilemma: The Negro Problem and Modern Democracy*. New York: Harper & Brothers.

Nakhleh, K. (1975) Cultural determinants of Palestinian collective identity: the case of the Arabs in Israel. *New Outlook*, 18, 31–40.

National Advisory Committee on Civil Disorders (1968) Washington, DC: U.S. Government Printing Office.

National Institute of Education (1977) Resegregation: a second generation school desegregation issue. Unpublished manuscript, Desegregation Studies Unit. Washington, DC.

Newcomb, T. M. (1956) The prediction of interpersonal attraction. *American Psychologist*, 11, 575–87.

Newcomb, T. M. (1961) *The Acquaintance Process*. New York: Holt, Rinehart & Winston.

Norvell, N. and Worchel, S. (1981) A re-examination of the relation between equal status contact and intergroup attraction. *Journal of Personality and Social Psychology*, *41*, 902–8.

No Sizwe (1979) *One Azania, One Nation*. London: Zed Press.

Orpen, C. (1975) Authoritarianism revisited: A critical examination of 'expressive' theories of prejudice. In S. J. Morse and C. Orpen (eds), *Contemporary South Africa*. Cape Town: Juta, pp. 103–11.

Palmore, E. B. (1955) The introduction of Negroes into white departments. *Human Organization*, *14*, 27–8.

Park, B. M. and Rothbart, M. (1982) Perception of outgroup homogeneity and levels of social categorisation: memory for the subordinate attributions of ingroup and outgroup members. *Journal of Personality and Social Psychology*, *42*, 1051–68.

Park, R. E. (1950) *Race and Culture*. Glencoe, Ill.: The Free Press.

Parker, S. (1974) *Workplace Industrial Relations*. London: H.M.S.O.

Parkin, F. (1971) *Class Inequality and Political Order*. London: MacGibbon and Kee.

Patchen, M. (1982) *Black-White Contact in Schools: Its Social and Academic Effects*. West Lafayette, IN: Purdue University Press.

Peabody, D. (1970) Evaluative and descriptive aspects in personality perception: a reappraisal. *Journal of Personality and Social Psychology*, *16*, 639–46.

Peach, C. (1958) *West Indian Migration to Britain*. London: Oxford University Press.

Peled, T. (1980) *On Social Distance between Jews and Arabs*. Jerusalem: The Israel Institute of Applied Social Research, Research Report 1978–9, 19–21.

Peled, T. and Bar-Gal, D. (1983) *Intervention Activities in Arab-Jewish Relations: Conceptualization, Classification and Evaluation*. Jerusalem: The Israel Institute of Applied Social Research.

Pettigrew, T. F. (1958) Personality and sociocultural factors in intergroup attitudes: a cross-national comparison. *Journal of Conflict Resolution*, *2*, 29–42.

Pettigrew, T. F. (1961) Social psychology and desegregation research. *American Psychologist*, *16*, 105–12.

Pettigrew, T. F. (1967) Social evaluation theory: consequences and applications. In D. Levine (ed.), *Nebraska Symposium on Motivation*. Lincoln, Nebraska: University of Nebraska Press, vol. 15.

Pettigrew, T. F. (1969) Racially separate or together? *Journal of Social Issues*, *25*(1), 43–69.

Pettigrew, T. F. (1971) *Racially Separate or Together?* New York: McGraw-Hill.

Pettigrew, T. F. (1979a) Racial change and social policy. *Annals of the Academy of Political and Social Sciences*, *441*, 114–31.

Pettigrew, T. F. (1979b) The ultimate attribution error: extending Allport's cognitive analysis of prejudice. *Personality and Social Psychology Bulletin*, *4*, 461–76.

Pettigrew, T. F. (1982) Prejudice. In T. F. Pettigrew, G. M. Fredrickson, D. T. Knobel, N. Glazier and R. Ueda (eds), *Prejudice*. Cambridge, MA: Harvard University Press.

Pettigrew, T. F. (1985) Black American uniqueness: the danger of generalizing from a special case. Unpublished Paper given at the First Circum-Mediterranean Regional Conference of the International Association for Cross-Cultural Psychology: Ethnic Minority and Immigrant Research. Malmo, Sweden, 25 June, 1985.

Pettigrew, T. F. (1986) *Modern Racism: American Black-White Relations Since the 1960s*. Cambridge, MA: Harvard University Press.

Pettigrew, T. F., Useem, E., Norman, C. and Smith, M. S. (1973) Busing: a review of the evidence. *Public Interest, 30*, 88–118.

Phizacklea, A. and Miles, R. (1980) *Labour and Racism*. London: Routledge & Kegan Paul.

Platzky, L. and Walker, C. (1983) Review of relocation. In South African Research Service (eds), *South African Review 1*. Johannesburg: Ravan, pp. 83–96.

Pommerin, G. (1981) Klassenzeitungen – damit man sich besser kennenlernt. *Ausländerkinder in Schule und Kindergarten, 4*, 27–30.

Poole, M. A. (1982) Religious residential segregation in urban Northern Ireland. In F. W. Boal and J. N. H. Douglas (eds), *Integration and Division: Geographical Perspectives on the Northern Ireland Problem*. London: Academic Press.

Poole, M. A. (1983) The demography of violence. In J. Darby (ed.), *Northern Ireland: the Background to the Conflict*. Belfast: Appletree Press.

Popper, K. R. (1957) *The Poverty of Historicism*. London: Routledge & Kegan Paul. (Originally published in *Economica*, 1944–45.)

Popper, K. R. (1959) *The Logic of Scientific Discovery*. London: Hutchinson. (Originally published in German in 1934.)

Pratte, R. (1979) *Pluralism in Education*. Springfield, IL: Charles C. Thomas.

Price, G. (1950) *White Settlers and Native Peoples*. Melbourne: The Georgian House.

Pushkin, I. and Venness, T. (1973) The development of racial awareness and prejudice in young children. In P. Watson (ed.), *Psychology and Race*. Harmondsworth: Penguin.

Pyszczynski, T. A. and Greenberg, J. (1981) Role of disconfirmed expectancies in the instigation of attributional processing. *Journal of Personality and Social Psychology, 40*, 31–8.

Quattrone, G. A. and Jones, E. E. (1980) The perception of variability within ingroups and outgroups: implications for the law of small numbers. *Journal of Personality and Social Psychology, 38*, 141–52.

Randall, P. (ed.) (1971) *Towards Social Change*. Johannesburg: SPROCAS.

Read, F. (1975) Judicial evolution of the law of school integration since Brown v. Board of Education. *Law and Contemporary Problems, 39*(1), 7–49.

Reed, B. A. (1947) Accommodation between Negro and white employees in a West Coast aircraft industry, 1942–1944. *Social Forces, 26*, 76–84.

Regan, D. T., Straus, E. and Fazio, R. (1947) Liking and the attribution process. *Journal of Experimental Social Psychology, 10*, 385–97.

Reicher, S. D. (1984) The St. Pauls riot: an explanation of the limits of crowd action in terms of a social identity model. *European Journal of Social Psychology*, *14*, 1–21.

Reid, F. J. and Sumiga, L. (1984) Attitudinal politics in intergroup behaviour: interpersonal vs. intergroup determinants of attitude change. *British Journal of Social Psychology*, *23*, 335–40.

Revans, F. W. (1956) Industrial morale and size of unit. *Political Quarterly*, *27*, 303–11.

Rich, P. B. (1984) *White Power and the Liberal Conscience*. Johannesburg: Ravan.

Riley, R. T. and Pettigrew, T. F. (1976) Dramatic events and attitude change. *Journal of Personality and Social Psychology*, *34*, 1004–15.

Riordan, C. (1978) Equal status interracial contact: a review and revision of the concept. *International Journal of Intercultural Relations*, *2*, 161–85.

Riordan, C. and Ruggiero, J. (1980) Producing equal status interracial interaction: a replication. *Social Psychology Quarterly*, *43*, 131–6.

Rist, R. (1978) *The Invisible Children*. Cambridge, MA: Harvard University Press.

Roberts, H. W. (1953) The impact of military service upon the racial attitudes of Negro servicemen in World War II. *Social Problems*, *1*, 65–9.

Rogers, M., Hennigan, K., Bowman, C. and Miller, N. (1984) Intergroup acceptance in classrooms and playground settings. In N. Miller and M. B. Brewer (eds), *Groups in Contact: The Psychology of Desegregation*. New York: Academic Press.

Rokeach, M. (ed.) (1960) *The Open and Closed Mind*. New York: Basic Books.

Rokeach, M., Smith, P. W. and Evans, R. I. (1960) Two kinds of prejudice or one? In M. Rokeach (ed.), *The Open and Closed Mind*. New York: Basic Books.

Rose, P. (1972) *Nation of Nations: The Ethnic Experience and the Racial Crisis*. Random House: New York.

Rose, R. (1971) *Governing without Consensus: An Irish Perspective*. London: Faber and Faber.

Rose, T. L. (1981) Cognitive and dyadic processes in intergroup contact. In D. L. Hamilton (ed.), *Cognitive Processes in Stereotyping and Intergroup Behavior*. Hillsdale, N.J.: Erlbaum.

Rosen, H. W. (1970) *The Arabs and Jews in Israel: The Reality, the Dilemma, the Promise*. Jerusalem: Keter Press.

Rossell, C. (1978) School desegregation and community change. *Law and Contemporary Problems*, *42*(3), 133–83.

Rothbart, M. (1981) Memory processes and social beliefs. In D. L. Hamilton (ed.), *Cognitive Processes in Stereotyping and Intergroup Behavior*. Hillsdale, NJ: Erlbaum.

Rothbart, M., Dawes, R. and Park, B. (1984) Stereotyping and sampling biases in intergroup perception. In J. R. Eiser (ed.), *Attitudinal Judgment*. New York: Springer-Verlag.

Rothbart, M., Evans, M. and Fulero, S. (1979) Recall for confirming events: memory processes and the maintenance of social stereotypes. *Journal of Experimental Social Psychology*, *15*, 343–55.

Rothstein, D. (1972) Culture creation and social reconstruction: the sociocultural dynamics of intergroup contact. *American Sociological Review*, *37*, 671–8.

Roy, D. (1952) Quota restriction and goldbricking in a machine shop. *American Journal of Sociology*, *57*, 427–42.

Roy, D. (1954) Efficiency and 'the fix': informal intergroup relations in a piecework machine shop. *American Journal of Sociology*, *60*, 225–66.

Russell, M. J. (1961) *Study of a South African Inter-Racial Neighbourhood.* Institute for Social Research: University of Natal, Durban.

Saenger, G. and Gilbert, E. (1950) Customer reactions to the integration of Negro sales personnel. *International Journal of Opinion and Attitude Research*, *4*, 57–76.

Sagar, H. A. and Schofield, J. W. (1980) Racial and behavioral cues in black and white children's perceptions of ambiguously aggressive acts. *Journal of Personality and Social Psychology*, *39*(4), 590–8.

Sagar, H. A. and Schofield, J. W. (1984) Integrating the desegregated school: problems and possibilities. In M. Maehr and D. Bartz (eds), *Advances in Motivation and Achievement: A Research Annual.* Greenwich, CT: JAI Press.

Salamone, F. A. and Swanson, C. H. (1979) Identity and ethnicity: ethnic groups and interactions in a multi-ethnic society. *Ethnic groups*, *2*, 167–83.

Savage, M. (1975) Major patterns of group interaction in South African society. In L. Thompson and J. Butler (eds), *Change in Contemporary South Africa.* University of California Press, pp. 280–302.

Schaeffer, R. T. (1973) Contacts between immigrants and Englishmen. *New Community*, *2*, 358–71.

Schlemmer, L. (1976) White voters and change in South Africa. *Optima*, *27*, 62–83.

Schofield, J. W. (1979) The impact of positively structured contact on intergroup behavior: does it last under adverse conditions? *Social Psychology Quarterly*, *42*(3), 280–4.

Schofield, J. W. (1982) *Black and White in School: Trust, Tension or Tolerance?* New York: Praeger.

Schofield, J. W. (in press). Causes and consequences of the color-blind perspective. In S. Gaertner and J. Dovidio (eds), *Prejudice and Discrimination.* New York: Academic Press.

Schofield, J. W. and McGivern, E. (1979) The development of interracial bonds in a desegregated school. In R. Blumberg and J. Roye (eds), *Interracial Bonds.* New York: General Hall.

Schofield, J. W. and Sagar, H. A. (1977) Peer interaction patterns in an integrated middle school. *Sociometry*, *40*(2), 130–8.

Schofield, J. W. and Sagar, H. A. (1979) The social context of learning in an interracial school. In Ray Rist (ed.), *Inside Desegregated Schools: Appraisals of an American Experiment.* San Francisco: Academic Press.

Schofield, J. W. and Snyder, H. (1980) The effect of intimacy on co-worker preference in a desegregated school. Paper presented at the meeting of the American Psychological Association, Montreal.

Schönbach, P., Gollwitzer, P., Stiepel, G. and Wagner, U. (1981) *Education and*

Intergroup Attitudes. London: Academic Press.

Schwarzwald, J. and Amir, Y. (1984) Interethnic relations and education: an Israeli perspective. In N. Miller and M. B. Brewer (eds), *Groups in Contact: The Psychology of Desegregation*. New York: Academic Press.

Schwarzwald, J., Cohen, S. and Hoffman, M. (1985) Carry-over of contact effects from acquainted to unacquainted targets. *Journal of Multilingual and Multicultural Development*, in press.

Sears, D. O. and Allen, H. M. (1984) The trajectory of local desegregation controversies and whites' opposition to busing. In N. Miller and M. B. Brewer (eds), *Groups in Contact: The Psychology of Desegregation*. New York: Academic Press.

Segal, M. (1981) Das Bild vom Gastarbeiter in der Presse. Eine inhaltsanalytische Untersuchung von Printmedien in Salzburg und München. Unpublished doctoral dissertation, Salzburg.

Sharan, S. (1980) Cooperative learning in teams: recent methods and effects on achievement, attitudes and ethnic relations. *Review of Educational Research*, 5(2), 241–72.

Shaw, M. E. (1973) Changes in sociometric choices following forced integration of an elementary school. *Journal of Social Issues*, 29, 143–57.

Sherif, M. (1966a) *Group Conflict and Cooperation*. London: Routledge & Kegan Paul.

Sherif, M. (1966b) *In Common Predicament*. Boston: Houghton Mifflin.

Sherif, M. and Hovland, C. I. (1961) *Social Judgment: Assimilation and Contrast Effects in Communication and Attitude Change*. New Haven/London: Yale University Press.

Sherif, M. and Sherif, C. W. (1965) Research on intergroup relations. In O. Klineberg and R. Christie (eds), *Perspectives in Social Psychology*. New York: Holt, Rinehart & Winston.

Simard, L. M. (1981) Cross-cultural interaction: potential invisible barriers. *Journal of Social Psychology*, *113*, 171–92.

Simard, L. M. and Taylor, D. M. (1973) The potential for bicultural communication in a dyadic situation. *Canadian Journal of Behavioural Science*, 5, 211–25.

Simon, B. (1985) Stereotyping and homogenization of ingroup and outgroup in minority–Majority contexts. Diplompsychologe dissertation, Universität Münster.

Simpson, G. E. and Yinger, J. M. (1972) *Racial and Cultural Minorities: An Analysis of Prejudice and Discrimination*. New York: Harper & Row.

Slavin, R. (1977) How student learning teams can integrate the desegregated classroom. *Integrated Education*, *15*, 56–8.

Slavin, R. E. (1983) *Cooperative learning*. New York: Longman.

Smith, F. T. (1943) An experiment in modifying attitudes toward the Negro. Unpublished doctoral dissertation. Columbia University Teachers' College.

Smith, M. W. (1981) Improving intergroup relations: the impact of two types of small group encounters between Israeli Arabs and Jewish youth. Unpublished doctoral dissertation, Temple University, Philadelphia, PA.

Smooha, S. (1980a) Existing and alternative policy toward the Arabs in Israel. *Megamot*, 26, 30–52.

Smooha, S. (1980b) *The Orientation and Politization of the Arab Minority in Israel*. Occasional papers on the Middle East (new series). Haifa: University of Haifa, The Jewish–Arab Center, no. 2.

Smooha, S. and Hofman, J. E. (1976/77) Some problems of Arab-Jewish coexistence in Israel. *Middle-East Review*, 9(2), 5–14.

Smooha, S. and Peretz, D. (1982) The Arabs in Israel. *Journal of Conflict Resolution*, 26, 451–84.

Snyder, M. (1981) On the self-perpetuating nature of social stereotypes. In D. L. Hamilton (ed.), *Cognitive Processes in Stereotyping and Intergroup Behavior*. Hillsdale, NJ: Erlbaum.

Snyder, M. and Swann, W. B. (1978a) Hypothesis-testing processes in social interaction. *Journal of Personality and Social Psychology*, 36, 1202–12.

Snyder, M. and Swann, W. B. (1978b) Behavioral confirmation in social interaction: from social perception to social reality. *Journal of Experimental Social Psychology*, 14, 148–62.

Spangenberg, J. and Nel, E. M. (1983) Effect of equal-status contact on ethnic attitudes. *Journal of Social Psychology*, 121, 173–80.

Sparks, C. (1980) *Never Again!* London: Bookmarks.

Statistisches Jahrbuch 1983 für die Bundesrepublik Deutschland (1983). Stuttgart: Kohlhammer.

Steinfield, M. (1970) *Cracks in the Melting Pot*. Beverly Hills: Glencoe Press.

Stephan, W. G. (1978) School desegregation: an evaluation of predictions made in Brown v. Board of Education. *Psychological Bulletin*, 85, 217–38.

Stephan, W. G. and Rosenfield, D. (1978) Effects of desegregation on racial attitudes. *Journal of Personality and Social Psychology*, 36, 795–804.

Stephan, W. G. and Rosenfield, D. (1982) Racial and ethnic stereotyping. In A. G. Millar (ed.), *In the Eye of the Beholder: Contemporary Issues in Stereotyping*. New York: Praeger.

Stephan, W. G. and Stephan, C. W. (1984) The role of ignorance in intergroup relations. In N. Miller and M. B. Brewer (eds), *Groups in Contact*. New York: Academic Press.

Stephenson, G. M. and Brotherton, C. J. (1979) *Industrial Relations: A Social Psychological Approach*. Chichester, UK: Wiley.

Stephenson, G. M., Brotherton, C. J., Skinner, M. R. and Delafield, G. (1983) Size of organisation and attitudes at work. *Industrial Relations Journal*, 14(2), 28–40.

Stolz, L. and Tjaden, N. (1980) Gemeinsamer Kunstunterricht einer deutschen und türkischen Grundschulklasse. 'Deutschland Arbeitsland, die Türkei Reiseland'. *Kunst und Unterricht*, 62, 17–23.

Stouffer, S. A., Suchman, E. A., DeVinney, L. C., Star, S. A. and Williams, R. M., Jr. (1949a) *The American Soldier*. Princeton, NJ: Princeton University Press, vol. 1.

Stouffer, S. A., Lumsdaine, A. A., Lumsdaine, M. H., Williams, R. M., Smith, M. B., Janis, I. L., Starr, S. A. and Cottrell, L. S. (1949b) *The American*

Soldier. Princeton NJ: Princeton University Press, vol. 2.

Studlar, D. T. (1977) Social context and attitudes toward coloured immigrants. *British Journal of Sociology*, *28*, 168–84.

Suzman, A. (1960) Race classification and definition in the legislation of the Union of South Africa 1910–1960. *Acta Juridica*, 339–67.

Tajfel, H. (ed.) (1978a) *Differentiation Between Social Groups*. London: Academic Press.

Tajfel, H. (1978b) Interindividual behaviour and intergroup behaviour. In H. Tajfel (ed.), *Differentiation between Social Groups: Studies in social psychology of intergroup relations*. London: Academic Press.

Tajfel, H. (1981) *Human Groups and Social Categories: Studies in Social Psychology*. Cambridge: Cambridge University Press.

Tajfel, H. (1982a) *Social Identity and Intergroup Relations*. Cambridge/Paris: Cambridge University Press/Maison des Science de l'Homme.

Tajfel, H. (1982b) Social Psychology of intergroup relations. *Annual Review of Psychology*, *33*, 1–39.

Tajfel, H. (ed.) (1984) *The Social Dimension: European Developments in Social Psychology* (2 vols). Cambridge: Cambridge University Press.

Tajfel, H., Flament, C., Billig, M. and Bundy, R. P. (1971) Social categorisation and intergroup behaviour. *European Journal of Social Psychology*, *1*, 149–78.

Tajfel, H. and Forgas, J. P. (1981) Social categorization: cognitions, values and groups. In J. P. Forgas (ed.), *Social Cognition*. London: Academic Press.

Talacchi, S. (1960) Organisation size, individual attitudes and behaviour: an empirical study. *Administrative Science Quarterly*, *5*(3), 398–420.

Taylor, D. G., Sheatsley, P. B. and Greeley, A. M. (1978) Attitudes toward racial integration. *Scientific American*, *238*(6), 42–9.

Taylor, D. M., Meynard, R. and Rheault, E. (1977) Threat to ethnic identity and second language learning. In H. Giles (ed.), *Language, Ethnicity and Intergroup Relations*. London/New York: Academic Press.

Taylor, D. M., Simard, L. M. and Papineau, D. (1978) Perceptions of cultural difference and language use: a field study in a bilingual environment. *Canadian Journal of Behavioural Science*, *10*, 181–91.

Taylor, D. M., Simard, L. M., McKirnan, D. J. and Bellerose, J. (1982) Anglophone and francophone managers' perceptions of cultural differences in approaches to work. *Canadian Journal of Behavioural Science*, *14*, 144–51.

Taylor, D. M., Wong-Rieger, D., McKirnan, D. J. and Bercusson, T. (1982) Interpreting and coping with threat in the context of intergroup relations. *Journal of Social Psychology*, *117*, 257–69.

Taylor, D. M. and Simard, L. (1979) Ethnic identity and intergroup relations. In D. J. Lee (ed.), *Emerging Ethnic Boundaries*. Ottawa: University of Ottawa Press.

Taylor, D. M. and Dubé-Simard, L. (1984) Language planning and intergroup relations: anglophone and francophone attitudes toward Bill 101. In R. Y. Bourhis (ed.), *Conflict and Language Planning in Quebec*. Clevedon, England: Multilingual Matters.

Taylor, S. E. (1981) A categorization approach to stereotyping. In D. L.

Hamilton (ed.), *Cognitive Processes in Stereotyping and Intergroup Behavior*. Hillsdale, NJ: Erlbaum.

Taylor, S. E., Fiske, S. T., Etcoff, N. and Ruderman, A. (1978) The categorical and contextual bases of person memory and stereotyping. *Journal of Personality and Social Psychology*, 36, 778–93.

Thibaut, J. W. and Kelley, H. H. (1959) *The Social Psychology of Groups*. New York: Wiley.

Thomas, W. I. and Thomas, D. S. (1928) *The Child in America: Behavior Problems and Programs*. New York: Knopf.

Trew, K. (1983a) Group identification in a divided society. In J. Harbison (ed.), *Children of the Troubles: Children in Northern Ireland*. Belfast: Stranmillis.

Trew, K. (1983b) A sense of national identity: fact or artefact? *The Irish Journal of Psychology*, 6, 28–36.

Trew, K. (1985) Evaluating children's community holidays. Paper presented at Conference on Contact and the Reconciliation of Conflict, Northern Ireland Regional Office of the British Psychological Society, Belfast.

Trew, K. (in press) The dual education systems. In L. McWhirter and K. Trew (eds), *The Northern Ireland Conflict: Myth and Reality*. Ormskirk: Hesketh.

Trew, K., McWhirter, L., Finnegan, A., Maguire, A., Hinds, J. and Semrau, G. (1984) Irish children's summer program in Greensboro: evaluation 1984–85 (Preliminary report). Department of Psychology, Queen's University of Belfast.

Triandis, H. C. (1971) *Attitude and Attitude Change*. New York: Wiley.

Triandis, H. C. (1972) *The Analysis of Subjective Culture*. New York: Wiley.

Triandis, H. C. (1976) The future of pluralism. *Journal of Social Issues*, 32, 179–91.

Triandis, H. C. and Davis, E. E. (1965) Race and belief as determinants of behavior intentions. *Journal of Personality and Social Psychology*, 2, 715–25.

Triandis, H. C. and Vassiliou, V. (1967) Frequency of contact and stereotyping. *Journal of Personality and Social Psychology*, 7, 316–28.

Turner, J. C. (1978) Social categorisation and social discrimination in the minimal group paradigm. In H. Tajfel (ed.), *Differentiation between Social Groups: Studies in the Social Psychology of Intergroup Relations*. London: Academic Press.

Turner, J. C. (1981) The experimental social psychology of intergroup behavior. In J. C. Turner and H. Giles (eds), *Intergroup Behaviour*. Oxford: Basil Blackwell.

Turner, J. C. (1982) Towards a cognitive redefinition of the social group. In H. Tajfel (ed.), *Social Identity and Intergroup Relations*. Cambridge/Paris: Cambridge University Press/Maison des Sciences de l'Homme.

Turner, J. C. and Giles, H. (1981) Introduction: the social psychology of intergroup behaviour. In J. C. Turner and H. Giles (eds), *Intergroup Behaviour*. Oxford: Basil Blackwell.

United States Commission on Civil Rights (1982) *Statement on School Desegrega-*

tion. Washington, DC: United States Commission on Civil Rights Clearing-house (Publication 76).

University of Liverpool (1954) *The Dock Worker*. University Press: Liverpool.

Unsöld, W. (1978) Lehrereinstellung und Schülervorurteil, Frankfurt am Main: Lang.

Urbach, P. (1985) Good and bad arguments against historicism. In G. Currie and A. Musgrave (eds), *Popper and the Human Sciences*. Dordrecht: Martinus Nijhoff.

Van den Berghe, P. L. (1971) Racial segregation in South Africa: degrees and kinds. In H. Adam (ed.), *South Africa: Sociological Perspectives*. London: Oxford University Press, pp. 37–49.

van Knippenberg, A. (1978) Status differences, comparative relevance and intergroup differentiation. In H. Tajfel (ed.), *Differentiation between Social Groups*. London: Academic Press.

van Knippenberg, A. and van Oers, H. (1984) Social identity and equity concerns in intergroup perceptions. *British Journal of Social Psychology*, 23, 351–61.

Wagner, U. (1983) Soziale Schichtzugehörigkeit, formales Bildungsniveau und ethnische Vorurteile. Berlin: Express.

Wagner, U., Baumhold, B. and Keuth, U. (1983) Gemeinsame Familienseminare für Ausländer und Deutsche. Überlegungen und Erfahrungen. *ISS-Informationsdienst zur Ausländerarbeit*, 2/3, 120–2.

Wagner, U., Hewstone, M. and Machleit, U. (in preparation) Contact and liking among German and Turkish pupils in Germany.

Walker, K. F. (1979) Psychology and industrial relations: a general perspective. In G. M. Stephenson and C. J. Brotherton (eds), *Industrial Relations: A Social Psychological Approach*. Chichester: Wiley.

Walker, I. and Pettigrew, T. F. (1984) Relative deprivation theory: an overview and conceptual critique. *British Journal of Social Psychology*, 23, 301–10.

Ward, C. (1979) Where race didn't divide: some reflections on slum clearance in Moss Side. In R. Miles and A. Phizacklea (eds), *Racism and Political Action in Britain*. London: Routledge & Kegan Paul.

Ward, C. and Hewstone, M. (1985) Ethnicity, language and intergroup relations in Malaysia and Singapore: a social psychological analysis. *Journal of Multilingual and Multicultural Development*, in press.

Warr, P. B. (1973) *Psychology and Collective Bargaining*. London: Hutchinson.

Watson, G. (1947) *Action for Unity*. New York: Harper.

Watson, G. (1970) *Passing for White*. London: Tavistock.

Weber, R. and Crocker, J. (1983) Cognitive processes in the revision of stereotypic beliefs. *Journal of Personality and Social Psychology*, 45, 961–77.

Weitz, S. (1972) Attitude, voice and behavior: a repressed affect model of interracial interaction. *Journal of Personality and Social Psychology*, 24, 14–21.

Wenninger, G. (1978) Ausländische Arbeitnehmer im Urteil ihrer deutschen Kollegen. Unpublished doctoral dissertation. München.

220   *References*

Westie, F. R. (1964) Race and ethnic relations. In E. L. Faris (ed.), *Handbook of Modern Sociology*. Chicago: Rand McNally.

Whitley, B. E., Schofield, J. W. and Snyder, H. N. (1984) Peer preferences in a desegregated school: a round robin analysis. *Journal of Personality and Social Psychology*, 46, 799–810.

Wilder, D. A. (1978) Perceiving persons as a group: effects on attributions of causality and beliefs. *Social Psychology*, 41, 13–23.

Wilder, D. A. (1981) Perceiving persons as a group: categorization and intergroup relations. In D. L. Hamilton (ed.), *Cognitive Processes in Stereotyping and Intergroup Behaviour*. Hillsdale, NJ: Erlbaum.

Wilder, D. A. (1984) Intergroup contact: the typical member and the exception to the rule. *Journal of Experimental Social Psychology*, 20, 177–94.

Wilder, D. A. and Thompson, J. G. (1980) Intergroup contact with independent manipulations of ingroup and outgroup interaction. *Journal of Personality and Social Psychology*, 38, 589–603.

Williams, R. M. (1947) *Reduction of Intergroup Tensions*. New York: Social Science Research Council.

Williams, R. M. (1964) *Strangers Next Door: Ethnic Relations in American Communities*. Englewood Cliffs, NJ: Prentice-Hall.

Wilner, D. M., Walkley, R. P. and Cook, S. W. (1952) Residential proximity and intergroup relations in public housing projects. *Journal of Social Issues*, 8, 45–69.

Wilner, D. M., Walkley, R. and Cook, S. W. (1955) *Human Relations in Interracial Housing: A Study of the Contact Hypothesis*, Minneapolis, MN: University of Minnesota Press.

Winter, G. and Klein, P. (1975) Urteile deutscher Arbeitnehmer über Völker in Relation zur Zahl ihrer ausländischen Bekannten. V. Arbeits- und Freizeitkontakte der Befragten im Ausland im Vergleich mit analogen Kontakten in der Bundesrepublik Deutschland. *Psychologische Beiträge*, 17, 527–55.

Wisdom, J. (1975) Random remarks on the role of social sciences in the judicial decision-making process in school desegregation cases. *Law and Contemporary Problems*, 39(1), 135–49.

Worchel, S. (1979) Co-operation and the reduction of intergroup conflict: some determining factors. In W. G. Austin and S. Worchel (eds), *The Social Psychology of Intergroup Relations*. Monterey, Ca.: Brooks/Cole.

Worchel, S. and Norvell, N. (1980) Effect of perceived environmental conditions during co-operation on intergroup attraction. *Journal of Personality and Social Psychology*, 38, 764–72.

Worchel, S., Andreoli, V. A. and Folger, R. (1977) Intergroup co-operation and intergroup attraction: the effect of previous interaction and outcome of combined effort. *Journal of Experimental Social Psychology*, 13, 131–40.

Worchel, S., Axsom, D., Ferris, F., Samaha, G. and Schweizer, S. (1978) Determinants of the effect of intergroup co-operation on intergroup attraction. *Journal of Conflict Resolution*, 22, 429–39.

Works, E. (1961) The prejudice-interaction hypothesis from the point of view of the Negro minority group. *American Journal of Sociology*, 67, 47–52.

Zemach, M. (1980) *Attitudes of the Jewish Majority in Israel toward the Arab Minority*. Jerusalem: The Van Leer Foundation.

Zimbardo, P. G. (1970) The human choice: individuation, reason, and order versus deindividuation, impulse, and chaos. In W. J. Arnold and D. Levine (eds), *Nebraska Symposium on Motivation*. Lincoln, Neb.: University of Nebraska Press, vol. 17.

Index of Names

Index of Subjects

WITHDRAWN